Knox Press
www.knoxpress.com

Third edition, first printing
Copyright © 2021 by American Battlefield Trust
Washington, D.C.

Printed in the United States of America
BOOK DESIGN by Steven Stanley
TEXT by Kristopher D. White
MAPS by Steven Stanley

Library of Congress Catalog Card Number: 2019918270
ISBN: 978-1-68261-934-6

Published by:
Knox Press
Princeton, New Jersey

AMERICAN BATTLEFIELD TRUST ★ ★ ★

PRESERVE. EDUCATE. INSPIRE.

BATTLE MAPS OF THE CIVIL WAR: THE EASTERN THEATER VOLUME 1

FOREWORD

"David, can I tell you something?
I just love those maps you guys send to me."

THE MAPS I REFER TO ARE, OF COURSE, THE **SPECIALLY** created ones we began including in our battlefield fundraising mail appeals nearly 20 years ago, and if I had a dollar for every time someone said those words to me, well, the American Battlefield Trust could have preserved twice as much battlefield land than the 53,000 acres we have saved to date!

The maps—which are created by graphic designer and cartographer Steven Stanley, in close consultation with our battlefield preservation experts—are designed to show potential donors, at a glance, the specific piece(s) of battlefield land we are attempting to save, and the historic significance of that hallowed ground. Over the years, however, they have evolved into something more than just maps of regiments and brigades, charges and retreats, high ground and gullies. These simple maps have become a personal connection between the generous supporters of this great cause and the ground they have personally help to save. Again, I cannot tell you how many times people have told me they collect Trust maps in binders and have them in hand when they visit the battlefields, often to walk the very ground they have made personal gifts to preserve—and across which their ancestors tread so many decades ago.

Next to the preserved land itself, our maps are the best visual evidence of the tangible and measurable nature of our mission. Unlike most nonprofit organizations, we can show our supporters exactly—to the 100th of an acre—what their philanthropy is accomplishing, the precise land their donations are helping to preserve forever and why it is important to our history as a nation. To track our progress through the maps, over time, as the Trust saves more and more land, and essentially completes the preservation of many of our nation's most important battlefields, is extremely satisfying.

Many times over the years, members have also told me that they wished we would publish a book

of our maps. We were reluctant to do this because, first, we are in the land-preservation business, not the book business, and I demand that we stay focused on our core mission. Second, we know that, with a tempo of 30–40 land transactions each year, any book of maps we publish is liable to be outdated before it leaves the press. Third, we are ever-mindful of being good stewards of our members' contributions, so to spend money on a book—unless we were certain it would generate additional revenue we could use to support our mission—is a decision we take seriously. To address this last concern, we have decided to revive a book-selling model popular in earlier times, that of the "subscription model," meaning that we take orders for the book to help pay for it up front, and mail it to readers when it is ready. We all just have to bite the bullet and live with the fact that—until we stop saving land, which will not happen for many, many years—any map book will be somewhat outdated, but it will still give readers a better understanding of how we are succeeding in our vital mission.

We currently envision a series of books highlighting the battles of the Eastern and Western Theaters of the Civil War, as well as a book on the battles of the Revolutionary War, which is now a crucial part of our mission. My greatest hope is that this first volume will fill you with pride for all you have done for the cause of battlefield preservation, and that, by keeping it close at hand and referring to it often, it will inspire you to continue to make the preservation of American hallowed ground an important part of your personal legacy. Thank you.

David

David Duncan
President
American Battlefield Trust

WHAT GOES INTO MAKING A "NEW" MAP?

By Steven Stanley

THIS IS A TOPIC THAT COULD BE THE BASIS FOR AN ENTIRE BOOK in and of itself. Map creation is a topic that fascinates many history buffs. So much so that I have an entire 45-minute talk and PowerPoint presentation dedicated to how I create my battle maps. In a nutshell, the process is straightforward, but it's also labor and research intensive, while being wildly rewarding.

The first thing I do is actually find the battlefield. This might sound silly, but it is easier said than done for the majority of the battles I map. Granted, most people can locate Gettysburg, Vicksburg and Antietam, but do they know where the Natural Bridge Battlefield is located? I didn't either when I was first assigned the task of creating a battle map for land the Trust was preserving. I'll give you a hint, the battlefield is located in the Sunshine State.

Once I have located the battlefield, I then start pulling together all of the source materials I can find. For some battles, the list of materials is extensive; for others, not so much. I use primary sources first— letters, diaries, books—and then gather contemporary sources, too. After this step, I try to locate any existing maps; these are in the form of both primary and contemporary sources.

The existing maps help to get me started on locating the troops on the battlefield proper. Some of these maps are right on the money, and some are not. Now that I have this wealth of material spread across my office desk and floor, my wife knows that I am getting deeply involved in creating a new map by the mess around me.

Next, I will locate the oldest topographical (Topo) map of the battlefield. This topographical map gives me a better sense on how the battlefield looked around or at the time of the battle. As we all know, the topography of battlefields can change greatly after 150 or more years due to man and Mother Nature.

Using the old topographical map as a base, I then overlay a modern United States Geological Survey (USGS) map over the historical map. Before USGS reworked its modern Topo maps to be more user-friendly, I used to hand draw each and every Topo line on the maps. The Virginia Peninsula battles weren't too bad to draw because the terrain is fairly flat, but for the Shenandoah Valley battles you have mountains to contend with. Some maps take a couple of hours to hand draw, whereas others take a couple of days.

Using the historical and contemporary maps as guides, I start adding in the historical and modern roads, using different symbols for each. Sometimes the historical and modern roads coexist, which makes my job slightly easier. Then on to adding in the water features. They could be just small streams that were there at the time of the battle to huge rivers, bays, and sometimes, the Atlantic Ocean. After adding in the water, it is now time to add in historical features such as houses, commercial buildings, churches and other elements that make up the battlefield. Finally, I add in the historical treeline.

Once the base map is complete, I can truly add in the location of the troops. Using the sources I have collected, I add in where a unit entered the battle, and then follow the said unit's subsequent movements during the battle. The primary and contemporary resources I have collected get the troops moving in the correct direction.

After I feel I have the troops in the correct positions and moving the correct way, I send the maps to a historian for that battle and have them check my work. I will take any and all suggestions or corrections to heart and adjust the maps accordingly.

Once all the adjustments and corrections are made to the map, I deliver it to the American Battlefield Trust, which, in turn, delivers it to supporters and preservationists such as yourself.

INTRODUCTION

THE CIVIL WAR WAS THE SEMINAL EVENT OF 19TH-CENTURY AMERICA. There was hardly a household in the United States not touched by the conflict in some capacity. In the more than four years of war, Union and Confederate forces clashed in excess of 10,000 times. Engagements ranged from raids in Missouri, Mississippi and Vermont—to full-scale battles at Shiloh, Chancellorsville and Spotsylvania. The names of seemingly nondescript watercourses and towns, such as Antietam, Chickamauga and Gettysburg, were forever etched into the psyche of generations of Americans.

By the end of 1865, and this monumental clash of arms, the nation was reunited, and more than 3.9 million slaves were now, and forever, free. Reunification and freedom, though, came at a high price. The war had cost the nation an estimated $5.2 billon and some 620,000 lives—and the cultural, political and natural landscapes of the nation were changed forevermore.

From the United States Constitution to the battlefield parks created by the veterans of the war as open-air classrooms, the Civil War continues to impact the daily lives of Americans. Each year, millions of visitors from across the world travel to the sites associated with America's bloodiest conflict to reflect upon, learn from and remember the sacrifice of so many.

The importance of Civil War battlefields, and what happened on those fields, cannot be understated. To that end, and now more than 30 years ago, a group of concerned citizens and historians banded together to help preserve the threatened battlefields of the American Civil War. Since those early days of the modern preservation movement, the American Battlefield Trust has grown in size and strength to accomplish what no other organization of its kind could—saving battlefields associated with the Revolutionary War, War of 1812 and American Civil War. To date, the American Battlefield Trust has saved more than 53,000 acres of battlefield land in 24 states associated with 143 battles spanning the first 100 years of our nation's history.

Due to the sheer number of battlefields that we have saved, we cannot fit every map we have ever produced into this volume. Thus, we have focused on some of the major actions of the Eastern Theater of the American Civil War, which spanned from central Pennsylvania south to the Virginia–North Carolina border, east to the Atlantic Ocean and west into modern-day West Virginia. This theater of war alone witnessed some 3,000 engagements, of which more than 2,000 took place in the Commonwealth of Virginia.

The true "star" of this work is the battle maps. We have provided the reader with some brief overview text to bring them up to speed on the battle action, and then we allowed the maps to tell the rest of the story. The reader should keep in mind that the maps contained within this book are only a fraction of the hundreds of maps we have available on our website: www.battlefields.org. To include all of our maps would have been burdensome to the reader and cost prohibitive to the buyer.

It is our sincere hope that this collection of maps will give you a better understanding of the major actions of the Eastern Theater of the American Civil War, as well as an appreciation for the tens of thousands of acres of hallowed ground our members have helped preserve over the last three decades.

FIRST BATTLE *of* MANASSAS

(FIRST BULL RUN)

JULY 21, 1861

ON JULY 16, 1861, THE NEWLY ORGANIZED UNION ARMY IN WASHINGTON, DC, marched from the capital toward a Confederate army under the command of Brig. Gen. Pierre G. T. Beauregard, drawn up behind Bull Run—a creek just to the west of Centreville, Virginia. Beauregard's men defended the strategic railroad junction at Manassas, a few miles to the southwest of a stone bridge that crossed Bull Run.

On July 18, the Federal commander, Brig. Gen. Irvin McDowell, sent a small force across Bull Run at Blackburn's Ford to test the strength of the Confederate defenses. A brief skirmish ensured, with light casualties and little result.

Looking to maintain the initiative, and with pressure from the politicians in Washington to end the war quickly, McDowell made plans to attack the Rebel army. The Federal commander sought to attack the left end of Beauregard's line, while making a simultaneous demonstration where the Warrenton Turnpike crossed Bull Run at the stone bridge to hold the Confederates in place.

Early on the 21st, two of McDowell's divisions crossed at Sudley Ford and attacked the Confederate left flank on Matthews Hill, initiating the first major land battle of the Civil War. Fighting raged throughout the morning, as outnumbered Confederate forces were driven back southward to Henry Hill.

By early afternoon, Confederate reinforcements from Brig. Gen. Joseph Johnston's army in the Shenandoah Valley arrived at Manassas Junction in force, via the railroad. Johnston's soldiers bolstered the Rebel fortunes in the Henry Hill sector of the battlefield—centered around an all-Virginia brigade led by Brig. Gen. Thomas J. Jackson.

Jackson set up his infantry in a reverse slope position, which offered cover and concealment from the enemy. The old artillerist that he was, Jackson also set some 13 cannon along the ridge. These guns formed the backbone for the Confederate rallying point.

Soon, two batteries of Union guns rolled into position, and a close-in artillery duel ensued. Morning Union success now gave way to the weight of a concerted Confederate counterattack.

By 5 p.m., the Federals were in full retreat, and the combined Confederate armies of Beauregard and Johnston held the field.

Although victorious, Confederate forces were too disorganized and far too green to pursue the Federals. By July 22, the shattered Union army reached the safety of Washington. The First Battle of Bull Run convinced the nation that the Civil War would be a long and costly affair. McDowell was relieved of command and replaced by Maj. Gen. George B. McClellan, who set about reorganizing and training the troops for the long road ahead.

✳ ✳ PRESERVATION ✳ ✳

To date, the **American Battlefield Trust** has saved **373 acres** at Manassas Battlefield.

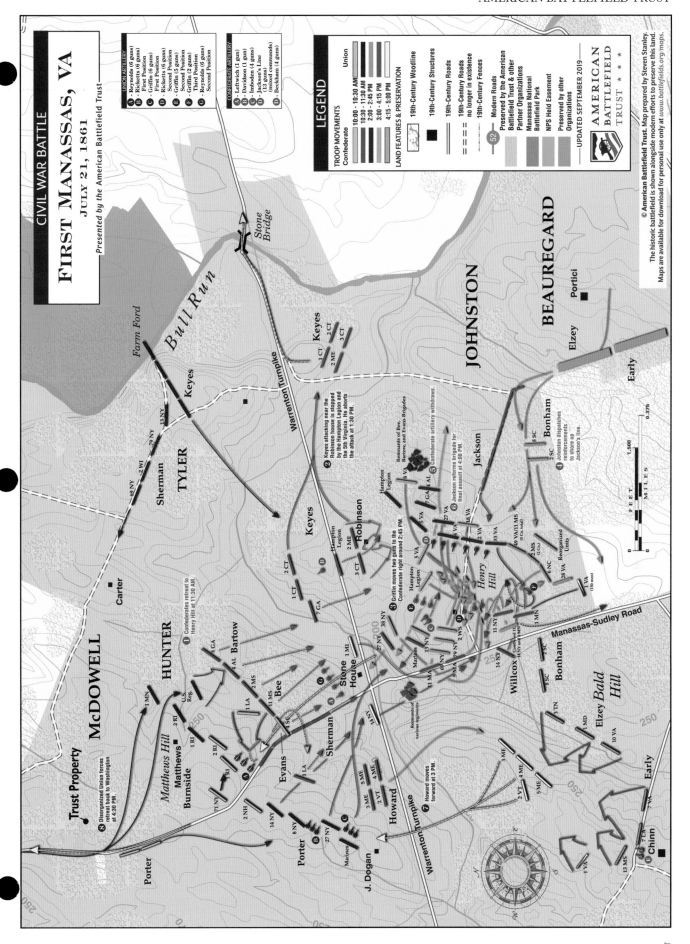

CIVIL WAR BATTLE

FIRST MANASSAS, VA
JULY 21, 1861

Presented by the American Battlefield Trust

UNION ARTILLERY
- Reynolds (6 guns)
- Ricketts (6 guns) First Position
- Griffin (6 guns) First Position
- Ricketts (6 guns) Second Position
- Griffin (5 guns) Second Position
- Griffin (2 guns) Third Position
- Reynolds (6 guns) Second Position

CONFEDERATE ARTILLERY
- Leftwich (1 gun)
- Davidson (1 gun)
- Imboden (4 guns)
- Jackson's Line (13 guns) (four commands)
- Beckham (4 guns)

LEGEND

TROOP MOVEMENTS
Confederate   Union
- 10:00 - 10:30 AM
- 10:30 - 11:30 AM
- 2:00 - 2:45 PM
- 3:00 - 4:15 PM
- 4:15 - 5:00 PM

LAND FEATURES & PRESERVATION
- 19th-Century Woodline
- 19th-Century Structures
- 19th-Century Roads
- 19th-Century Roads no longer in existence
- 19th-Century Fences
- Modern Roads
- Preserved by the American Battlefield Trust & other Partner Organizations
- Manassas National Battlefield Park
- NPS Held Easement
- Preserved by other Organizations

—UPDATED SEPTEMBER 2019—

AMERICAN BATTLEFIELD TRUST ★★★★

© American Battlefield Trust. Map prepared by Steven Stanley. The historic battlefield is shown alongside modern efforts to preserve this land. Maps are available for download for personal use only at www.battlefields.org/maps.

Map labels:

Stone Bridge

Bull Run

Farm Ford

JOHNSTON

BEAUREGARD

Portici

Elzey

Early

Bonham

8 SC

2 SC

Jackson

① Johnston dispatches reinforcements to shore up Jackson's line.

⑤ Jackson reforms brigade for final assault at 4:00 PM.

⑥ Confederate artillery withdraws.

Remnants of Bee, Bartow, and Evans Brigades

8 VA

7 GA AL

② Keyes attacking near the Robinson house is stopped by the Hampton Legion and the 5th Virginia. He aborts the attack at 1:30 PM.

Keyes
2 ME
1 CT
3 CT

Warrenton Turnpike

Keyes

MCDOWELL

TYLER

Sherman

60 NY
2 WI
79 NY
13 NY

① Confederate retreat to Henry Hill at 11:30 AM.

Carter

Robinson

Hampton Legion
2 ME

Henry Hill

④ Griffin moves two guns to the Confederate right around 2:45 PM.

27 VA
2 VA
4 VA
33 VA
5 VA
49 VA/11 MS (5 Co. total)
2 MS
6 NC
28 VA
1 VA (150 men)

Manassas-Sudley Road

Bonham
2 SC

Willcox
8 SC

Elzey
13 TN
MD
10 VA

Bald Hill

7 GA

1 MI
38 NY
27 NY
13 NY
14 NY
11 NY
14 NY
Marines
5 MA/1 MN
11 MA
69 NY
6 MA
2 MN

HUNTER

4 AL Bartow
5 GA
4 AL
2 MS
1 LA
11 MS
8 SC
Bee

Matthews Hill
Matthews
Burnside
1 MN
2 RI
1 RI
2 RI
7 NY
14 NY
2 NH

Stone House

Sherman
1 MI
A

Evans
1 LA
B

Trust Property

⑧ Disorganized Union forces retreat back to Washington at 4:30 PM.

Porter
8 NY
27 NY
Marines

Howard
3 ME
5 ME
2 VT
4 ME
3 ME
2 VT
5 ME

③ Howard moves forward at 3 PM.

Porter

J. Dogan

Warrenton Turnpike

J. Dogan

Early
7 LA
7 VA
13 MS
1 VA

⑨ Chinn

N

FEET   1,500   0
MILES   0.375

BATTLE *of* HAMPTON ROADS

(BATTLE OF THE *MONITOR* AND THE *MERRIMACK*)

MARCH 8-9, 1862

WHEN VIRGINIA SECEDED IN APRIL 1861, MANY OF THE vessels, guns and repair facilities of the U.S. Navy at the Gosport Naval Yard in Portsmouth, Virginia, were hastily scuttled, destroyed or abandoned, only for the Confederates to capture and repurpose them. Among the captured items was the steam frigate USS *Merrimack*. Initially scuttled and burned to the waterline, the ship sank pier side, but only her upperworks were destroyed by fire. The fledgling Confederate navy raised the ship, moved her into the graving dock and replaced her wooden superstructure with an iron-covered citadel mounting 10 guns and a massive 1,500-pound iron ram. The new behemoth was dubbed the CSS *Virginia*.

By early March 1862, the principal Union army in the east, the Army of the Potomac, was preparing to make its way from Washington, DC, to the Virginia Peninsula, where it would drive toward the Confederate capital of Richmond. The 121,500-man army would move via water, in a combined army-navy operation that would carry the troops to Fortress Monroe—located on the tip of the Virginia Peninsula at Hampton Roads.

On March 8, one week prior to the departure of the Union flotilla, the CSS *Virginia* steamed down the Elizabeth River, seeking to interdict Federal naval operations at Hampton Roads. Under the command of Flag Officer Franklin Buchanan, the CSS *Virginia* headed straight for the USS *Cumberland* off Newport News. Around 2 p.m. on March 8, 1862, the CSS *Virginia* struck the *Cumberland* with its iron ram, smashing a huge hole in its wooden hull. However, in delivering a mortal blow to the *Cumberland*, the CSS *Virginia* lost its ram, which had become entangled within the shredded hull of its opponent.

The *Virginia* next turned its sights on the nearby USS *Congress*. Seeking to avoid the same fate that had befallen the *Cumberland*, the crew of the USS *Congress* purposely ran aground on a nearby shoal. Unable to maneuver, the *Congress* was quickly wrecked by Confederate fire. At 4 p.m., the USS *Congress* lowered its flag and surrendered. Hoping to accept the USS *Congress'* formal surrender, Franklin Buchanan, who had come out onto his ship's deck, was wounded by a musket ball fired from shore. With daylight waning and its captain needing medical attention, the *Virginia* broke off its attack and returned to shore.

In the midst of the growing panic of the Federal fleet, a new and innovative ship had silently slipped into Hampton Roads during the night of March 8, 1862. The USS *Monitor*, the radical invention of John Ericsson commanded by Lt. John L. Worden, prepared to defend the rest of the Federal fleet from the seemingly invincible *Virginia*.

The next morning, the Virginia prepared for another assault. As she approached the USS *Minnesota*, her crew noticed a strange raft-like vessel by the Minnesota's side. With the USS *Monitor* now bearing down on the *Virginia*, the Confederate ironclad shifted its fire to this newcomer with the large rotating turret. Over the next few hours, the two ironclads traded shots in a close-range slugfest.

After several hours of close combat, the USS *Monitor* disengaged and headed for the safety of shallower waters. The CSS *Virginia*, short on ammunition and concerned over the lowering tide, also broke off and headed for the safety of Norfolk. The world's first battle between steam-powered, ironclad warships ended in a draw, but its impact on the future of naval warfare was profound.

✳ ✳ PRESERVATION ✳ ✳

The **American Battlefield Trust** has not saved any land in the Hampton Roads area.

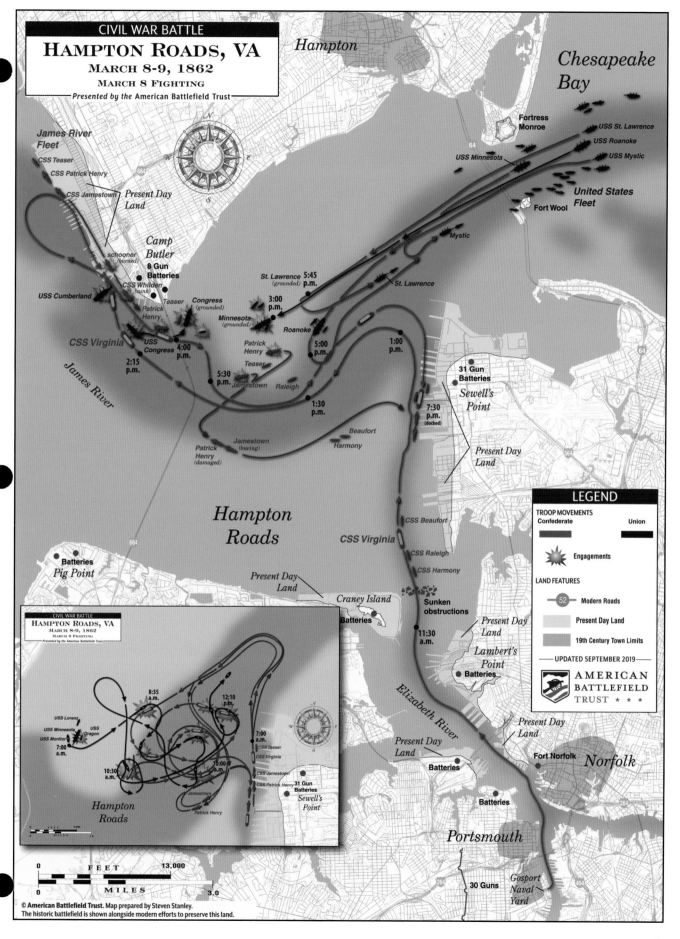

CIVIL WAR BATTLE
HAMPTON ROADS, VA
MARCH 8-9, 1862
MARCH 8 FIGHTING
Presented by the American Battlefield Trust

Hampton

Chesapeake Bay

James River Fleet

Fortress Monroe

USS St. Lawrence
USS Roanoke
USS Mystic

USS Minnesota

CSS Teaser
CSS Patrick Henry
CSS Jamestown

Present Day Land

United States Fleet

Fort Wool

schooner (burned)

Camp Butler

Mystic

8 Gun Batteries

St. Lawrence 5:45 (grounded) p.m.

CSS Whilden (sunk)

Teaser

Congress (grounded)

3:00 p.m.

St. Lawrence

USS Cumberland

Patrick Henry

Minnesota (grounded)

Roanoke

CSS Virginia

USS Congress 4:00 p.m.

2:15 p.m.

5:00 p.m.

1:00 p.m.

31 Gun Batteries

Sewell's Point

James River

5:30 p.m.
Jamestown

Patrick Henry

Teaser

Raleigh

1:30 p.m.

7:30 p.m. (docked)

Present Day Land

Patrick Henry (damaged)

Jamestown (towing)

Beaufort

Harmony

Hampton Roads

Batteries
Pig Point

Present Day Land

Craney Island

Batteries

CSS Beaufort

Sunken obstructions

CSS Raleigh

11:30 a.m.

Present Day Land

CSS Virginia

CSS Harmony

Lambert's Point

Batteries

LEGEND

TROOP MOVEMENTS

Confederate   Union

Engagements

LAND FEATURES

52 Modern Roads

Present Day Land

19th Century Town Limits

— UPDATED SEPTEMBER 2019 —

AMERICAN BATTLEFIELD TRUST ★ ★ ★

Elizabeth River

Present Day Land

Fort Norfolk

Norfolk

Batteries

Batteries

Portsmouth

30 Guns

Gosport Naval Yard

CIVIL WAR BATTLE
HAMPTON ROADS, VA
MARCH 8-9, 1862
MARCH 9 FIGHTING
Presented by the American Battlefield Trust

8:35 a.m.

12:10 p.m.

USS Lorenz

USS Minnesota

USS Dragon

USS Monitor

7:00 a.m.

7:00 a.m.

CSS Teaser

CSS Virginia

10:30 a.m.

10:00 a.m.

CSS Jamestown

CSS Patrick Henry 31 Gun Batteries

Jamestown

Sewell's Point

Patrick Henry

Hampton Roads

0   13,000
FEET

0   MILES   3.0

© **American Battlefield Trust.** Map prepared by Steven Stanley.
The historic battlefield is shown alongside modern efforts to preserve this land.

BATTLE *of* WILLIAMSBURG

MAY 5, 1862

AFTER LANDING HIS ARMY OF THE POTOMAC AT FORT MONROE, George McClellan initiated his now-famous Peninsula Campaign, the first major Union offensive on Richmond, Virginia.

The first roadblock on the way to the Confederate capital was Yorktown, Virginia, the scene of the famous British surrender to George Washington during the Revolutionary War. For nearly a month, McClellan's men besieged the Confederate forces in and around the historic town.

By May 1, 1862, Confederate Gen. Joseph E. Johnston found his position at Yorktown untenable. Two days later, he withdrew his army from the Warwick-Yorktown line—retreating in the direction of Richmond.

Surprised by the sudden turn of events, McClellan ordered a pursuit of the Rebel army. Muddy roads hampered the movement of both armies, yet the Federals managed to catch up with the Confederates near Williamsburg on May 5.

Johnston deployed Maj. Gen. James Longstreet's division as a rear guard some four miles to the southeast of the town. Longstreet, in turn, utilized earthen Fort Magruder (named for Confederate Gen. John "Prince John" Magruder) and the fort's support trenches to establish a defensive position.

In the vanguard of the Union pursuit were the divisions of Gens. Joseph Hooker and Philip Kearny, two of the most aggressive generals in McClellan's army.

Hooker pressed forward, leading an unsupported assault on Fort Magruder. During the fight, Hooker was unhorsed by an artillery shell that spooked his mount. The now muddy and hatless division commander called for reinforcements as Confederates began to counterattack out of their fortifications.

Muddy roads, rain and poor leadership initially held back Union reinforcements from other units, but Kearny's division arrived in a timely manner to help his fellow III Corps division commander.

The Confederates countered by reinforcing Longstreet with Maj. Gen. Daniel Harvey Hill's division. As a brigade of the Union IV Corps, commanded by Brig. Gen. Winfield Scott Hancock, arrived in support of Hooker's right, Hancock's brigade occupied two abandoned redoubts on the Confederate left flank. The Confederates counterattacked Hancock unsuccessfully, but his localized success was not exploited, as neither McClellan nor his second-in-command were on the field.

Johnston continued his withdrawal up the peninsula that evening. McClellan miscategorized the battle as a "brilliant victory" over superior forces—but he did correctly categorize Hancock as "superb."

In the end, neither commander had committed his entire army to the fight. McClellan scored his second tactical victory of the week. Williamsburg proved to be the largest engagement of the Peninsula Campaign until Seven Pines (Fair Oaks) three weeks later.

✳ ✳ PRESERVATION ✳ ✳

To date, the **American Battlefield Trust** has saved **69 acres** at Williamsburg Battlefield.

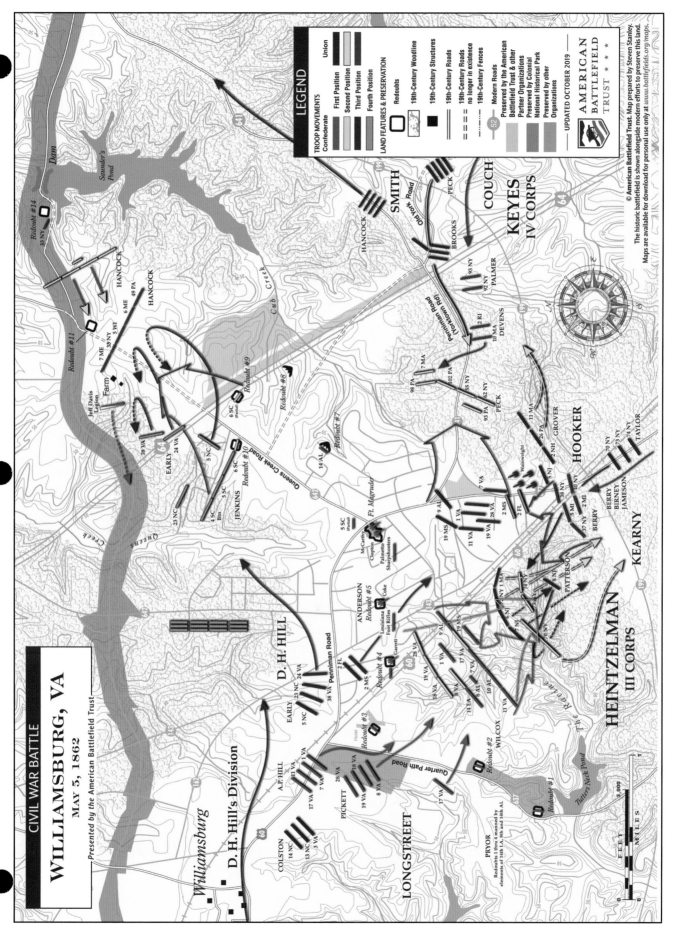

CIVIL WAR BATTLE

WILLIAMSBURG, VA

MAY 5, 1862

Presented by the American Battlefield Trust

BATTLE *of* GAINES' MILL

JUNE 27, 1862

FOLLOWING THE BATTLE OF SEVEN PINES (FAIR OAKS), MAY 31–JUNE 1, 1862, and the wounding of Joseph Johnston, command of the principal Confederate army in the east fell to Gen. Robert E. Lee. Largely unknown outside inner army circles, Lee was viewed by those who did know him as a disappointment thus far in the Civil War. That perception would change with his rise to army command.

With their backs against their own capital, Lee's newly dubbed Army of Northern Virginia looked to wrestle the strategic initiative from George McClellan and drive the Yankees from the Richmond area. As Lee's men dug trenches around Richmond, and the soldiers and civilians grumbled about "Granny Lee" being the "King of Spades," Lee bolstered his army and planned a massive offensive.

With 92,000 men, Lee initiated the Seven Days Battles (June 25–July 1). The Chickahominy River split the Union army in two, and Lee sought to engage and destroy the Federals in detail. Sending the bulk of his army across the river, he struck the Union V Corps on the right, while the remainder of his army held the rest of the Federals in place south of the river.

The first Confederate blow landed at Beaver Dam Creek on June 26. Although victorious, the Federals retreated south and east toward the Chickahominy River. On June 27, Maj. Gen. Fitz John Porter's V Corps established a new defensive line along Boatswain's Creek, just north of the Chickahominy. Porter's orders from Maj. Gen. George B. McClellan were to hold off Robert E. Lee's army long enough for McClellan to begin moving the Army of the Potomac south toward the James River. Porter, with around 34,000 men, was outnumbered by Lee's nearly 60,000 men and his back was to the Chickahominy.

The clear, high ground south of Boatswain's Creek around the Watt Family farm provided Porter with excellent ground to place his artillery, and his infantry used the banks of the creek to its advantage— setting up a three-line defense-in-depth. Anxious to renew his assaults from the day before, Lee sent the bulk of his force forward late on the 27th, with the intention of destroying Porter's force. The Federals beat back successive waves of disjointed attacks, inflicting some of the heaviest casualties the war had yet seen.

By dusk, however, Lee's Confederates were more organized. With daylight fading, the Southern divisions of James Longstreet, Richard Ewell, A. P. Hill and others assaulted Porter's entire defensive line in the largest coordinated attack in the Eastern Theater of the Civil War. The assault sent the Northerners fleeing toward the Chickahominy. During the night, the Federals limped across the river and burned the bridges behind them. Gaines' Mill was the third in the Seven Days Battles and initiated a series of rearguard actions as McClellan moved his army to the safety of the James River—handing over the strategic initiative to Robert E. Lee.

✳ ✳ PRESERVATION ✳ ✳

To date, the **American Battlefield Trust** has saved **346 acres** at Gaines' Mill Battlefield.

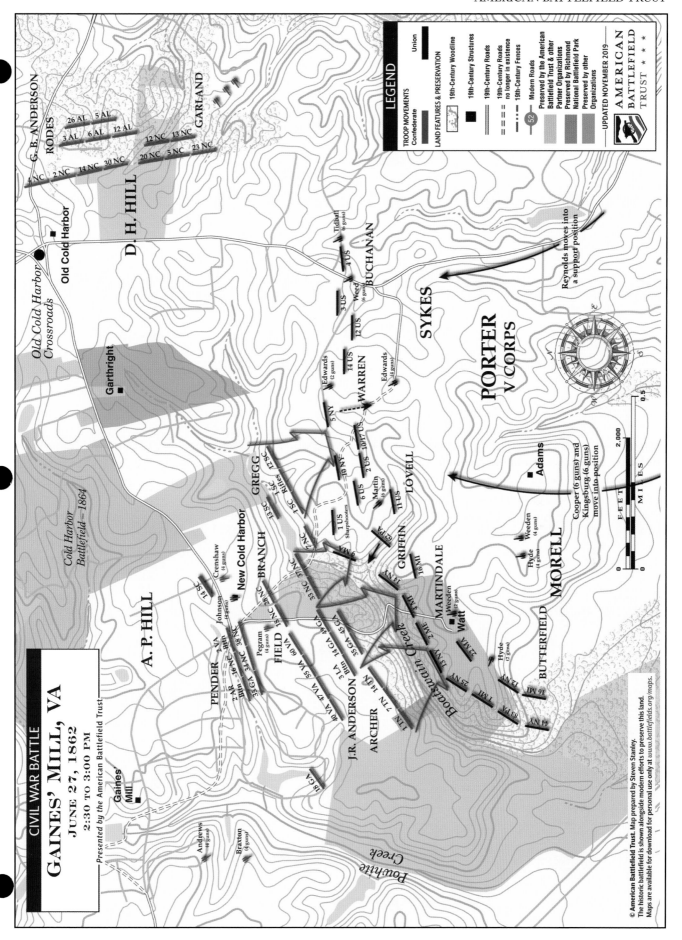

CIVIL WAR BATTLE
GAINES' MILL, VA
JUNE 27, 1862
2:30 TO 3:00 PM
Presented by the American Battlefield Trust

LEGEND

TROOP MOVEMENTS
Confederate — Union

LAND FEATURES & PRESERVATION
- 19th-Century Woodline
- 19th-Century Structures
- 19th-Century Roads
- 19th-Century Roads no longer in existence
- 19th-Century Fences
- Modern Roads
- Preserved by the American Battlefield Trust & other Partner Organizations
- Preserved by Richmond National Battlefield Park
- Preserved by other Organizations

— UPDATED NOVEMBER 2019 —

AMERICAN BATTLEFIELD TRUST ★ ★ ★

© American Battlefield Trust. Map prepared by Steven Stanley.
The historic battlefield is shown alongside modern efforts to preserve this land.
Maps are available for download for personal use only at *www.battlefields.org/maps*.

13

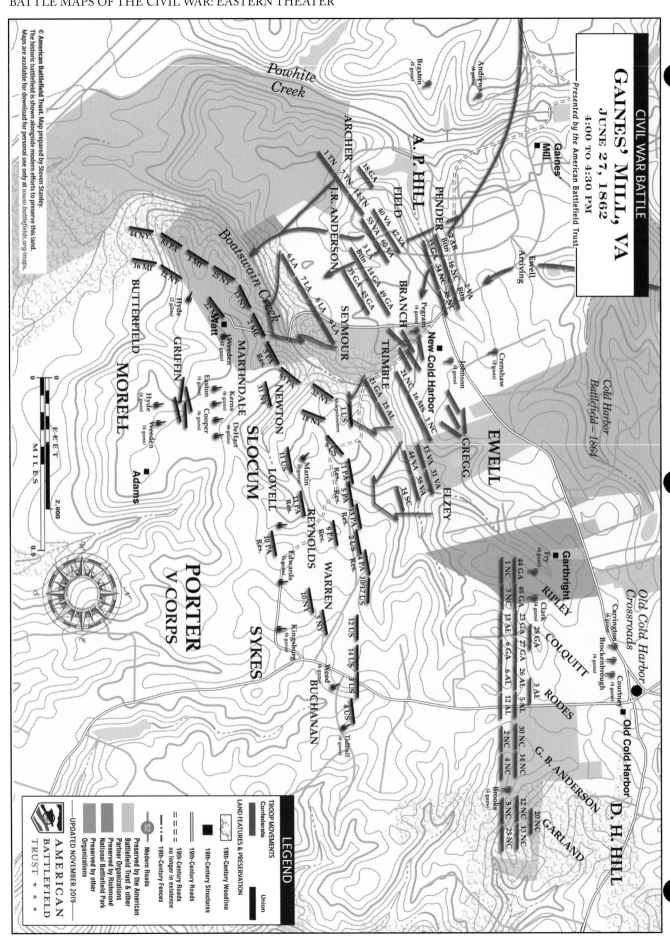

CIVIL WAR BATTLE

GAINES' MILL, VA

JUNE 27, 1862
4:00 TO 4:30 PM

Presented by the American Battlefield Trust

LEGEND

LAND FEATURES & PRESERVATION

- 19th-Century Structures
- 19th-Century Woodline
- Modern Roads
- 19th-Century Roads
- 19th-Century Roads no longer in existence
- 19th-Century Fences

- Preserved by the American Battlefield Trust & other Partner Organizations
- Preserved by Richmond National Battlefield Park
- Preserved by other Organizations

TROOP MOVEMENTS

- Confederate
- Union

UPDATED NOVEMBER 2019

AMERICAN BATTLEFIELD TRUST ★★★

© American Battlefield Trust. Map prepared by Steven Stanley. The historic battlefield is shown alongside modern efforts to preserve this land. Maps are available for download for personal use only at www.battlefields.org/maps.

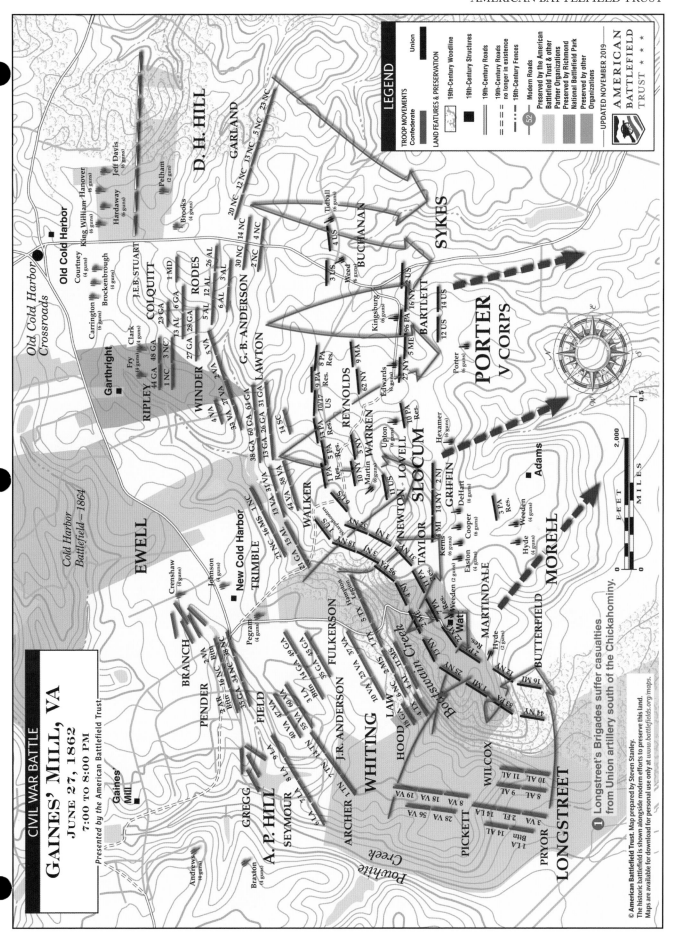

CIVIL WAR BATTLE

GAINES' MILL, VA

JUNE 27, 1862
7:00 TO 8:00 PM

Presented by the American Battlefield Trust

LEGEND

TROOP MOVEMENTS
Confederate   Union

LAND FEATURES & PRESERVATION
19th-Century Woodline
19th-Century Structures

19th-Century Roads
19th-Century Roads no longer in existence
19th-Century Fences
52   Modern Roads

Preserved by the American Battlefield Trust & other Partner Organizations
Preserved by Richmond National Battlefield Park
Preserved by other Organizations

—UPDATED NOVEMBER 2019—

AMERICAN BATTLEFIELD TRUST ★ ★ ★

① Longstreet's Brigades suffer casualties from Union artillery south of the Chickahominy.

© American Battlefield Trust. Map prepared by Steven Stanley.
The historic battlefield is shown alongside modern efforts to preserve this land.
Maps are available for download for personal use only at *www.battlefields.org/maps.*

15

BATTLE *of* GLENDALE

(BATTLE OF FRAZIER'S FARM)

JUNE 30, 1862

ROBERT E. LEE LOOKED TO KEEP THE MOMENTUM as the Seven Days Battles (June 25–July 1) wore on. He also sought to secure Richmond and to destroy the Union army before it could slip away to the safety of Federal gunboats on the James River.

After the Battle of Gaines' Mill, Lee shifted the left wing of his army to the south side of the Chickahominy River. With the Army of the Potomac in full retreat, Lee intended to take advantage of his enemy and to cut the Federal host in two by thrusting the largest portion of his army—six divisions, totaling 44,800 men—against the Yankees then gathered near Glendale. At the same time, Stonewall Jackson's four divisions were to engage the Union rear guard at White Oak Swamp.

Plagued by poor coordination among its senior commanders, and the reliance on overly complicated battleplans and marching orders, the Army of Northern Virginia struggled to land the killing blow on McClellan's army throughout the Seven Days Battles. And the pending battle on June 30 proved to be more of the same.

After five days of constant fighting and marching, the Confederate divisions of Maj. Gens. Benjamin Huger, James Longstreet and A. P. Hill converged on the retreating Union army in the vicinity of Glendale. Longstreet's and Hill's fierce attacks penetrated the Union defense near Willis Church, routing Brig. Gen. George A. McCall's Pennsylvania Reserve division near the Frayser Farm. McCall was captured, and a little-known brigade commander, Brig. Gen. George G. Meade, was severely wounded. Union counterattacks by the hard-hitting divisions of Joseph Hooker and Phillip Kearny sealed the breach and saved the Union line of retreat along the Willis Church Road. The Federal soldiers were further aided by Benjamin Huger's slow-moving Confederate division. Huger's men wasted hours cutting a new road through the thick woods and never participated in the battle. Failing to bring their full force to bear on the Federals, the Confederate offensive ground to a halt.

On the Union right, two divisions of Union infantry and six batteries under the temporary command of Brig. Gen. William Franklin guarded the Union army's northern flank along White Oak Swamp. Stonewall Jackson made feeble and sluggish efforts to cross White Oak Swamp. Bogged down in a fruitless artillery duel, Jackson ordered his weary soldiers to needlessly rebuild a bridge across the swamp, rather than having them utilize nearby fords. While Jackson tied down a portion of the Federal forces from entering the battle, he and his men did not materially contribute to the day's action. It was yet another missed opportunity for the Confederate high command.

The battle at Glendale was Lee's best chance to cut off the Union army from the James River. That night, McClellan pulled the Union army back to the south and established a strong defensive position on Malvern Hill, where the fighting continued the next day.

✳ ✳ **PRESERVATION** ✳ ✳

To date, the **American Battlefield Trust** has saved **726 acres** at Glendale Battlefield.

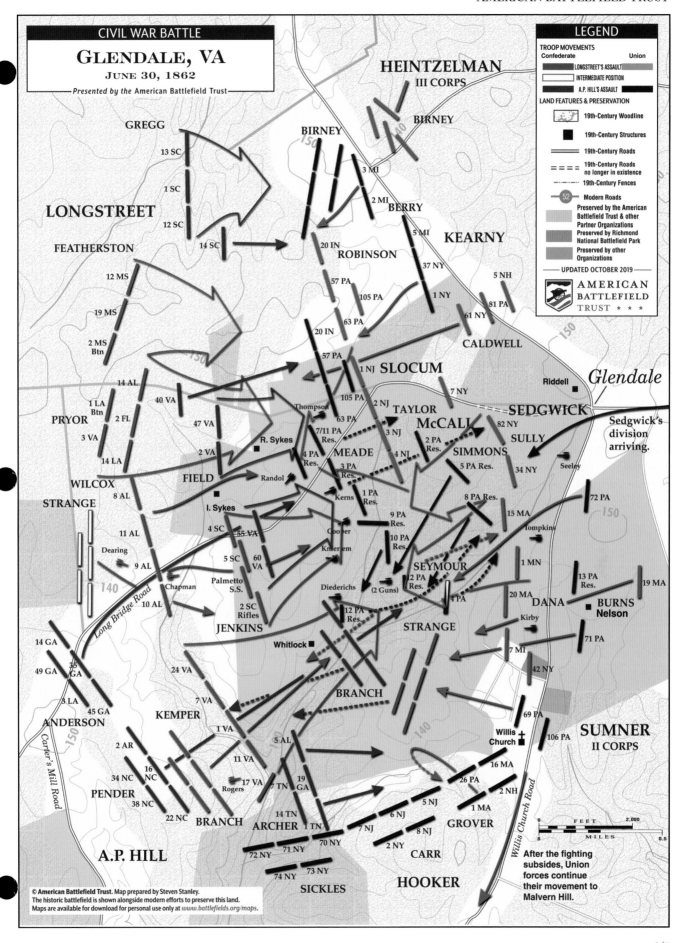

CIVIL WAR BATTLE

GLENDALE, VA

JUNE 30, 1862

Presented by the American Battlefield Trust

LEGEND

TROOP MOVEMENTS
Confederate · Union
LONGSTREET'S ASSAULT
INTERMEDIATE POSITION
A.P. HILL'S ASSAULT

LAND FEATURES & PRESERVATION
19th-Century Woodline
19th-Century Structures
19th-Century Roads
19th-Century Roads no longer in existence
19th-Century Fences
52 Modern Roads
Preserved by the American Battlefield Trust & other Partner Organizations
Preserved by Richmond National Battlefield Park
Preserved by other Organizations

— UPDATED OCTOBER 2019 —

AMERICAN BATTLEFIELD TRUST ★ ★ ★

Glendale

Sedgwick's division arriving.

After the fighting subsides, Union forces continue their movement to Malvern Hill.

FEET 2,000
MILES 0.5

© American Battlefield Trust. Map prepared by Steven Stanley.
The historic battlefield is shown alongside modern efforts to preserve this land.
Maps are available for download for personal use only at *www.battlefields.org/maps.*

17

BATTLE *of* MALVERN HILL

JULY 1, 1862

ON THE LATE AFTERNOON OF JUNE 30, THE RETREATING Federal Army of the Potomac finally stopped at the James River. Now within the supporting range of U.S. Navy gunboats, the bulk of McClellan's army took up a defensive position atop Malvern Hill.

The 130-foot-high Malvern Hill offered some of the best defensive terrain of the entire Civil War. The plateau-like hill was flanked to the east by the ironically named Western Run, while to the west, Crewes Run and the Malvern Bluffs offered natural defensive barriers. Directly to the south lay the James River. To the north, gently rolling ground offered clear fields of fire with few ravines or defilades for the enemy to utilize on the attack.

Colonel Henry J. Hunt, McClellan's chief of artillery, posted 171 guns facing west, north and east on the hill. Federal infantry of the V, III and IV Corps was in close support of the guns, with more infantry reserves nearby. Union gunboats prowled the James River, well within close supporting distance.

Robert E. Lee yearned to apply pressure to the enemy forces and destroy them against the James River. It was not to be. Poor maps, poor communication, confusing road names, another overly complicated battle plan and another lackluster showing by Stonewall Jackson all worked in concert to doom the Confederate assault before it could get off the ground.

The Confederates sought to counter the massed Federal artillery and soften the Union infantry with "grand batteries" of their own. Around 1:00 p.m., both sides opened an artillery duel, but poor coordination and an effective Union counterbattery fire doomed Lee's gunners.

Lee next ordered in the infantry. In the course of a few hours, some 20 separate brigades under seven division commanders clashed with the Federals. The attacks were not coordinated properly and advanced across the open ground at different times; most were stalled well short of the hill's crest. For each Confederate advance, the effectiveness of the Federal artillery was the deciding factor, repulsing attack after attack, resulting in a tactical Union victory. Confederate Gen. D. H. Hill surveyed the carnage on the bloody field and remarked after the war, disgustedly, "[I]t was not war, it was murder."

On July 2, McClellan withdrew the army to Harrison's Landing on the James River, ending the Seven Days Battles and the first Union drive on Richmond. It would take almost two more years and cost tens of thousands of lives before the Federals were this close to Richmond again.

Following the campaign, McClellan commenced a six-week period of recovery and rehabilitation for his army. In the meantime, Lee pressed his newly won advantage and carried the war from central into northern Virginia, and beyond. The high casualties and lessons learned at Malvern Hill and the Seven Days Battles raised both the military and political stakes of the war in profound ways.

✳ ✳ **PRESERVATION** ✳ ✳

To date, the **American Battlefield Trust** has saved **1,426 acres** at Malvern Hill Battlefield.

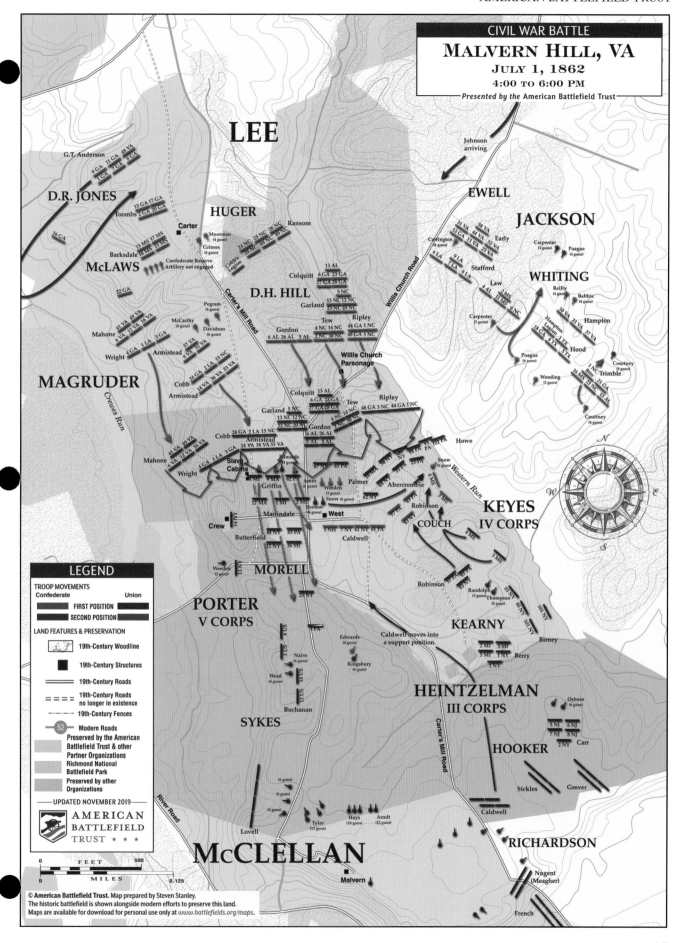

LEE

JACKSON

EWELL

D.R. JONES

HUGER

WHITING

McLAWS

D.H. HILL

MAGRUDER

KEYES
IV CORPS

COUCH

MORELL

KEARNY

PORTER
V CORPS

HEINTZELMAN
III CORPS

HOOKER

SYKES

RICHARDSON

McCLELLAN

LEGEND

TROOP MOVEMENTS

Confederate   Union

FIRST POSITION

SECOND POSITION

LAND FEATURES & PRESERVATION

19th-Century Woodline

19th-Century Structures

19th-Century Roads

19th-Century Roads no longer in existence

19th-Century Fences

52   Modern Roads

Preserved by the American Battlefield Trust & other Partner Organizations

Richmond National Battlefield Park

Preserved by other Organizations

UPDATED NOVEMBER 2019

AMERICAN
BATTLEFIELD
TRUST ★ ★ ★

FEET   500

MILES   0.125

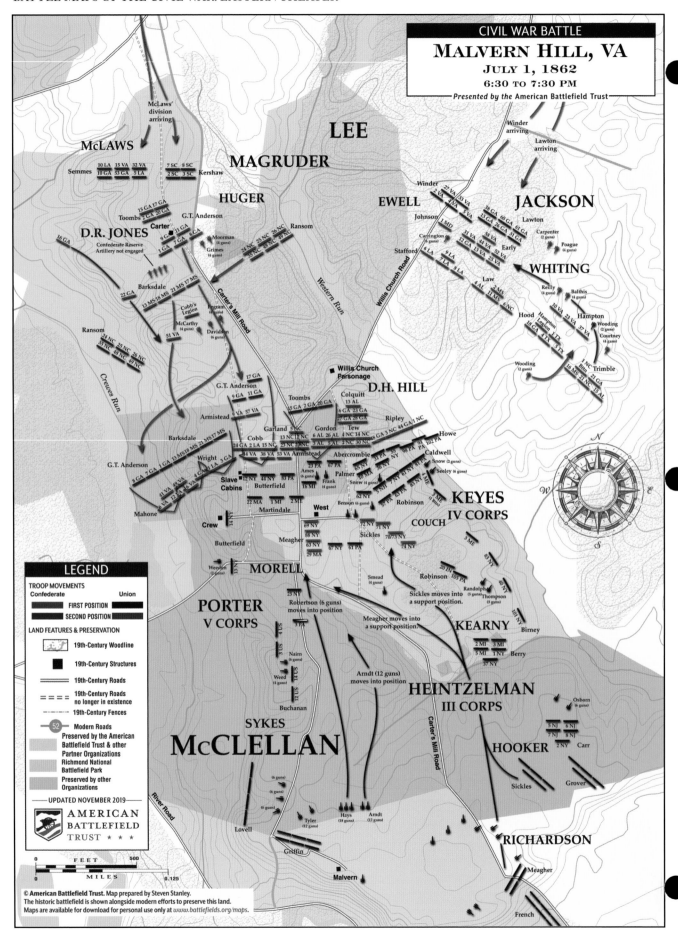

CIVIL WAR BATTLE
MALVERN HILL, VA
JULY 1, 1862
6:30 TO 7:30 PM
Presented by the American Battlefield Trust

LEGEND

TROOP MOVEMENTS

Confederate   Union

FIRST POSITION

SECOND POSITION

LAND FEATURES & PRESERVATION

19th-Century Woodline

19th-Century Structures

19th-Century Roads

19th-Century Roads no longer in existence

19th-Century Fences

52 Modern Roads

Preserved by the American Battlefield Trust & other Partner Organizations

Richmond National Battlefield Park

Preserved by other Organizations

UPDATED NOVEMBER 2019

AMERICAN BATTLEFIELD TRUST ★★★

FEET 500
MILES 0.125

© American Battlefield Trust. Map prepared by Steven Stanley.
The historic battlefield is shown alongside modern efforts to preserve this land.
Maps are available for download for personal use only at www.battlefields.org/maps.

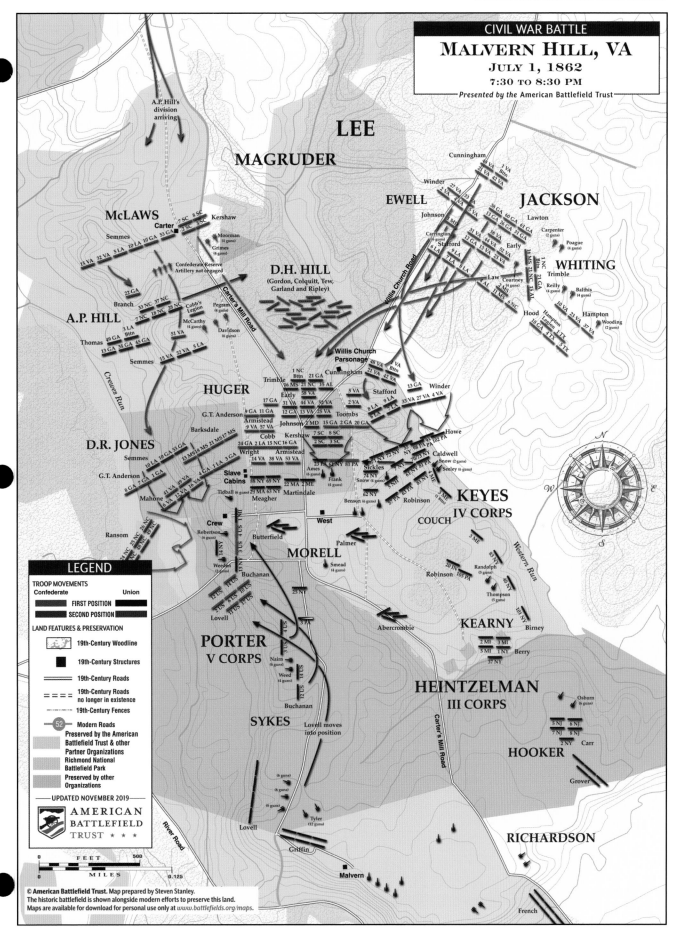

CIVIL WAR BATTLE

MALVERN HILL, VA

JULY 1, 1862
7:30 TO 8:30 PM

Presented by the American Battlefield Trust

LEE

MAGRUDER

A.P. Hill's division arriving

McLAWS

Carter
Kershaw
7 SC 8 SC
2 SC 3 SC

Semmes
Moorman (4 guns)
Grimes (4 guns)

15 VA 32 VA 5 LA 10 LA 10 GA 53 GA

Confederate Reserve Artillery not engaged

22 GA

D.H. HILL
(Gordon, Colquitt, Tew, Garland and Ripley)

Branch
33 NC 37 NC

A.P. HILL

7 NC 18 NC 28 NC
Cobb's Legion
Pegram (4 guns)
McCarthy (4 guns)
Davidson (6 guns)

Thomas 49 GA 3 LA Bttn
13 GA 35 GA 45 GA 51 VA

Semmes 15 VA 32 VA 5 LA

EWELL

JACKSON

Cunningham
44 VA 1 VA Bttn
21 VA 42 VA

Winder 27 VA 33 A
21 VA 33 A
Johnson
5 VA 38 GA 60 GA 61 GA
13 GA 26 GA 31 GA
Carrington (2 guns)
38 VA
6 LA 31 VA 44 VA 52 VA
Stafford 12 GA 13 VA 52 VA Early
9 LA
7 LA 8 LA

Lawton
Carpenter (2 guns)
Poague (4 guns)

WHITING

16 MS 1 NC Bttn
21 NC 21 GA
Trimble
Reilly (4 guns) Balthis (4 guns)
Law
Courtney (4 guns)
2 AL 4 AL
11 MS 6 NC
10 VA 23 VA Hampton
Hood Hampton Legion 1 TX
18 GA 4 TX 5 TX
Wooding (2 guns)

HUGER

Trimble 1 NC Bttn 21 GA Cunningham
16 MS 21 NC 15 AL
Early 58 VA
17 GA 31 VA 44 VA 52 VA
9 GA 11 GA
G.T. Anderson 12 GA 13 VA 25 VA Toombs
Armistead 9 VA 37 VA
Johnson 2 MD 15 GA 2 GA 20 GA
Barksdale Cobb Kershaw 7 SC 8 SC
24 GA 2 LA 15 NC 16 GA 2 SC 3 SC
Wright Armistead
14 VA 38 VA 53 VA
23 PA 61 NY 81 PA
Ames (6 guns)
Frank (4 guns)
Snow (2 guns)

45 VA VA Bttn
21 VA 42 VA
5 VA Stafford 13 GA Winder
8 LA 7 LA 33 VA 27 VA 4 VA
6 LA 2 VA
Howe

D.R. JONES

Semmes
10 LA GA 53 GA
33 MS 18 MS 21 MS17 MS
G.T. Anderson
4 GA 1 LA 3 GA
8 GA 7 GA 1 GA
Mahone
41 VA 49 VA
6 VA 12 VA 16 VA
Slave Cabins
Tidball (6 guns)
Ransom
24 NC 25 NC 26 NC
49 NC 35 NC

Sickles
74 NY
Snow (4 guns)
62 NY
71 NY 72 NY
70 NY 99 PA 102 PA
73 NY 5 NY
5 NY 74 NY 63 NY
Benson (6 guns)

KEYES
IV CORPS
Caldwell
Seeley (6 guns)
Howe
3 ME (6 guns)
Robinson
COUCH

88 NY 69 NY
29 MS 63 NY
22 MA 2 ME
Meagher Martindale

Crew
Robertson (6 guns)
Butterfield West
Weeden (3 guns) Buchanan
Palmer
MORELL
Smead (4 guns)
25 NY
Abercrombie
5 ME 3 ME
Randolph (5 guns)
20 IN
Robinson 105 PA
Thompson (5 guns)

KEARNY
2 MI 3 MI
5 MI 1 NY Berry
37 NY Birney
101 NY

LEGEND

TROOP MOVEMENTS
Confederate   Union
———— FIRST POSITION
———— SECOND POSITION

LAND FEATURES & PRESERVATION

🏞 19th-Century Woodline

■ 19th-Century Structures

≡ 19th-Century Roads

= = = 19th-Century Roads no longer in existence

——— 19th-Century Fences

52 Modern Roads

Preserved by the American Battlefield Trust & other Partner Organizations

Richmond National Battlefield Park

Preserved by other Organizations

— UPDATED NOVEMBER 2019 —

🛡 AMERICAN
BATTLEFIELD
TRUST ★ ★ ★

PORTER
V CORPS

Nairn (6 guns)
Weed (4 guns)
Buchanan

SYKES

Lovell moves into position

2 US 1 US
2 US 3 US 10 US
Lovell
4 US
5 US
1 US
4 US

(6 guns)
(6 guns)
(6 guns)
Tyler (12 guns)
Griffin
Lovell

HEINTZELMAN
III CORPS

Osborn (6 guns)

5 NJ 6 NJ
7 NJ 8 NJ
2 NY Carr

HOOKER

Grover

Malvern

RICHARDSON

French

BATTLE *of* CEDAR MOUNTAIN

AUGUST 9, 1862

ROBERT E. LEE FELT THAT RICHMOND WAS NEVER SAFER than when its defenders were not nearby. Meaning, when the enemy is not at the gates, the Confederate army does not need to be there either. With this idea in mind, and riding the wave of momentum created by the Seven Days Battles, Lee proposed to take the fight to the enemy. With McClellan's army bottled up at Harrison's Landing, Lee sent some 24,000 men northwest to the key rail junction of Gordonsville, Virginia. The move to Gordonsville would serve to test McClellan's intentions, open a new front that would relieve pressure on Richmond and counter President Abraham Lincoln's newly created Army of Virginia, now operating in northern Virginia.

Unlike McClellan, Lincoln was not sitting idly by awaiting the Confederates' next move. With the Federals compiling a stunning string of victories in the Western Theater, Lincoln sought to bring some of that good fortune to the East, in the form of Maj. Gen. John Pope. Pope had scored a recent western victory at Island Number 10. Thus, Lincoln tapped Pope to take over his new eastern army.

Once in the East, Pope set his sights on Gordonsville. By the second week of the month, Jackson knew that the three corps that comprised the "miscreant" Pope's army were nearing Culpeper, Virginia, just to the northeast of Gordonsville. The veteran Confederate commander planned to isolate the II Corps of the Army of Virginia and destroy it before Federal reinforcements could arrive.

In the sweltering August heat, Jackson's men trudged into Culpeper County, where the lead elements of his force—a brigade commanded by Brig. Gen. Jubal Early—made contact with the Federals near Cedar Run.

With the August temperatures soaring, the Confederates advanced their artillery to engage the Federal line. During the prolonged artillery duel, both Jackson and fellow Confederate Gen. Charles Winder participated in firing Confederate artillery pieces. Although it was called "the prettiest artillery duel ever witnessed during the war," it had significant consequences when Winder was mortally wounded by a shell.

Near 5:00 p.m, Federal corps commander Maj. Gen. Nathaniel P. Banks launched two attacks against the Confederate positions. One column of Federal troops moved against Confederate forces near the Cedars, while a second force advanced against the Rebel guns placed near the Crittenden Gate. At the crisis moment, Stonewall Jackson rode into the fray and attempted to draw his sword, which had rusted within its scabbard. Undaunted, Jackson waved a battle flag and his scabbard-encased sword over his head as he worked to rally his forces. Reinvigorated, the Confederates launched a counterattack that drove back the Union wave.

Meanwhile, on the Confederate left, soldiers collapsed the Federal right, as Richard Ewell's division drove back the left. By 7:00 p.m., the Union line was in full retreat.

The Battle at Cedar Mountain shifted the fighting in Virginia from the Peninsula to northern Virginia, solidifying Lee's strategic initiative for the remainder of the summer.

✳ ✽ PRESERVATION ✳ ✽

To date, the **American Battlefield Trust** has saved **498 acres** at Cedar Mountain Battlefield.

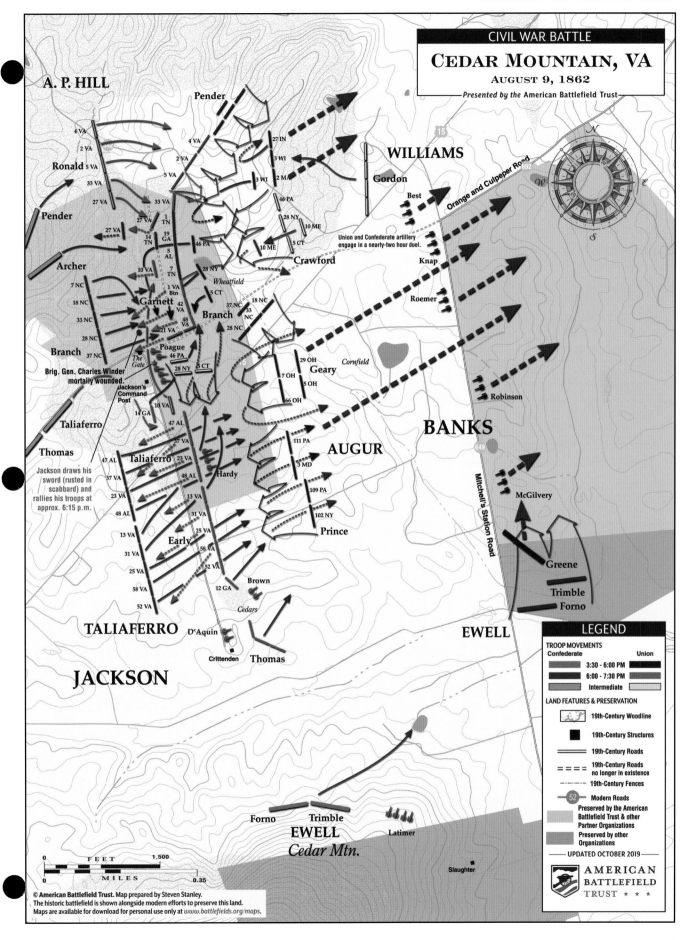

CIVIL WAR BATTLE

CEDAR MOUNTAIN, VA

AUGUST 9, 1862

Presented by the American Battlefield Trust

A. P. HILL

Pender

4 VA
2 VA

Ronald 5 VA

33 VA

27 VA

Pender

27 VA

Archer

7 NC

18 NC

33 NC

28 NC

Branch

37 NC

Branch

Brig. Gen. Charles Winder
mortally wounded.

Taliaferro

Thomas

Jackson draws his
sword (rusted in
scabbard) and
rallies his troops at
approx. 6:15 p.m.

4 VA

2 VA

5 VA

33 VA

27 VA

1 TN

14 TN

19 GA

5 AL

10 VA

7 TN

1 VA Btn

42 VA

48 VA

21 VA

Garnett

Poague
46 PA

The Gate

28 NY 5 CT

Jackson's
Command
Post

10 VA

14 GA

47 AL

37 VA

47 AL 23 VA

Taliaferro

37 VA

23 VA 48 AL

48 AL

13 VA

13 VA 31 VA

31 VA

25 VA

Early

25 VA 58 VA

58 VA 52 VA

52 VA

12 GA

Brown

Cedars

TALIAFERRO

D'Aquin

Crittenden

Thomas

JACKSON

27 IN

3 WI

3 WI 2 MA

46 PA

28 NY

10 ME

10 ME

5 CT

Crawford

Wheatfield

28 NY

5 CT

37 NC

33 NC

18 NC

28 NC

Branch

Hardy

WILLIAMS

Gordon

Best

Union and Confederate artillery
engage in a nearly-two hour duel.

Knap

Roemer

29 OH

7 OH

5 OH

66 OH

Geary

Cornfield

111 PA

3 MD

AUGUR

109 PA

102 NY

Prince

Robinson

BANKS

Orange and Culpeper Road

McGilvery

Greene

Trimble
Forno

EWELL

Forno   Trimble

EWELL

Cedar Mtn.

Latimer

Slaughter

LEGEND

TROOP MOVEMENTS

Confederate		Union
	3:30 - 6:00 PM	
	6:00 - 7:30 PM	
	Intermediate	

LAND FEATURES & PRESERVATION

- 19th-Century Woodline
- 19th-Century Structures
- 19th-Century Roads
- 19th-Century Roads no longer in existence
- 19th-Century Fences
- 52 Modern Roads
- Preserved by the American Battlefield Trust & other Partner Organizations
- Preserved by other Organizations

— UPDATED OCTOBER 2019 —

AMERICAN BATTLEFIELD TRUST ★ ★ ★

FEET   1,500
0
MILES   0.35

SECOND BATTLE *of* MANASSAS
(SECOND BULL RUN)

AUGUST 28-30, 1862

TAKING ADVANTAGE OF MCCLELLAN'S INACTIVITY **NEAR RICHMOND**, Lee attempted to follow up on what Jackson had started at Cedar Mountain. After shifting the bulk of his army to the Rappahannock River, above Culpeper, Lee unleashed Jackson and Confederate cavalry leader Maj. Gen. Jeb Stuart on a sweeping march around Pope's flank, to cut the Federals' communication line with Washington. This move would force Pope away from the Rappahannock River line and closer to Washington. Lee and his second-in-command, James Longstreet, would then trail Jackson by one day.

Initially misinterpreting Confederate intentions, Pope ignored first Jackson's and then Longstreet's movements, until word reached the Federal commander that Jackson and Stuart were threatening his rear. Pope countered the Rebel movements, and he had the opportunity to destroy Lee's army in detail. It was not to be.

Jackson took up a strong position on the old Manassas (Bull Run) Battlefield of 1861, north of the hill where he had received his nom de guerre, and inside an unfinished railroad bed. On August 28, Pope and Jackson clashed at Groveton (Brawner's Farm).

Believing that Jackson was attempting to escape, Pope directed his scattered forces to converge on the Confederate position. With reinforcements trickling in from McClellan's Army of the Potomac, Pope launched a series of fierce, but largely piecemeal attacks on Jackson's line throughout August 29. Although the Union assaults pierced Jackson's line on several occasions, the attackers were repulsed each time. Late in the morning, Lee arrived on the field with Longstreet's command, taking a position on Jackson's right. Also arriving in the vicinity of Longstreet's Wing were the veteran soldiers of the Union V Corps, commanded by George McClellan's most trusted subordinate Fitz John Porter.

Anxious to get Porter's men into the fight, Pope ordered a flanking movement by the Army of the Potomac's most seasoned corps commander. Porter would hit Jackson's right while part of Pope's Army of Virginia and elements of McClellan's army would hit Jackson's left and center. A series of communication errors and poor coordination on the Federal side played into the Confederates' hands, as Pope and his subordinates couldn't get out of their own way to launch an assault.

The next day, convinced that the Confederates were retreating, the Union commander ordered a pursuit near midday, but the advance quickly ended when skirmishers encountered Jackson's forces still ensconced behind the unfinished railroad. Pope's plans now shifted to a major assault on Jackson's line. However, with ample artillery support, the Confederate defenders repulsed the attack.

Lee and Longstreet seized the initiative and launched a massive counterattack against the Union left. Longstreet's wing, nearly 30,000 strong, swept eastward toward Henry Hill, where the Confederates hoped to cut off Pope's escape. Union forces mounted a tenacious defense on Chinn Ridge that bought time for Pope to shift enough troops onto Henry Hill and stave off disaster. After dark, Pope pulled his beaten army off the field and across Bull Run.

With Union forces in full retreat, Lee ordered Jackson to make another wide-sweeping march to cut off the retreating foe. The race toward Washington was on in earnest.

✳ ✳ **PRESERVATION** ✳ ✳

To date, the **American Battlefield Trust** has saved **373 acres** at Manassas Battlefield.

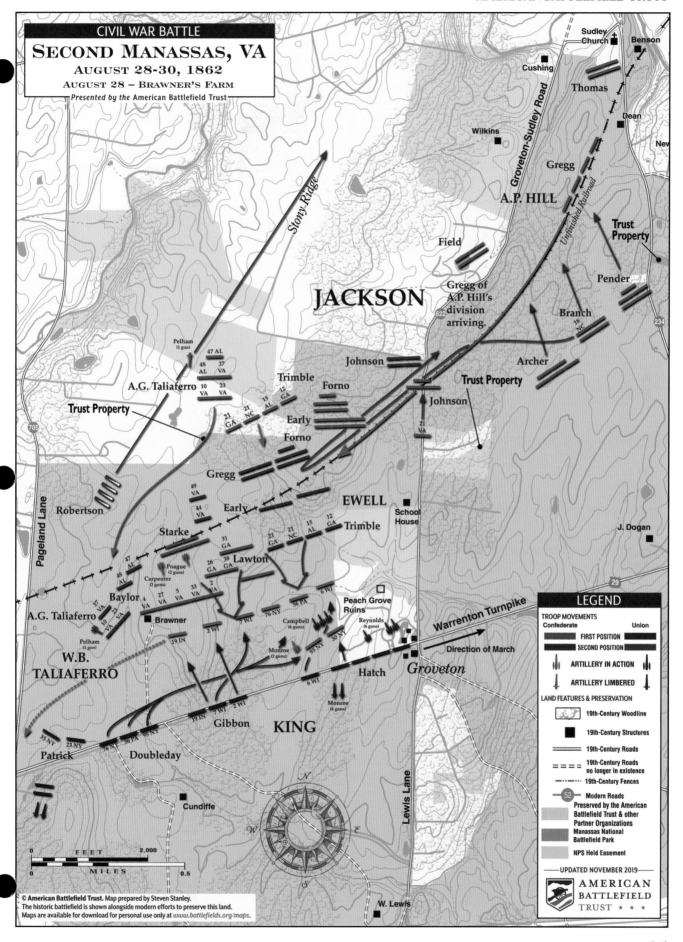

CIVIL WAR BATTLE
SECOND MANASSAS, VA
AUGUST 28-30, 1862
AUGUST 28 – BRAWNER'S FARM
Presented by the American Battlefield Trust

JACKSON

Stony Ridge

Groveton-Sudley Road

Unfinished Railroad

Sudley Church

Benson

Cushing

Thomas

Wilkins

Dean

New

A.P. HILL

Gregg

Field

Trust Property

Pender

Gregg of A.P. Hill's division arriving.

Branch

Archer

18 NC

Pelham (1 gun)

47 AL

48 AL   37 VA

10 VA   23 VA

A.G. Taliaferro

Trimble

12 GA

15 AL

Forno

Johnson

Trust Property

Johnson

21 VA

Trust Property

21 GA   21 NC

Early

Forno

Gregg

49 VA

44 VA

Early

EWELL

21 GA   21 NC   15 GA   12 GA

School House

J. Dogan

Robertson

Starke

31 GA

26 GA   38 GA   Lawton

2

21 GA   21 NC

Trimble

29

Poague (2 guns)

Carpenter (2 guns)

5   33 VA

27 VA

7 WI   76 NY

56 PA

Peach Grove Ruins

Reynolds (6 guns)

Warrenton Turnpike

LEGEND

47 AL

48 AL

Baylor

4

2

Brawner

Campbell (6 guns)

95 NY   30 NY

Hatch

Groveton

Direction of March

37 VA   23 VA

10 VA   23 VA

A.G. Taliaferro

Pelham (1 gun)

19 IN

2 WI

7 WI   2 WI

Monroe (2 guns)

95 NY

6 WI

Monroe (4 guns)

Lewis Lane

W.B. TALIAFERRO

95 NY   23 NY

Patrick

76 NY   56 PA   95 NY

Doubleday

19 IN   7 WI   2 WI

Gibbon

KING

Cundiffe

W. Lewis

Pageland Lane

705

234

622

TROOP MOVEMENTS
Confederate   Union
▬▬▬ FIRST POSITION
▬▬▬ SECOND POSITION
ARTILLERY IN ACTION
ARTILLERY LIMBERED

LAND FEATURES & PRESERVATION
19th-Century Woodline
■ 19th-Century Structures
═══ 19th-Century Roads
= = = 19th-Century Roads no longer in existence
—··— 19th-Century Fences
52 Modern Roads
Preserved by the American Battlefield Trust & other Partner Organizations
Manassas National Battlefield Park
NPS Held Easement

UPDATED NOVEMBER 2019

AMERICAN BATTLEFIELD TRUST ★ ★ ★

FEET   2,000
0
MILES   0.5

N   S   E   W

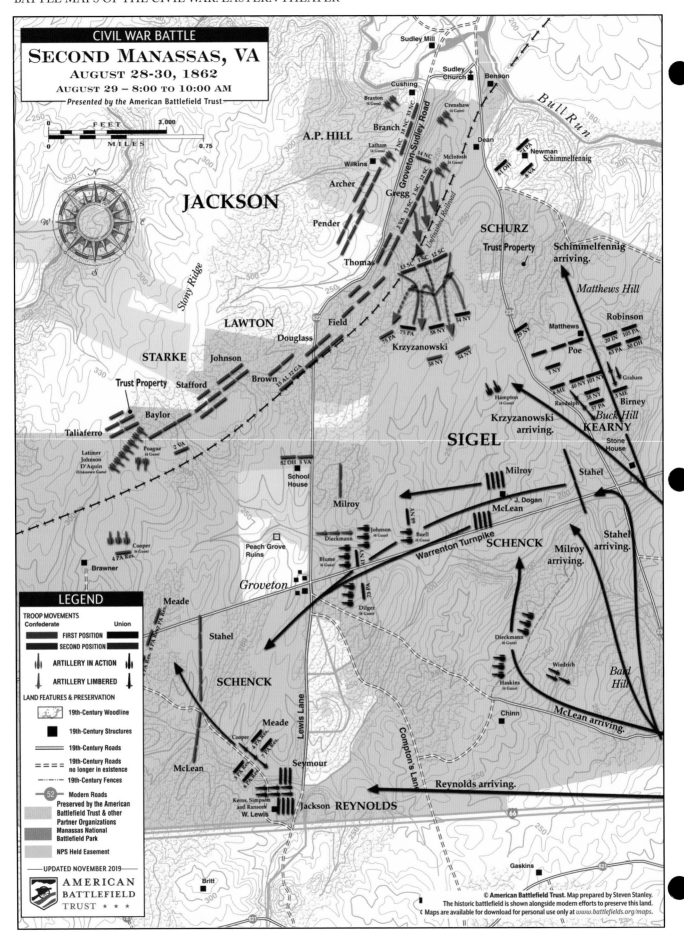

CIVIL WAR BATTLE
SECOND MANASSAS, VA
AUGUST 28-30, 1862
AUGUST 29 – 8:00 TO 10:00 AM
—Presented by the American Battlefield Trust—

FEET 3,000
MILES 0.75

JACKSON

A.P. HILL

Sudley Mill

Sudley Church

Benson

Braxton (4 Guns)

Cushing

Crenshaw (4 Guns)

Branch

18 NC 33 NC

7 NC

14 NC

Dean

73 PA
Newman
Schimmelfennig
61 OH
8 VA

Latham (4 Guns)

Wilkins

McIntosh (4 Guns)

Archer

Gregg

1 SC 12 SC

Pender

2 VA 13 SC 13 SC

SCHURZ

Trust Property

Schimmelfennig arriving.

Matthews Hill

Thomas

13 SC 1 SC 12 SC

LAWTON

Field

Robinson

Matthews

20 IN 105 PA

Poe

63 PA 30 OH

622

Douglass

75 PA 75 PA 58 NY 54 NY

1 NY

Krzyzanowski

STARKE

Johnson

58 NY 54 NY

4 ME 40 NY 101 NY

38 NY 3 ME

Graham

Brown

13 AL 12 GA

Hampton (4 Guns)

Randolph

57 PA

Birney

Trust Property

Stafford

Krzyzanowski arriving.

Buck Hill

Baylor

KEARNY

Taliaferro

Stone House

SIGEL

Latimer
Johnson
D'Aquin
(Unknown Guns)

Poague (4 Guns)

2 VA

Milroy

J. Dogan

Stahel

82 OH 5 VA

McLean

School House

Milroy

68 NY

Stahel arriving.

Cooper (6 Guns)

Johnson (6 Guns)

Buell (6 Guns)

Milroy arriving.

4 PA Res.

Dieckmann

41 NY

SCHENCK

Brawner

Peach Grove Ruins

Blume (6 Guns)

Warrenton Turnpike

Groveton

73 PA

Dieckmann (6 Guns)

Dilger (6 Guns)

Meade

Wiedrich

Bald Hill

Stahel

Haskins (6 Guns)

SCHENCK

Chinn

McLean arriving.

Meade

Lewis Lane

Cooper

4 PA Res.

McLean

7 PA Res.

Seymour

3 PA Res.

8 PA Res.

Kerns, Simpson and Ransom
W. Lewis

Jackson **REYNOLDS**

Reynolds arriving.

66

Britt

Gaskins

LEGEND
TROOP MOVEMENTS
Confederate / Union
- FIRST POSITION
- SECOND POSITION
- ARTILLERY IN ACTION
- ARTILLERY LIMBERED

LAND FEATURES & PRESERVATION
- 19th-Century Woodline
- 19th-Century Structures
- 19th-Century Roads
- 19th-Century Roads no longer in existence
- 19th-Century Fences
- 52 Modern Roads
- Preserved by the American Battlefield Trust & other Partner Organizations
- Manassas National Battlefield Park
- NPS Held Easement

— UPDATED NOVEMBER 2019 —

AMERICAN BATTLEFIELD TRUST ★ ★ ★

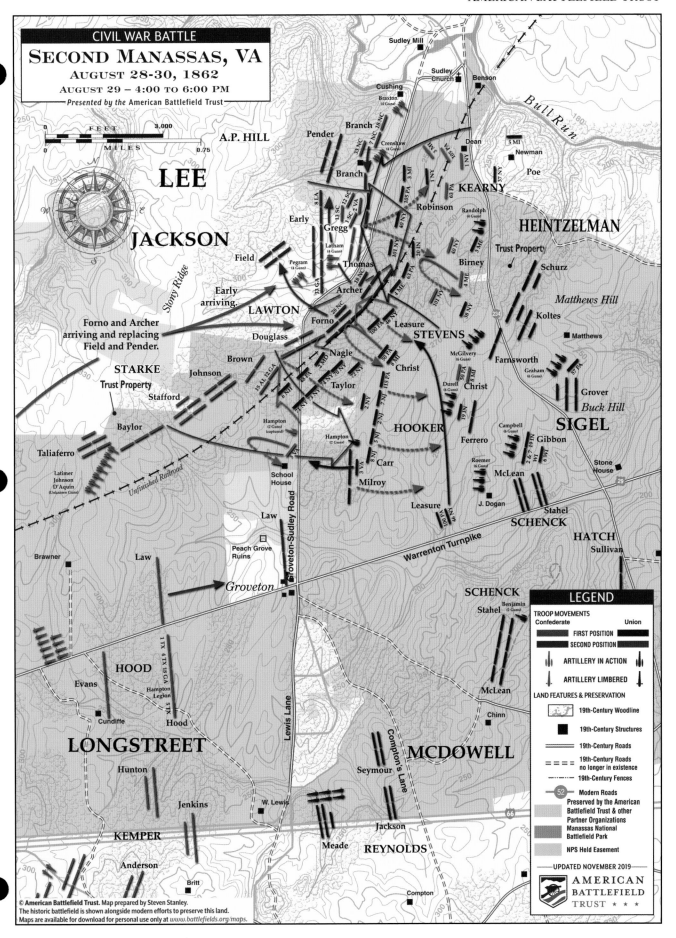

CIVIL WAR BATTLE

SECOND MANASSAS, VA

AUGUST 28-30, 1862

AUGUST 29 – 4:00 TO 6:00 PM

Presented by the American Battlefield Trust

FEET 3,000

MILES 0.75

A.P. HILL

LEE

JACKSON

Stony Ridge

Early arriving.

Forno and Archer arriving and replacing Field and Pender.

LAWTON

STARKE
Trust Property

Taliaferro

Latimer
Johnson
D'Aquin
(Unknown Guns)

Unfinished Railroad

Brawner

Law

LONGSTREET

HOOD

Evans

Cundiffe

Hood

Hunton

Jenkins

KEMPER

Anderson

Britt

Pender
Branch
Early
Gregg
Latham
(4 Guns)
Field
Pegram
(4 Guns)
Thomas
Archer
Forno
Douglass
Brown
Johnson
Nagle
Taylor
Stafford
Baylor
Hampton
(2 Guns)
(captured)
Hampton
(2 Guns)
School
House
Law
Peach Grove
Ruins
Groveton
Lewis Lane
W. Lewis

Cushing
Branch
Crenshaw
(4 Guns)
Robinson
Thomas
Leasure
Christ
Carr
Milroy
Leasure

STEVENS
HOOKER

Seymour

Meade

Compton's Lane

REYNOLDS

MCDOWELL

Jackson

Compton

Braxton
(4 Guns)
Dean
Newman
Poe

KEARNY

Birney

Randolph
(4 Guns)

HEINTZELMAN

Schurz
Koltes
Matthews

Matthews Hill

Trust Property

McGilvery
(6 Guns)
Farnsworth
Graham
(6 Guns)
Durell
(6 Guns)
Christ
Ferrero
Campbell
(6 Guns)
Roemer
(6 Guns)
McLean
J. Dogan

Grover
Buck Hill

SIGEL

Gibbon

Stone
House

Stahel
SCHENCK

HATCH
Sullivan

SCHENCK
Stahel
Benjamin
(2 Guns)

McLean

Chinn

Warrenton Turnpike

Sudley Mill

Sudley
Church
Benson

Bull Run

LEGEND

TROOP MOVEMENTS
Confederate   Union

FIRST POSITION

SECOND POSITION

ARTILLERY IN ACTION

ARTILLERY LIMBERED

LAND FEATURES & PRESERVATION

19th-Century Woodline

19th-Century Structures

19th-Century Roads

19th-Century Roads
no longer in existence

19th-Century Fences

52   Modern Roads
Preserved by the American
Battlefield Trust & other
Partner Organizations
Manassas National
Battlefield Park
NPS Held Easement

UPDATED NOVEMBER 2019

AMERICAN
BATTLEFIELD
TRUST ★ ★ ★

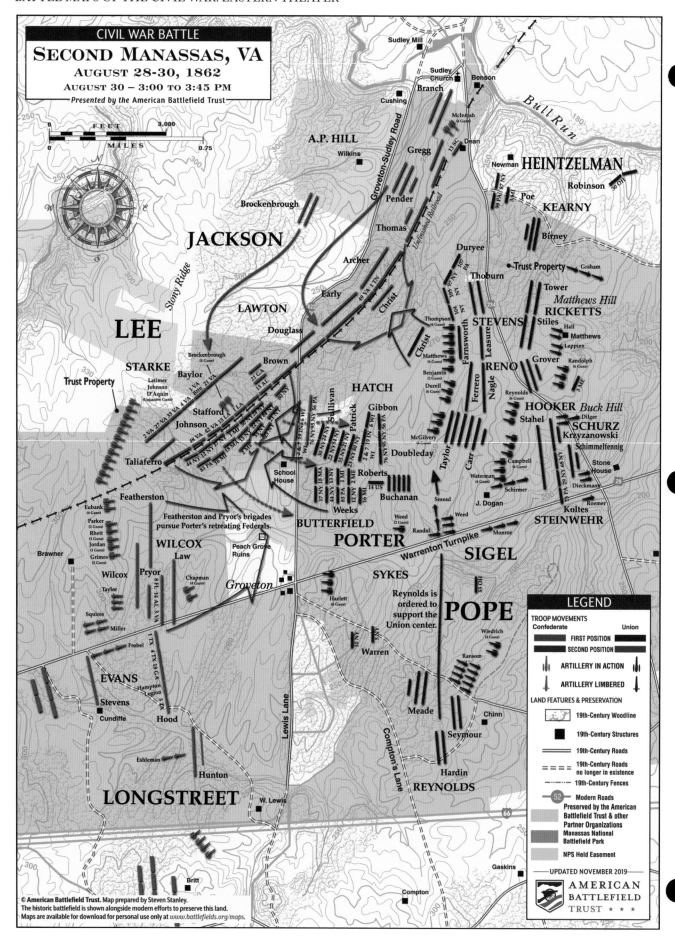

CIVIL WAR BATTLE
SECOND MANASSAS, VA
AUGUST 28-30, 1862
AUGUST 30 – 3:00 TO 3:45 PM
Presented by the American Battlefield Trust

FEET 3,000
MILES 0.75

Featherston and Pryor's brigades pursue Porter's retreating Federals.

Reynolds is ordered to support the Union center.

LEGEND
TROOP MOVEMENTS

Confederate		Union
	FIRST POSITION	
	SECOND POSITION	
	ARTILLERY IN ACTION	
	ARTILLERY LIMBERED	

LAND FEATURES & PRESERVATION

- 19th-Century Woodline
- 19th-Century Structures
- 19th-Century Roads
- 19th-Century Roads no longer in existence
- 19th-Century Fences
- 52 Modern Roads
- Preserved by the American Battlefield Trust & other Partner Organizations
- Manassas National Battlefield Park
- NPS Held Easement

UPDATED NOVEMBER 2019

AMERICAN BATTLEFIELD TRUST ★★★

© American Battlefield Trust. Map prepared by Steven Stanley.
The historic battlefield is shown alongside modern efforts to preserve this land.
Maps are available for download for personal use only at www.battlefields.org/maps.

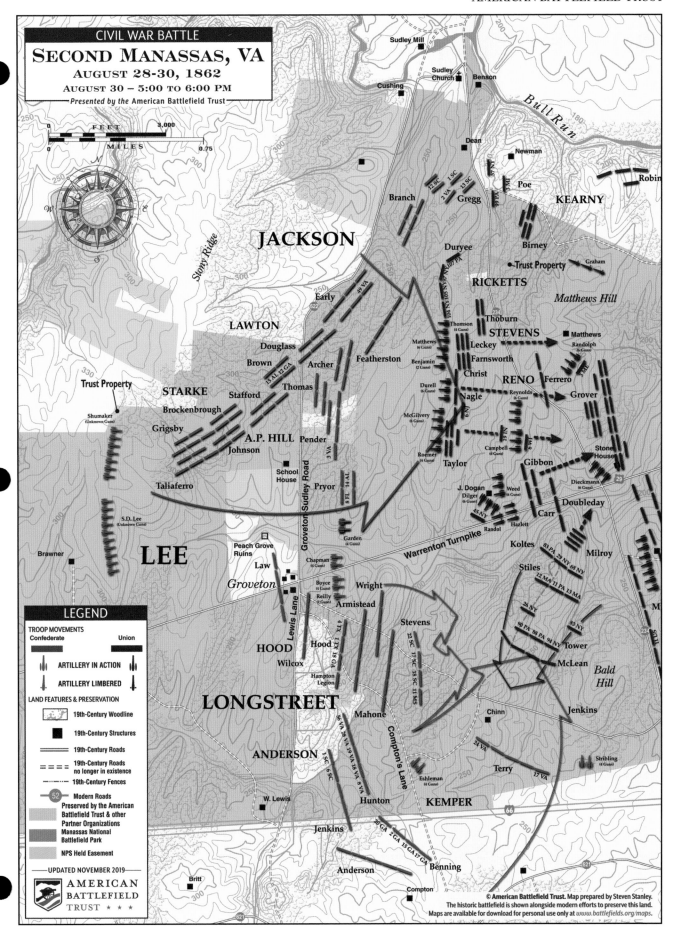

CIVIL WAR BATTLE

SECOND MANASSAS, VA

AUGUST 28-30, 1862

AUGUST 30 – 5:00 TO 6:00 PM

Presented by the American Battlefield Trust

FEET 3,000
MILES 0.75

LEGEND

TROOP MOVEMENTS
Confederate   Union

ARTILLERY IN ACTION
ARTILLERY LIMBERED

LAND FEATURES & PRESERVATION
19th-Century Woodline
19th-Century Structures
19th-Century Roads
19th-Century Roads no longer in existence
19th-Century Fences
52 Modern Roads
Preserved by the American Battlefield Trust & other Partner Organizations
Manassas National Battlefield Park
NPS Held Easement

— UPDATED NOVEMBER 2019 —

AMERICAN BATTLEFIELD TRUST ★ ★ ★

© American Battlefield Trust. Map prepared by Steven Stanley.
The historic battlefield is shown alongside modern efforts to preserve this land.
Maps are available for download for personal use only at www.battlefields.org/maps.

29

BATTLE *of* CHANTILLY
(BATTLE OF OX HILL)

SEPTEMBER 1, 1862

IT HAD BEEN A STUNNING TURN OF EVENTS THAT carried the Confederate Army of Northern Virginia from the outskirts of their capital at the end of June to Fairfax County, Virginia, near Washinton DC, in late August. Robert E. Lee's army strung together an impressive array of battle honors from the Seven Days Battles to Second Manassas. In the wake of the latter battlefield victory, Lee looked to land the killing blow on Maj. Gen. John Pope and the combined forces of the Federal Army of Virginia, and Army of the Potomac, as they withdrew toward the defenses of Washington. Once again, Lee ordered Stonewall Jackson to take his wing of the army and execute a sweeping movement around the Federal right. The Confederate commander hoped to cut off Pope's retreating army as they made their way to Jermantown (Germantown), where the two roads leading Pope's army to Washington converged.

By the early afternoon of September 1, Pope was aware of Jackson's threat to his flank and line of retreat. After dispatching a force under the command of Joseph Hooker to secure Jermantown, Pope ordered the IX Corps division of Brig. Gen. Issac Stevens to advance west along the Little River Turnpike to establish a forward defensive position. Stevens troops were supported by more IX men commanded by Maj. Gen. Jesse Reno, and III Corps troops commanded by Phil Kearny.

Stonewall Jackson, who had allowed his men to rest after the taxing marches of August, and the pitched battle of Second Manassas, received reports of Federals in his immediate vicinity. Near 4 p.m., Jackson dispatched a reconnaissance force to ascertain the enemy's strength and intentions, while also establishing a line of battle.

In the meantime, General Stevens deployed his Federals into a line of battle. Pressing two companies of his old regiment, the 79th New York Highlanders, forward as skirmishers, Stevens arrayed the remainder of his division and one brigade from Reno's division into a battleline. Amid a rainstorm, and in an attempt to clear the Little River Turnpike of Confederates, Stevens ordered his units forward. The Federals marched into the jaws of elements of three Confederate divisions. With his assault foundering, Stevens seized the flag of the 79th New York and urged the men forward. As he leaped over a fence, a Confederate bullet struck Stevens in the head, killing him instantly. Enraged, the Federals surged forward, breaching the Confederate position. The Union breakthrough was shortlived.

A lull in the fighting came across the field, as the rainstorm turned into a severe thunderstorm. Jackson took the time to reinforce and redeploy his men. This was a prudent decision on Jackson's part, as more Federals were marching toward his position.

Phil Kearny's III Corps division started in support of Stevens before the latter's death. Kearny's men engaged with Jackson's right flank. Outnumbered, Kearny rode off in search of support, but none was close at hand. Riding to the front, the one-armed Kearny found himself in the midst of a thunderstorm, and face-to-face with Col. Edward Thomas' Georgia brigade. Kearny wheeled his horse around as the Confederates called for his surrender. Shots rang out and Kearny was felled by a Rebel bullet that entered his hip and exited out of his shoulder. The general was dead before he hit the ground.

With two leaders killed in action, and a severe thunderstorm raging, the Battle of Chantilly came to an end. With Union forces in disarray, Lee grasped the opportunity to lead his army across the Potomac into Maryland for its first incursion into the North.

❋ ❋ PRESERVATION ❋ ❋

The loss of the Chantilly Battlefield was the catalyst for the modern battlefield preservation movement.

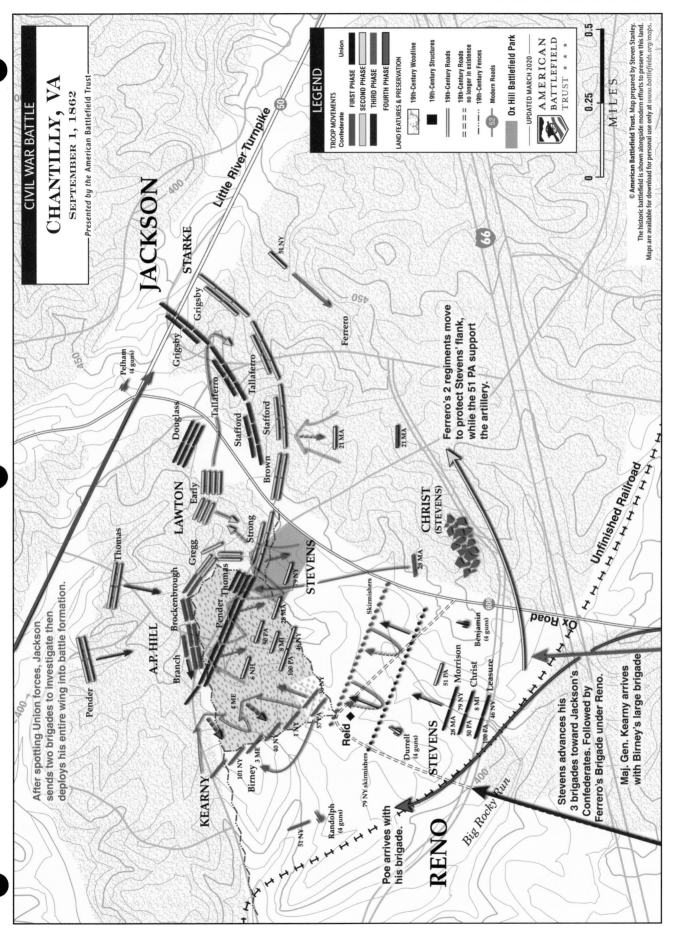

CIVIL WAR BATTLE

CHANTILLY, VA
SEPTEMBER 1, 1862

Presented by the American Battlefield Trust

JACKSON

STARKE

Little River Turnpike

50

400

450

450

Pelham (4 guns)

Grigsby

Grigsby

Douglass

Tallaferro

Tallaferro

Stafford

Stafford

Brown

Tallaferro

51 NY

Ferrero

21 MA

21 MA

LAWTON

Early

Thomas

Strong

Gregg

A.P. HILL

Brockenbrough

Pender

Thomas

Branch

79 NY

28 MA

50 PA

8 MI

100 PA

46 NY

6 NH

4 ME

STEVENS

CHRIST (STEVENS)

28 MA

Skirmishers

608

Morrison

Christ

Leasure

Benjamin (4 guns)

51 PA

79 NY

8 MI

46 NY

28 MA

50 PA

100 PA

KEARNY

101 NY

Birney

3 ME

40 NY

1 NY

57 PA

38 NY

Reid

Durrell (4 guns)

79 NY skirmishers

STEVENS

Pender

Thomas

Randolph (4 guns)

51 NY

RENO

Big Rocky Run

400

Ox Road

66

608

Unfinished Railroad

After spotting Union forces, Jackson sends two brigades to investigate then deploys his entire wing into battle formation.

Ferrero's 2 regiments move to protect Stevens' flank, while the 51 PA support the artillery.

Stevens advances his 3 brigades toward Jackson's Confederates. Followed by Ferrero's Brigade under Reno.

Maj. Gen. Kearny arrives with Birney's large brigade

Poe arrives with his brigade.

SIEGE *of* HARPERS FERRY

SEPTEMBER 12-15, 1862

SITUATED AT THE CONFLUENCE OF THE SHENANDOAH AND Potomac Rivers, Harpers Ferry, Virginia (today West Virginia), was already well known to most Americans by the fall of 1862. In October of 1859, the radical abolitionist John Brown had attempted to incite a slave rebellion in the area, and arm the newly freed slaves of his "army" with weapons procured at the Federal arsenal located in the town. The uprising was put down by the United States Marines, led by an army colonel named Robert E. Lee.

Harpers Ferry was captured in 1861, this time by Confederates. Union troops would later reoccupy the town.

Following the victory at Second Manassas, Lee carried his army across the Potomac River on September 3, and as he had done in the two previous campaigns, the now-veteran army commander split his forces. Lee outlined the details of the campaign for his key subordinates in his now-infamous Special Orders Number 191, later discovered by Federal soldiers outside Frederick, Maryland.

If the Army of Northern Virginia were to operate in this part of Maryland and Virginia, or if it were to march on Washington, DC, the more than 12,000–man Federal garrison at Harpers Ferry would have to be dealt with.

Thus, Lee dispatched three columns under Gen. Thomas "Stonewall" Jackson to Harpers Ferry, with the task of subduing the key river town and its garrison. In the meantime, the rest of the army marched toward Hagerstown, Maryland. Surrounded on three sides by steep heights, the terrain at Harpers Ferry made it nearly impossible to defend, a problem made worse by the Union commander, Col. Dixon S. Miles, who lacked experience leading troops in the field.

The defense of Harpers Ferry relied on holding Bolivar Heights, Maryland Heights and the 1,200-foot Loudoun Heights. Disregarding the advice of his subordinates, Miles divided his troops into four brigades, with the main force tasked with defending Bolivar Heights, a ridge two miles west of town on the southern bank of the Potomac River. Miles posted a lone brigade atop Maryland Heights. While he posted troops on Bolivar and Maryland Heights, he ignored Loudoun Heights, convinced that the oncoming Confederates would be unwilling or unable to secure artillery on the steep rise. On the highly strategic Maryland Heights, Miles deployed his weakest brigade, comprised of green soldiers.

Jackson's men easily ran the Federals off the key terrain. For three days, his troops placed artillery on the heights looking down on Harpers Ferry, and on the morning of September 15, Jackson ordered an artillery barrage that bombarded the small yet strategic town, followed by an infantry assault spearheaded by A. P. Hill's "Light Division."

Miles, believing the situation hopeless, decided to surrender the garrison and its more than 12,000 men, which proved to be the largest surrender of United States troops until the Second World War.

With Harpers Ferry now secure, Lee could give battle north of the Potomac River.

✳ ✳ PRESERVATION ✳ ✳

To date, the **American Battlefield Trust** has saved **542 acres** at Harpers Ferry Battlefield.

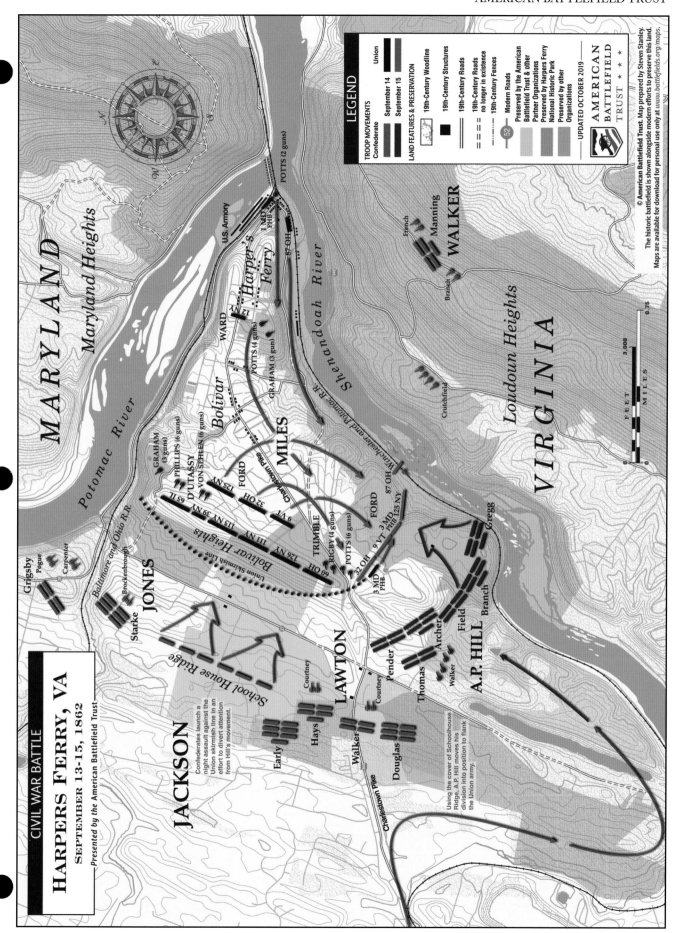

CIVIL WAR BATTLE

HARPERS FERRY, VA

SEPTEMBER 13-15, 1862

Presented by the American Battlefield Trust

MARYLAND

Maryland Heights

Potomac River

VIRGINIA

Loudoun Heights

Shenandoah River

Baltimore and Ohio R.R.

Winchester and Potomac R.R.

US. Armory

Harper's Ferry

POTTS (2 guns)

1 MD PHB

87 OH

WARD

12 NY

POTTS (4 guns)

GRAHAM (3 gun)

Bolivar

MILES

GRAHAM (3 guns)

PHILLIPS (6 guns)

VON SEHLEN (6 guns)

D'UTASSY

65 IL

32 OH

9 VT

125 NY

FORD

115 NY

39 NY

111 NY

126 NY

Bolivar Heights

Charlestown Pike

FORD

87 OH

125 NY

3 MD PHB

9 VT

3 MD PHB

TRIMBLE

RIGBY (4 guns)

POTTS (6 guns)

32 OH

60 OH

Union Skirmish Line

Gregg

Branch

Field

A.P. HILL

Archer

Pender

Thomas

Walker

Grigsby

Pogue

Carpenter

Starke

Brockenbrough

JONES

School House Ridge

JACKSON

Early

Hays

Courtney

Courtney

Walker

Douglas

LAWTON

French

Manning

Branch

WALKER

Crutchfield

Confederates launch a night assault against the Union skirmish line in an effort to divert attention from Hill's movement.

Using the cover of Schoolhouse Ridge, A.P. Hill moves his division into position to flank the Union army.

LEGEND

TROOP MOVEMENTS

Confederate	Union
September 14	
September 15	

LAND FEATURES & PRESERVATION

19th-Century Woodline

19th-Century Structures

19th-Century Roads

19th-Century Roads no longer in existence

19th-Century Fences

52 — Modern Roads

Preserved by the American Battlefield Trust & other Partner Organizations

Preserved by Harpers Ferry National Historic Park

Preserved by other Organizations

— UPDATED OCTOBER 2019 —

AMERICAN BATTLEFIELD TRUST ★ ★ ★

FEET   3,000

MILES   0.75

© American Battlefield Trust. Map prepared by Steven Stanley. The historic battlefield is shown alongside modern efforts to preserve this land. Maps are available for download for personal use only at *www.battlefields.org/maps*.

33

BATTLE *of* SOUTH MOUNTAIN
(CRAMPTON'S, TURNER'S AND FOX'S GAP)

SEPTEMBER 14, 1862

WITH JACKSON WORKING ON THE INVESTMENT OF Harpers Ferry, a new situation began to unfold to the east.

Following the defeat of John Pope at Second Manassas, a reluctant President Lincoln was forced to turn back to George B. McClellan and place him in charge of the Federal armies around Washington. Surprisingly, McClellan worked quickly to reorganize the mass of soldiers in and around Washington. From the capital, McClellan struck out with some 85,000 soldiers in search of Lee's army. Fortune smiled on the Federals when three men of the 27th Indiana found Lee's Special Orders No. 191 outside Frederick, Maryland.

Moving with uncharacteristic speed until the point of contact with the enemy, Little Mac drove west toward the South Mountain chain and Pleasant Valley beyond. To gain access to Pleasant Valley, as well as to relieve the pressure on Harpers Ferry, McClellan had to secure the gaps of the South Mountain range. From south to north, they were Crampton's, Fox's and Turner's Gaps.

Only an undersize Confederate force commanded by D. H. Hill protected Turner's and Fox's Gaps. Early on September 14, Brig. Gen. Jacob D. Cox's division of the Union IX Corps launched an attack against Brig. Gen. Samuel Garland's Tarheel brigade at Fox's Gap. Cox's Ohioans overran Garland's North Carolinians, driving the Southerners from behind a stone wall and mortally wounding Garland. With Fox's Gap now clear, Cox awaited reinforcements to further his gains.

While Union and Confederate commanders funneled troops into Fox's and Turner's Gaps, excessive caution plagued Maj. Gen. William B. Franklin's Federal VI Corps on its way to relieve the besieged garrison at Harpers Ferry. Roughly 1,000 Confederates held Crampton's Gap, yet Franklin was convinced the Rebels were a strong enough force to delay the advance of his 12,000-man corps. Around 4 p.m., some Federal commanders tired of waiting and launched an assault that dislodged the Confederates and secured the gap.

Meanwhile, at Turner's Gap, Hooker's corps had arrived on the field, and Burnside launched a coordinated assault. Union divisions made a relentless charge on the northern end of Turner's Gap. After a brutal firefight along a cornfield fence, Federals broke through the Rebel line, but darkness prevented the capture of Turner's Gap.

Back at Fox's Gap, the IX Corps mounted a separate effort to seize control of Turner's Gap but ran into stiff resistance from the Confederate divisions of John B. Hood and D. H. Hill. Casualties mounted, among them IX Corps commander Jesse Reno, who was shot down in almost the same spot as Samuel Garland had been that morning.

Though Lee, Longstreet and D. H. Hill agreed to abandon South Mountain before daylight on September 15, the bloody, daylong struggle bought the Confederate army valuable time to consolidate its position—and ready itself for the coming battle along Antietam Creek. McClellan had lost his best chance of destroying Lee's army in detail.

✳ ✳ **PRESERVATION** ✳ ✳

To date, the **American Battlefield Trust** has saved **704 acres** at South Mountain Battlefield.

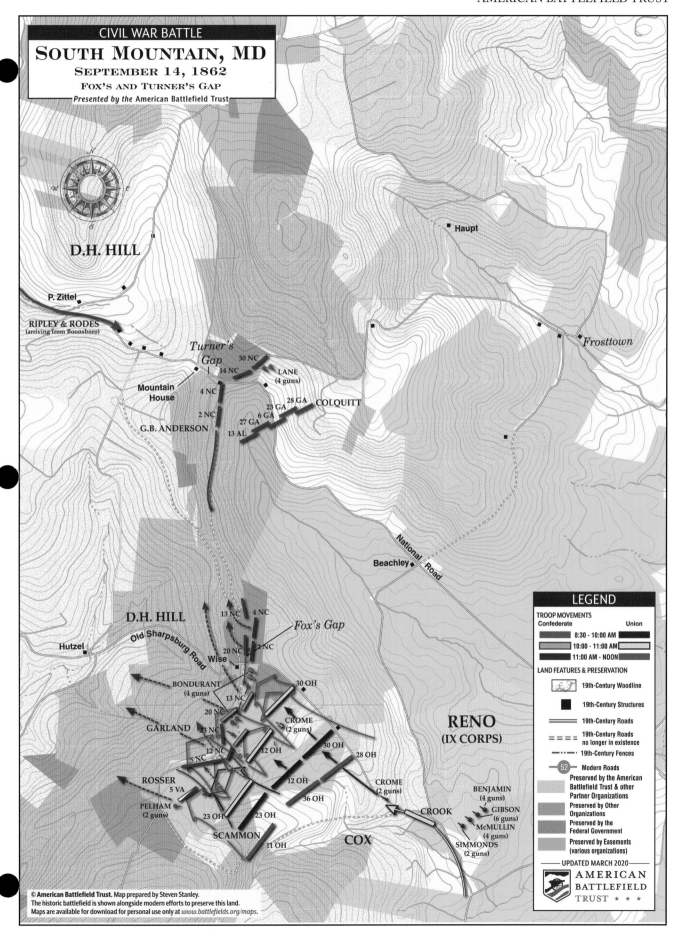

CIVIL WAR BATTLE

SOUTH MOUNTAIN, MD

SEPTEMBER 14, 1862

FOX'S AND TURNER'S GAP

Presented by the American Battlefield Trust

D.H. HILL

P. Zittel

RIPLEY & RODES
(arriving from Boonsboro)

Haupt

Frosttown

Turner's Gap

30 NC
14 NC
LANE
(4 guns)

Mountain House

4 NC
28 GA
23 GA
6 GA
2 NC
27 GA
13 AL
COLQUITT

G.B. ANDERSON

National Road

Beachley

D.H. HILL

13 NC   4 NC

Fox's Gap

Old Sharpsburg Road

20 NC   2 NC

Hutzel

Wise

BONDURANT
(4 guns)

30 OH

13 NC

20 NC

CROME
(2 guns)

GARLAND

23 NC

12 NC

5 NC

12 OH

30 OH

28 OH

RENO
(IX CORPS)

ROSSER
5 VA

12 OH

36 OH

CROME
(2 guns)

CROOK

BENJAMIN
(4 guns)

GIBSON
(6 guns)

McMULLIN
(4 guns)

SIMMONDS
(2 guns)

PELHAM
(2 guns)

23 OH   23 OH

SCAMMON

11 OH

COX

LEGEND

TROOP MOVEMENTS

Confederate	Union	
	8:30 - 10:00 AM	
	10:00 - 11:00 AM	
	11:00 AM - NOON	

LAND FEATURES & PRESERVATION

19th-Century Woodline

19th-Century Structures

19th-Century Roads

19th-Century Roads no longer in existence

19th-Century Fences

52 Modern Roads

Preserved by the American Battlefield Trust & other Partner Organizations

Preserved by Other Organizations

Preserved by the Federal Government

Preserved by Easements (various organizations)

— UPDATED MARCH 2020 —

AMERICAN BATTLEFIELD TRUST ★ ★ ★

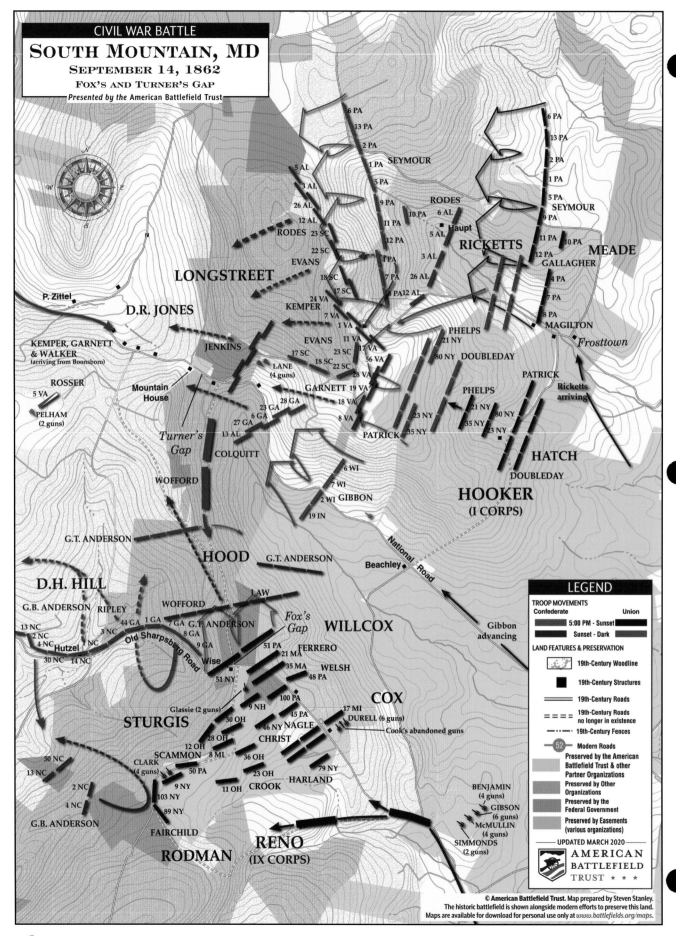

CIVIL WAR BATTLE
SOUTH MOUNTAIN, MD
SEPTEMBER 14, 1862
FOX'S AND TURNER'S GAP
Presented by the American Battlefield Trust

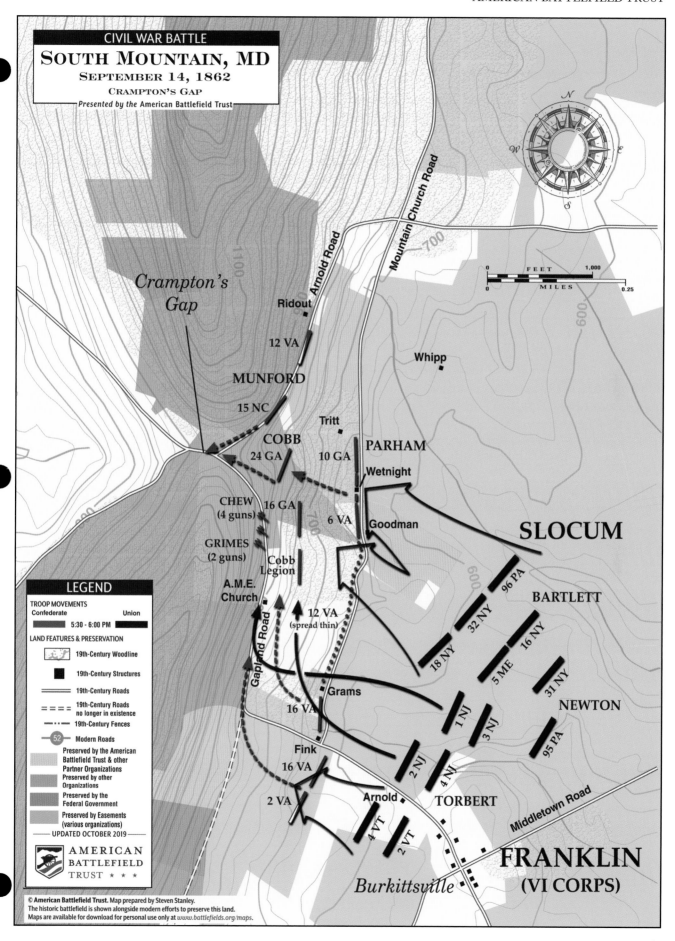

CIVIL WAR BATTLE
SOUTH MOUNTAIN, MD
SEPTEMBER 14, 1862
CRAMPTON'S GAP
Presented by the American Battlefield Trust

Crampton's Gap

Ridout

12 VA

MUNFORD

15 NC

Tritt

COBB
24 GA

PARHAM
10 GA

Wetnight

Whipp

CHEW
(4 guns)

16 GA

6 VA

Goodman

SLOCUM

GRIMES
(2 guns)

Cobb
Legion

A.M.E.
Church

96 PA

32 NY

BARTLETT

16 NY

12 VA
(spread thin)

18 NY

5 ME

31 NY

NEWTON

1 NJ

95 PA

3 NJ

Grams

16 VA

2 NJ

4 NJ

Fink

16 VA

Arnold

TORBERT

2 VA

4 VT

2 VT

Burkittsville

FRANKLIN
(VI CORPS)

Middletown Road

LEGEND

TROOP MOVEMENTS
Confederate   Union
5:30 - 6:00 PM

LAND FEATURES & PRESERVATION

19th-Century Woodline

19th-Century Structures

19th-Century Roads

19th-Century Roads
no longer in existence

19th-Century Fences

52   Modern Roads

Preserved by the American
Battlefield Trust & other
Partner Organizations

Preserved by other
Organizations

Preserved by the
Federal Government

Preserved by Easements
(various organizations)

UPDATED OCTOBER 2019

AMERICAN
BATTLEFIELD
TRUST ★ ★ ★

37

BATTLE *of* ANTIETAM
(BATTLE OF SHARPSBURG)

SEPTEMBER 17, 1862

WITH THE FALL OF HARPERS FERRY AND THE ABANDONMENT of his position along the South Mountain gaps, Lee next moved his army to the banks of Antietam Creek, near Sharpsburg, Maryland.

On the morning of September 17, Union soldiers of Joseph Hooker's I Corps began moving toward the Confederate left flank along the West Woods and Hagerstown Pike. The Federals struck the line of Stonewall Jackson's Southerners, and a ferocious firefight ensued in and around David Miller's 40-acre cornfield.

More Federals arrived in the form of Maj. Gen. Joseph K. Mansfield's XII Corps. As Mansfield deployed some green troops into a line of battle on the left of the Federal line, the corps commander fell, mortally wounded. He had been on the field for roughly 15 minutes. Yankees and Rebels surged back and forth through the now-famous East Woods and West Woods. The men of the XII Corps made a deep lodgment into the Confederate lines at the Dunker Church, but the inroads made there were short-lived.

More Federals poured onto the field. Some of the men of the Union II Corps were led to their doom in the West Woods, while others veered toward a sunken farm lane manned by Confederate soldiers utilizing this ready-made trench in a reverse slope position. The Confederates allowed many of the Federals to advance to within 50–75 yards of their position before mowing them down with small-arms fire. Severe casualties and an errant order forced the Confederates to abandon their position, but not before inflicting grievous casualties of their own, in the road now simply known as the "Bloody Lane."

Farther to the south and along the banks of Antietam Creek, the Union IX Corps attempted to cross the Rohrbach Bridge. A delay in orders, and then mismanagement of assaults on the bridge cost the Federals in both time and lives. By 1 p.m., a Pennsylvania and New York regiment forced its way across the bridge, while other Federals crossed downstream at Snavley's Ford.

In the late afternoon, thousands of Federals began their final drive on Sharpsburg. At the height of the crisis, Confederate soldiers fresh off parole duty in Harpers Ferry arrived at the right place at the right time. A. P. Hill's Light Division slammed into the Union troops, sending them reeling back toward the creek and ending the battle.

On the 18th, both sides remained in place, too bloodied to advance. Late that evening and on the 19th, Lee withdrew from the battlefield and slipped back across the Potomac into Virginia. Antietam gave President Abraham Lincoln the victory he desired before issuing the preliminary Emancipation Proclamation five days later—a document that changed the face of the war and American history.

✳ ✳ PRESERVATION ✳ ✳

To date, the **American Battlefield Trust** has saved **461 acres** at Antietam Battlefield.

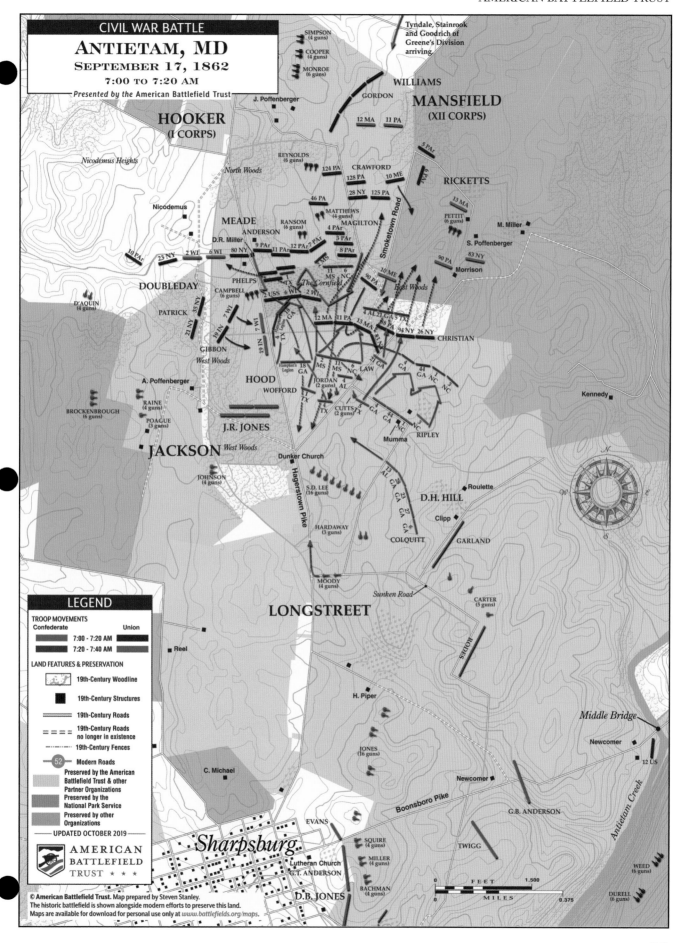

CIVIL WAR BATTLE

ANTIETAM, MD
SEPTEMBER 17, 1862
7:00 TO 7:20 AM
Presented by the American Battlefield Trust

Tyndale, Stainrook and Goodrich of Greene's Division arriving.

SIMPSON (4 guns)
COOPER (4 guns)
MONROE (6 guns)

WILLIAMS
GORDON
12 MA   11 PA

MANSFIELD
(XII CORPS)

HOOKER
(I CORPS)

J. Poffenberger

Nicodemus Heights

North Woods

Nicodemus

REYNOLDS (6 guns)
124 PA
128 PA
46 PA
28 NY

CRAWFORD
10 ME
125 PA

RICKETTS

5 PA
6 PA
13 MA

PETTIT (6 guns)

M. Miller

MEADE
ANDERSON
D.R. Miller
10 PAr   23 NY   2 WI   6 WI   80 NY   9 PAr   11 PAr   12 PA 7 PAr
MATTHEWS (4 guns)
RANSOM (6 guns)
MAGILTON
4 PAr
3 PAr
8 PAr

S. Poffenberger
90 PA   83 NY
Morrison

DOUBLEDAY
PHELPS
CAMPBELL (6 guns)
PATRICK
21 NY   35 NY   7 WI   19 IN
D'AQUIN (4 guns)

GIBBON
West Woods

2 USS   6 WI   2 WI
The Cornfield
11 MS
6 NC
90 PA
10 ME
East Woods

4 TX   14 WI
19 IN

12 MA   11 PA
13 MA
4 AL 21 GA 5 TX
5 TX
94 NY   26 NY
CHRISTIAN

18 GA
2 MS   11 MS 6 NC LAW
21 GA
GA
44 GA   3 NC
NC

Hampton's Legion
JORDAN (2 guns)
4 AL
4 TX

HOOD
WOFFORD

A. Poffenberger
RAINE (4 guns)
POAGUE (3 guns)
BROCKENBROUGH (6 guns)

J.R. JONES

CUTTS (2 guns)
5 GA   44 GA NC
Mumma
RIPLEY

Kennedy

JACKSON   West Woods
Dunker Church

JOHNSON (4 guns)
S.D. LEE (16 guns)

13 AL
26 GA
23 GA   28 GA
27 GA   6
HARDAWAY (3 guns)
COLQUITT

D.H. HILL

Roulette
Clipp

GARLAND

Hagerstown Pike

MOODY (4 guns)

LONGSTREET

Sunken Road

CARTER (5 guns)

ROHRS

Reel

H. Piper

Middle Bridge

Newcomer
12 US

JONES (16 guns)

Newcomer

C. Michael

Sharpsburg

EVANS

SQUIRE (4 guns)
MILLER (4 guns)

Boonsboro Pike

G.B. ANDERSON

Lutheran Church
G.T. ANDERSON

BACHMAN (4 guns)

TWIGG

WEED (6 guns)

Antietam Creek

D.B. JONES

DURELL (6 guns)

LEGEND

TROOP MOVEMENTS

Confederate	Union
7:00 - 7:20 AM	
7:20 - 7:40 AM	

LAND FEATURES & PRESERVATION

19th-Century Woodline

19th-Century Structures

19th-Century Roads

19th-Century Roads no longer in existence

19th-Century Fences

52 Modern Roads

Preserved by the American Battlefield Trust & other Partner Organizations

Preserved by the National Park Service

Preserved by other Organizations

— UPDATED OCTOBER 2019 —

AMERICAN
BATTLEFIELD
TRUST ★ ★ ★

FEET   1,500

MILES   0.375

© **American Battlefield Trust.** Map prepared by Steven Stanley.
The historic battlefield is shown alongside modern efforts to preserve this land.
Maps are available for download for personal use only at *www.battlefields.org/maps.*

39

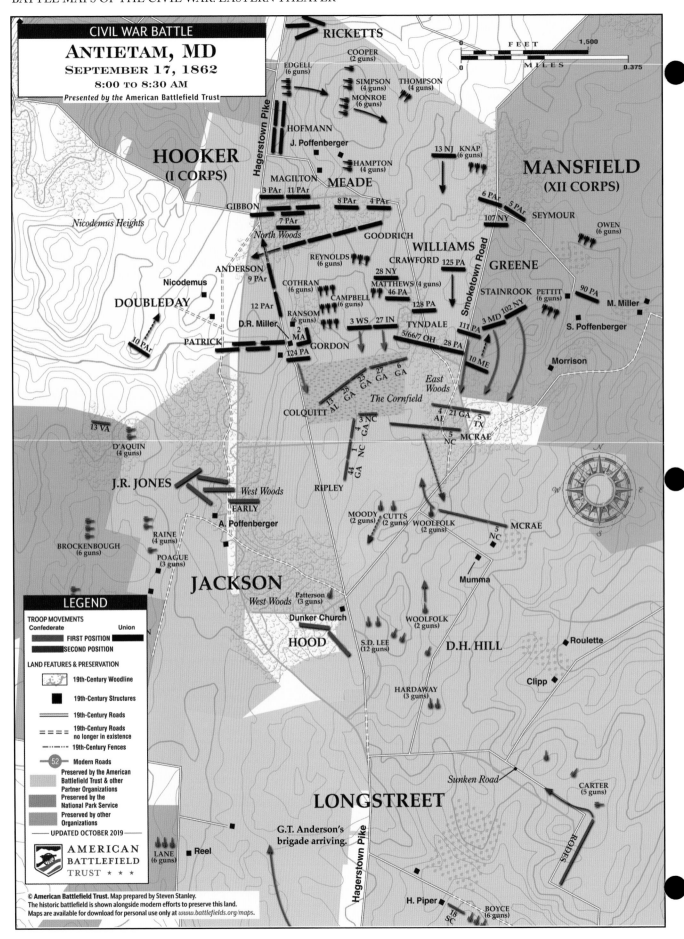

CIVIL WAR BATTLE
ANTIETAM, MD
SEPTEMBER 17, 1862
8:00 TO 8:30 AM
Presented by the American Battlefield Trust

RICKETTS

COOPER
(2 guns)

EDGELL
(6 guns)

SIMPSON
(4 guns)

THOMPSON
(4 guns)

MONROE
(6 guns)

FEET   1,500

MILES   0.375

HOFMANN

J. Poffenberger

13 NJ   KNAP
(6 guns)

HOOKER
(I CORPS)

HAMPTON
(4 guns)

MANSFIELD
(XII CORPS)

MAGILTON

MEADE

3 PAr 11 PAr

8 PAr 4 PAr

6 PAr 5 PAr

SEYMOUR

OWEN
(6 guns)

GIBBON

107 NY

Nicodemus Heights

7 PAr

North Woods

GOODRICH

WILLIAMS

GREENE

ANDERSON
9 PAr

REYNOLDS
(6 guns)

CRAWFORD

125 PA

Nicodemus

DOUBLEDAY

COTHRAN
(6 guns)

MATTHEWS (4 guns)

28 NY

46 PA

STAINROOK

PETTIT
(6 guns)

90 PA

M. Miller

12 PAr

CAMPBELL
(6 guns)

128 PA

3 MD 102 NY

RANSOM
(6 guns)

S. Poffenberger

10 PAr

D.R. Miller

2
MA

3 WS   27 IN

TYNDALE

111 PA

PATRICK

124 PA

GORDON

5/66/7 OH   28 PA

10 ME

Morrison

13
AL

28
GA

23
GA

27
GA

6
GA

*East
Woods*

13 VA

The Cornfield

COLQUITT

4
AL

21 GA

5
TX

3 NC

D'AQUIN
(4 guns)

4
GA

5
NC

MCRAE

44
GA

J.R. JONES

West Woods

RIPLEY

MOODY
(2 guns)

CUTTS
(2 guns)

WOOLFOLK
(2 guns)

5

MCRAE

5
NC

EARLY

A. Poffenberger

RAINE
(4 guns)

BROCKENBOROUGH
(6 guns)

POAGUE
(3 guns)

Mumma

JACKSON

West Woods

Patterson
(3 guns)

Dunker Church

WOOLFOLK
(2 guns)

D.H. HILL

Roulette

HOOD

S.D. LEE
(12 guns)

WOOLFOLK
(2 guns)

Clipp

LEGEND

HARDAWAY
(3 guns)

TROOP MOVEMENTS

Confederate   Union

FIRST POSITION

SECOND POSITION

LAND FEATURES & PRESERVATION

19th-Century Woodline

19th-Century Structures

19th-Century Roads

19th-Century Roads
no longer in existence

19th-Century Fences

52 Modern Roads

Preserved by the American
Battlefield Trust & other
Partner Organizations

Preserved by the
National Park Service

Preserved by other
Organizations

UPDATED OCTOBER 2019

Sunken Road

CARTER
(5 guns)

LONGSTREET

G.T. Anderson's
brigade arriving.

**AMERICAN
BATTLEFIELD
TRUST** ★ ★ ★

LANE
(6 guns)

Reel

Hagerstown Pike

© **American Battlefield Trust.** Map prepared by Steven Stanley.
The historic battlefield is shown alongside modern efforts to preserve this land.
Maps are available for download for personal use only at *www.battlefields.org/maps*.

H. Piper

18
SC

BOYCE
(6 guns)

40

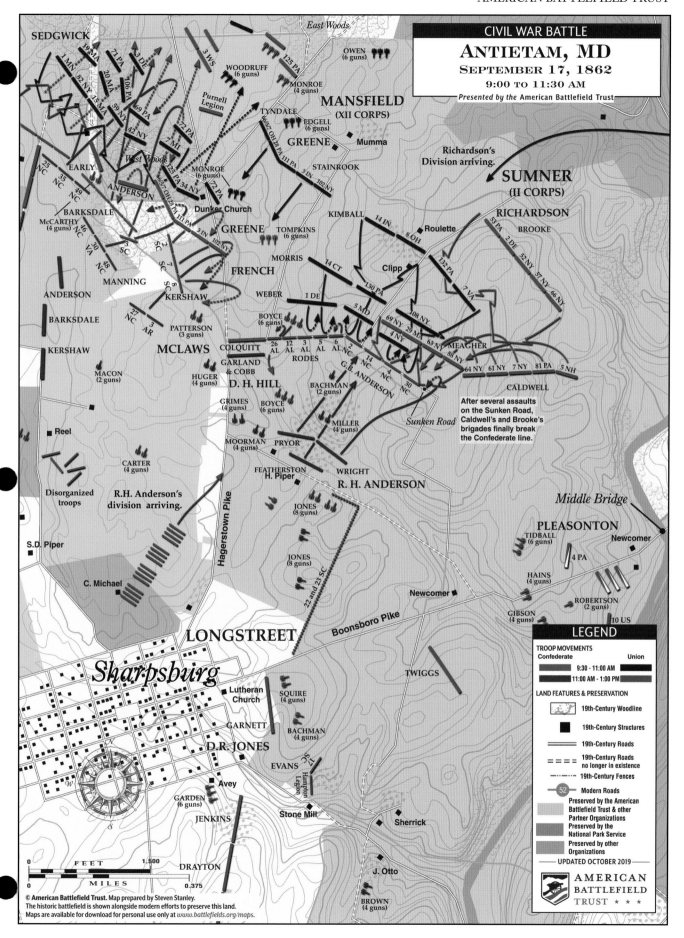

CIVIL WAR BATTLE

ANTIETAM, MD
SEPTEMBER 17, 1862
9:00 TO 11:30 AM
Presented by the American Battlefield Trust

LEGEND

TROOP MOVEMENTS
Confederate | Union
9:30 - 11:00 AM
11:00 AM - 1:00 PM

LAND FEATURES & PRESERVATION

- 19th-Century Woodline
- 19th-Century Structures
- 19th-Century Roads
- 19th-Century Roads no longer in existence
- 19th-Century Fences
- 52 Modern Roads
- Preserved by the American Battlefield Trust & other Partner Organizations
- Preserved by the National Park Service
- Preserved by other Organizations
- UPDATED OCTOBER 2019

AMERICAN BATTLEFIELD TRUST ★ ★ ★

After several assaults on the Sunken Road, Caldwell's and Brooke's brigades finally break the Confederate line.

Richardson's Division arriving.

R.H. Anderson's division arriving.

Disorganized troops

© American Battlefield Trust. Map prepared by Steven Stanley.
The historic battlefield is shown alongside modern efforts to preserve this land.
Maps are available for download for personal use only at *www.battlefields.org/maps*.

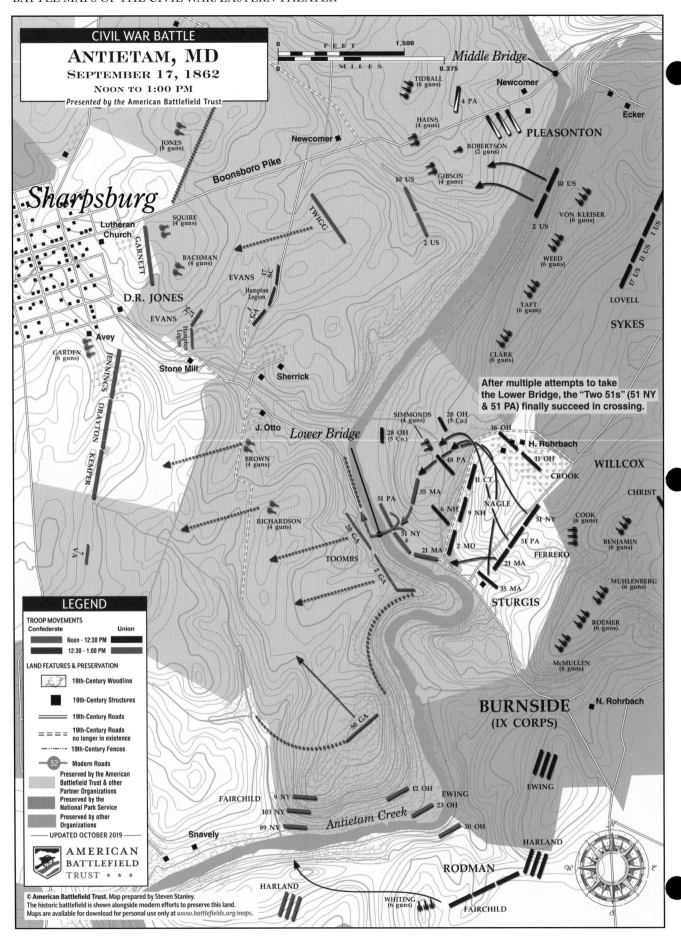

CIVIL WAR BATTLE
ANTIETAM, MD
SEPTEMBER 17, 1862
NOON TO 1:00 PM
Presented by the American Battlefield Trust

FEET 1,500

MILES 0.375

Middle Bridge

Sharpsburg

Boonsboro Pike

Lutheran Church

Lower Bridge

Antietam Creek

After multiple attempts to take the Lower Bridge, the "Two 51s" (51 NY & 51 PA) finally succeed in crossing.

BURNSIDE
(IX CORPS)

PLEASONTON

SYKES

WILLCOX

STURGIS

FERRERO

RODMAN

LEGEND
TROOP MOVEMENTS
Confederate   Union
- Noon - 12:30 PM
- 12:30 - 1:00 PM

LAND FEATURES & PRESERVATION
- 19th-Century Woodline
- 19th-Century Structures
- 19th-Century Roads
- 19th-Century Roads no longer in existence
- 19th-Century Fences
- 52 Modern Roads
- Preserved by the American Battlefield Trust & other Partner Organizations
- Preserved by the National Park Service
- Preserved by other Organizations

— UPDATED OCTOBER 2019 —

AMERICAN BATTLEFIELD TRUST ★ ★ ★

© American Battlefield Trust. Map prepared by Steven Stanley.
The historic battlefield is shown alongside modern efforts to preserve this land.
Maps are available for download for personal use only at *www.battlefields.org/maps*.

Unit labels on map: TIDBALL (6 guns), 4 PA, Newcomer, Ecker, HAINS (4 guns), ROBERTSON (2 guns), JONES (8 guns), Newcomer, 10 US, GIBSON (4 guns), 10 US, VON KLEISER (6 guns), SQUIRE (4 guns), TWIGG, 2 US, 2 US, 17 US, 1 US, WEED (6 guns), BACHMAN (4 guns), EVANS, 17 SC, Hampton Legion, GA, LOVELL, D.R. JONES, EVANS, GARNETT, 17 SC, Hampton Legion, TAFT (6 guns), CLARK (6 guns), Avey, GARDEN (6 guns), JENNINGS, DRAYTON, KEMPER, Stone Mill, Sherrick, SIMMONDS (4 guns), 28 OH (5 Co.), 36 OH, H. Rohrbach, 11 OH, CROOK, CHRIST, COOK (6 guns), J. Otto, BROWN (4 guns), 28 OH (5 Co.), 48 PA, 35 MA, 11 CT, NAGLE, 51 NY, 51 PA, BENJAMIN (6 guns), RICHARDSON (4 guns), 51 PA, 6 NH, 9 NH, 20 GA, 51 NY, 2 MD, 21 MA, MUHLENBERG (6 guns), VA, TOOMBS, 21 MA, 35 MA, 2 GA, ROEMER (6 guns), McMULLEN (6 guns), N. Rohrbach, 50 GA, EWING, 12 OH, EWING, 9 NY, 23 OH, FAIRCHILD, 103 NY, 89 NY, 30 OH, HARLAND, Snavely, RODMAN, HARLAND, WHITING (6 guns), FAIRCHILD

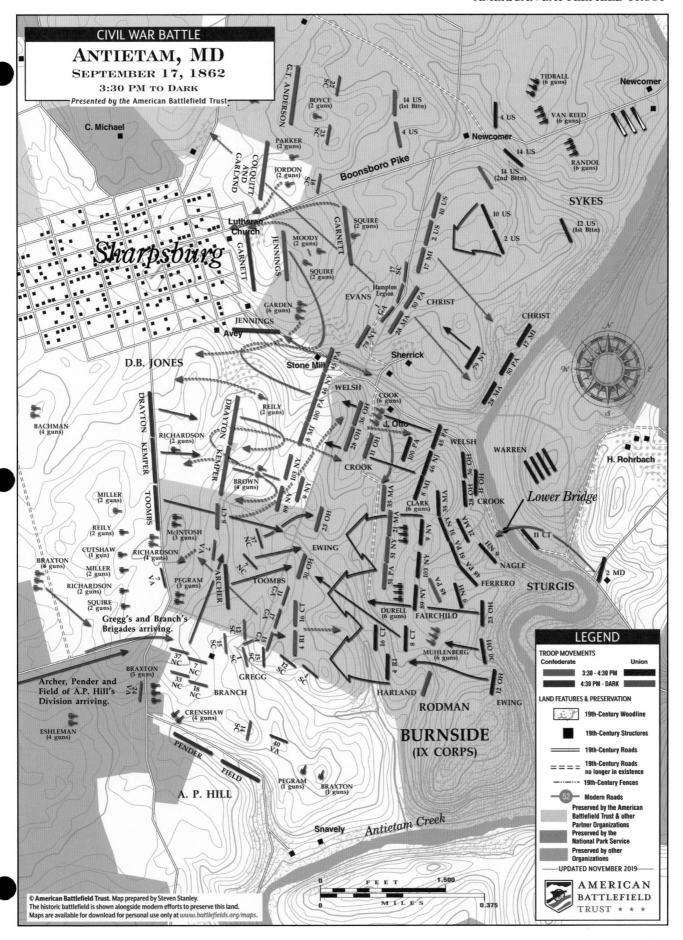

CIVIL WAR BATTLE
ANTIETAM, MD
SEPTEMBER 17, 1862
3:30 PM TO DARK
Presented by the American Battlefield Trust

C. Michael

Sharpsburg

Lutheran Church

D.B. JONES

BACHMAN
(4 guns)

MILLER
(2 guns)

REILY
(2 guns)

CUTSHAW
(1 gun)

MILLER
(2 guns)

BRAXTON
(6 guns)

RICHARDSON
(2 guns)

SQUIRE
(2 guns)

Gregg's and Branch's
Brigades arriving.

Archer, Pender and
Field of A.P. Hill's
Division arriving.

BRAXTON
(5 guns)

ESHLEMAN
(4 guns)

PENDER

FIELD

A. P. HILL

CRENSHAW
(4 guns)

PEGRAM
(1 guns)

BRAXTON
(1 guns)

Snavely

Antietam Creek

McINTOSH
(3 guns)

RICHARDSON
(4 guns)

PEGRAM
(3 guns)

ARCHER

TOOMBS

37
NC

7
NC

33
NC

18
NC

14
SC

40
VA

1
SC

GREGG

BRANCH

12
SC

15
SC

13
SC

12
GA

15
GA

17
GA

11
GA

16 CT

4 RI

BROWN
(4 guns)

DRAYTON
KEMPER

DRAYTON
KEMPER

RICHARDSON
(2 guns)

REILY
(2 guns)

G.T. ANDERSON

BOYCE
(2 guns)

PARKER
(2 guns)

JORDON
(2 guns)

COLQUITT AND GARLAND

22
SC

23
SC

18
SC

Boonsboro Pike

MOODY
(2 guns)

SQUIRE
(2 guns)

GARNETT

JENNINGS

GARNETT

GARDEN
(6 guns)

JENNINGS

Avey

Stone Mill

WELSH

REILY
(2 guns)

8 MI

28 OH

11 OH

36 OH

103
NY

9 NY

69 NY

CROOK

35
NC

7
NC

7
VA

TOOMBS

EWING

30 OH

23
OH

16 CT

14
US
(1st Bttn)

4 US

4 US

Newcomer

14 US

14 US
(2nd Bttn)

SQUIRE
(2 guns)

17
SC

17 MI

EVANS

Hampton
Legion

1
GA

79 NY

28 MA

17 MI

50 PA

CHRIST

Sherrick

COOK
(6 guns)

J. Otto

45 PA

46 NY

45 PA

100 PA

WELSH

CLARK
(6 guns)

35 MA

2 US

10 US

10 US

2 US

SYKES

12 US
(1st Bttn)

CHRIST

79 NY

50 PA

17 MI

23 MA

WARREN

CROOK

H. Rohrbach

Lower Bridge

11 CT

2 MD

NAGLE

FERRERO

STURGIS

21 MA

51 NY

51 PA

9 NY

103 NY

48 PA

48 PA

HN 9

89 NY

8 CT

DURELL
(6 guns)

FAIRCHILD

23 OH

30 OH

30 OH

12 OH

4 RI

MUHLENBERG
(6 guns)

HARLAND

RODMAN

EWING

BURNSIDE
(IX CORPS)

TIDBALL
(6 guns)

Newcomer

VAN REED
(6 guns)

RANDOL
(6 guns)

LEGEND

TROOP MOVEMENTS

Confederate	Union
3:30 - 4:30 PM	
4:30 PM - DARK	

LAND FEATURES & PRESERVATION

19th-Century Woodline

19th-Century Structures

19th-Century Roads

19th-Century Roads
no longer in existence

19th-Century Fences

52 Modern Roads

Preserved by the American
Battlefield Trust & other
Partner Organizations

Preserved by the
National Park Service

Preserved by other
Organizations

— UPDATED NOVEMBER 2019 —

AMERICAN
BATTLEFIELD
TRUST ★ ★ ★

FEET   1,500

MILES   0.375

BATTLE *of* FREDERICKSBURG

DECEMBER 11-13, 1862

ON NOVEMBER 7, 1862, ABRAHAM LINCOLN RELIEVED George McClellan of command of the Army of the Potomac. Three days later, Little Mac left his beloved army for the final time. Stepping in to replace McClellan was his close friend Ambrose Burnside. Burnside had had big shoes to fill and a timetable and Mother Nature working against him. Lincoln charged Burnside, along with two other army commanders, with securing Federal victories before the close of 1862. With waning support from the voters and the Emancipation Proclamation set to take effect on January 1, 1863, Lincoln yearned to win back public support, and he felt the battlefield offered the best prospects to right the proverbial ship.

Burnside quickly formulated a plan that was approved by the high command. His 123,000-man army would move from the Warrenton, Virginia, area to Fredericksburg, 40 miles distant. Once arrived, the Federals would secure the railroad and two key roads that ran through the city and 50 miles south to Richmond.

After a quick march through terrible weather, Burnside sat across the Rappahannock River from the city itself, held by fewer than 1,000 Confederates. Unfortunately, the pontoon bridges Burnside ordered to be awaiting his army were not there, and so he waited. For 10 days. And in those 10 days, the 78,000 man Confederate Army of Northern Virginia materialized before him.

With the enemy now in a blocking position, Burnside informed President Lincoln that he would attack Lee at Fredericksburg because the Rebel leader would be surprised by the audacity of such a move.

On December 11, the Federals attempted to lay their pontoon bridges at three locations along the river. Rebel soldiers contested the crossing and threw off Burnside's timetable by nearly two full days.

On the morning of December 13, Burnside planned to make a massive assault on the Confederate right flank at Prospect Hill. Nearly 60,000 Federals amassed in the fields in front of the objective. Union soldiers were to advance and seize Prospect Hill, and then push the Confederates to the west and north—away from Richmond—while at the same time, a heavy reserve of Federals would be ready to move at a moment's notice toward Richmond. A supporting attack would take place out of the city and assault a series of five hills collectively known as Marye's Heights. By the end of the day, 30,000 Federals attacked the Confederate position in the Marye's Heights sector.

A breakdown in communications and orders doomed the Federals. Amazingly, an undersized Union force of 8,000 men breached the Confederate line of 38,000 at and around Prospect Hill. It was a short-lived gain. At an open field now known as the Slaughter Pen Farm, Federals and Confederates grappled in a death struggle. The heroism displayed there produced no less than five Medal of Honor recipients. At Marye's Heights, seven futile assaults attacked a stone wall and sunken road. Not one Federal touched the wall, and not one made it into the road. Only darkness ended the battle. Two days later, the Federals withdrew across the Rappahannock, ending the campaign.

✷ ✷ PRESERVATION ✷ ✷

To date, the **American Battlefield Trust** has saved **248 acres** at Fredericksburg Battlefield.

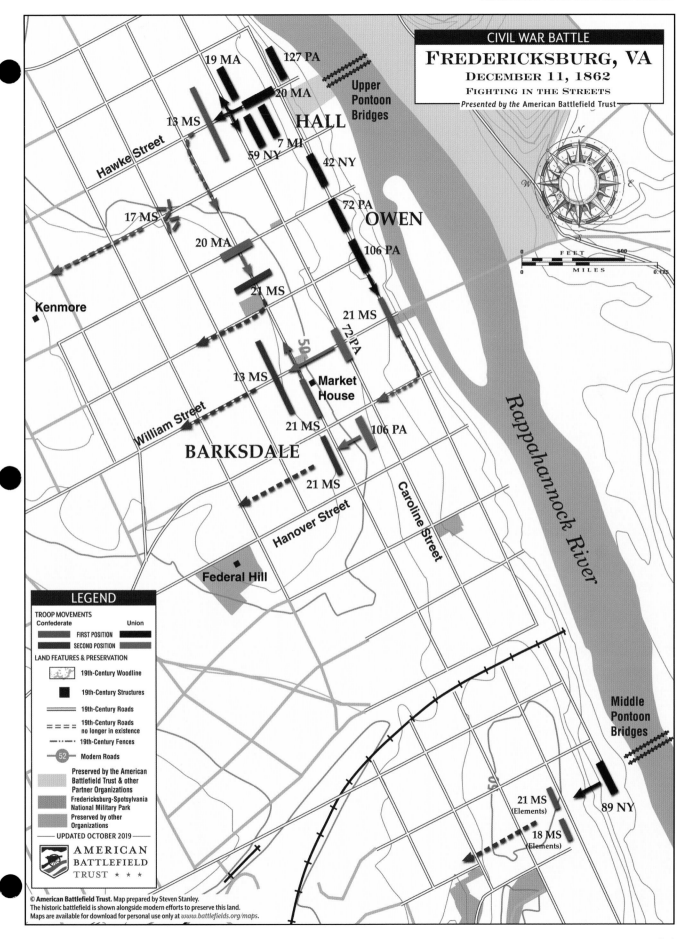

CIVIL WAR BATTLE
FREDERICKSBURG, VA
DECEMBER 11, 1862
FIGHTING IN THE STREETS
Presented by the American Battlefield Trust

19 MA
127 PA
Upper Pontoon Bridges
20 MA
HALL
13 MS
7 MI
59 NY
42 NY
72 PA
OWEN
17 MS
106 PA
20 MA
21 MS
21 MS
Kenmore
72 PA
50
13 MS
Market House
21 MS
BARKSDALE
106 PA
21 MS
Hanover Street
Caroline Street
Rappahannock River
Federal Hill

Hawke Street
William Street

LEGEND

TROOP MOVEMENTS
Confederate   Union
FIRST POSITION
SECOND POSITION

LAND FEATURES & PRESERVATION
19th-Century Woodline
19th-Century Structures
19th-Century Roads
19th-Century Roads no longer in existence
19th-Century Fences
52 Modern Roads
Preserved by the American Battlefield Trust & other Partner Organizations
Fredericksburg-Spotsylvania National Military Park
Preserved by other Organizations
UPDATED OCTOBER 2019

AMERICAN BATTLEFIELD TRUST ★ ★ ★

Middle Pontoon Bridges

21 MS (Elements)
89 NY
18 MS (Elements)

© American Battlefield Trust. Map prepared by Steven Stanley.
The historic battlefield is shown alongside modern efforts to preserve this land.
Maps are available for download for personal use only at www.battlefields.org/maps.

45

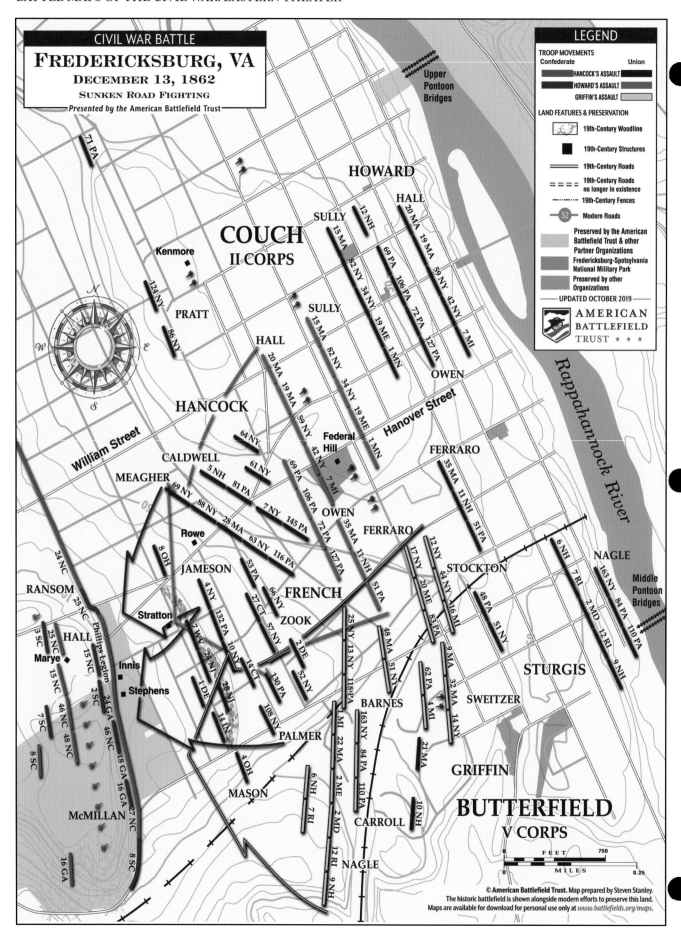

CIVIL WAR BATTLE
FREDERICKSBURG, VA
DECEMBER 13, 1862
SUNKEN ROAD FIGHTING
Presented by the American Battlefield Trust

LEGEND

TROOP MOVEMENTS
Confederate   Union

HANCOCK'S ASSAULT
HOWARD'S ASSAULT
GRIFFIN'S ASSAULT

LAND FEATURES & PRESERVATION

19th-Century Woodline

19th-Century Structures

19th-Century Roads

19th-Century Roads
no longer in existence

19th-Century Fences

52 Modern Roads

Preserved by the American
Battlefield Trust & other
Partner Organizations

Fredericksburg-Spotsylvania
National Military Park

Preserved by other
Organizations

— UPDATED OCTOBER 2019 —

AMERICAN
BATTLEFIELD
TRUST ★★★

© American Battlefield Trust. Map prepared by Steven Stanley.
The historic battlefield is shown alongside modern efforts to preserve this land.
Maps are available for download for personal use only at www.battlefields.org/maps.

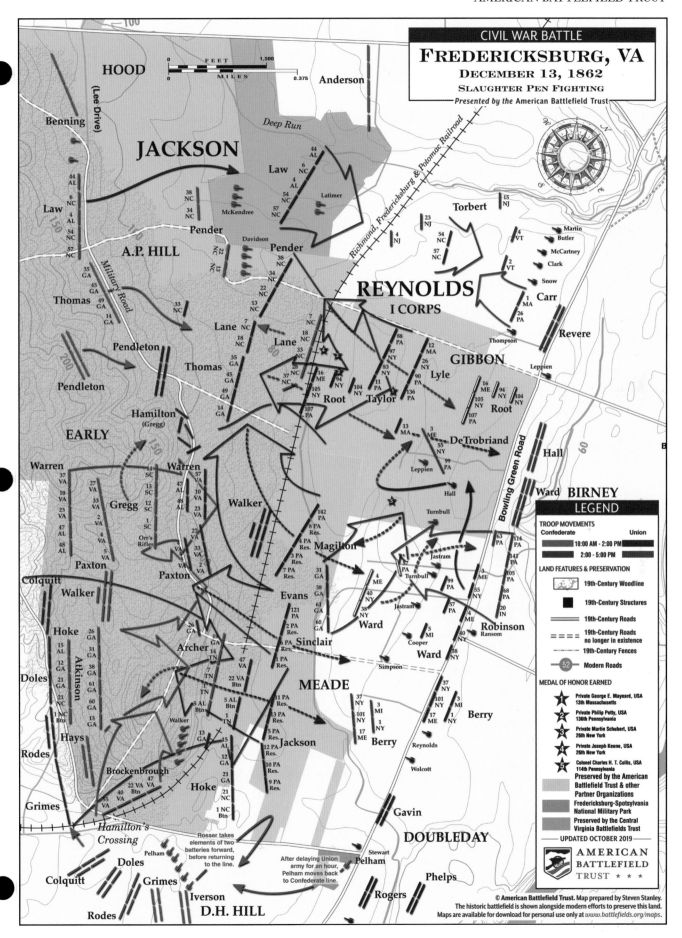

CIVIL WAR BATTLE
FREDERICKSBURG, VA
DECEMBER 13, 1862
SLAUGHTER PEN FIGHTING
Presented by the American Battlefield Trust

FEET
0 — 1,500
MILES
0 — 0.375

LEGEND

TROOP MOVEMENTS

	Confederate	Union
10:00 AM - 2:00 PM		
2:00 - 5:00 PM		

LAND FEATURES & PRESERVATION

- 19th-Century Woodline
- 19th-Century Structures
- 19th-Century Roads
- 19th-Century Roads no longer in existence
- 19th-Century Fences
- 52 — Modern Roads

MEDAL OF HONOR EARNED

1. Private George E. Maynard, USA — 13th Massachusetts
2. Private Philip Petty, USA — 136th Pennsylvania
3. Private Martin Schubert, USA — 26th New York
4. Private Joseph Keene, USA — 26th New York
5. Colonel Charles H. T. Collis, USA — 114th Pennsylvania

Preserved by the American Battlefield Trust & other Partner Organizations

Fredericksburg-Spotsylvania National Military Park

Preserved by the Central Virginia Battlefields Trust

— UPDATED OCTOBER 2019 —

AMERICAN BATTLEFIELD TRUST ★ ★ ★

Rosser takes elements of two batteries forward, before returning to the line.

After delaying Union army for an hour, Pelham moves back to Confederate line.

BATTLE *of* CHANCELLORSVILLE

APRIL 30 - MAY 6, 1863

FOLLOWING THE DISASTROUS FREDERICKSBURG CAMPAIGN, Lincoln again changed army commanders in the East. This time he turned to Joseph Hooker.

By mid-April, the Federal army was ready for action. Hooker's plan for the spring campaign was simple in design, but complex to execute. Nearly one half of the Union army would draw Lee's attention south of Fredericksburg with grand maneuvering and a river crossing. In the meantime, three Federal infantry corps would make an extended circuitous march around Lee's army, crossing the Rapidan River at two points and pressing into the Confederate rear. The final piece of Hooker's plan involved his newly reorganized Cavalry Corps. Around 10,000 troopers would slice into the Confederate rear, threaten Richmond, destroy railroads, sever communication lines and cause as much havoc as possible. Hooker felt that Lee would have two choices: retreat toward Richmond or be destroyed between the two wings of Hooker's army. Lee found a third option, however: come out swinging—and that is exactly what he did.

After discerning that Hooker's feint below Fredericksburg was just that, Lee divided his army and dispatched Stonewall Jackson to the west with a portion of the army. There, on May 1, Jackson engaged with Hooker's wing of the army sweeping into the Confederate rear near Chancellorsville. After a sharp fight east of the Chancellorsville crossroads, Hooker gave up the initiative and set up a defensive line in an area known as the Wildernesss.

With the initiative in hand, Lee decided to divide his army again and send Jackson on a march to strike Hooker's right flank. The following evening, Jackson's men assailed Maj. Gen. Oliver O. Howard's XI Corps and caved in the right of the Union line. That night, while riding between the lines, Jackson was wounded by friendly fire. He succumbed to pneumonia eight days later.

With Jeb Stuart assuming command of Jackson's corps, Lee renewed his attack early on May 3. Jackson's flank attack had left the Confederates in a vulnerable position, split in two, with an aroused enemy between the wings. Grand maneuvering gave way to a slugging match, and by 10 a.m., Hooker was wounded, the Chancellor Mansion was on fire and Lee was nearly master of the field.

At the zenith of his victory, word came in from Fredericksburg that the Federal feint had turned into a full-blown attack.

Splitting his army for the third time, Lee held Hooker's wing at bay, while a force marched six miles to the east and engaged with Federal units at the Salem Church. The Confederates brought the advance to a standstill there. Although victorious on May 1–3, the losses in men and leaders proved too much for the Army of Northern Virginia, and it could not land the killing blow to its perennial foe. Stalled on two fronts and suffering the effects of a concussion, Hooker decided to retreat and abandon his campaign on the night of May 5. The victory emboldened Lee and inspired him to launch a second northern invasion in June 1863.

❋ ❋ PRESERVATION ❋ ❋

To date, the **American Battlefield Trust** has saved **1,322 acres** at Chancellorsville Battlefield.

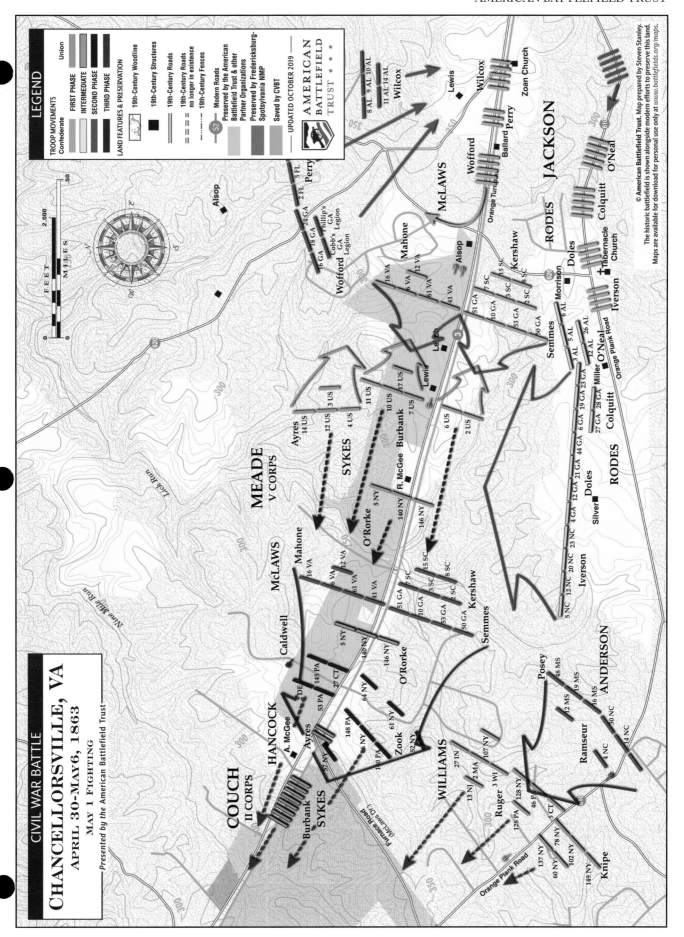

LEGEND

TROOP MOVEMENTS

Confederate | Union

FIRST PHASE
INTERMEDIATE
SECOND PHASE
THIRD PHASE

LAND FEATURES & PRESERVATION

19th-Century Woodline

19th-Century Structures

19th-Century Roads

19th-Century Roads no longer in existence

19th-Century Fences

52 — Modern Roads

Preserved by the American Battlefield Trust & other Partner Organizations

Preserved by Fredericksburg-Spotsylvania NMP

Saved by CVBT

— UPDATED OCTOBER 2019

AMERICAN BATTLEFIELD TRUST ★ ★ ★

CIVIL WAR BATTLE

CHANCELLORSVILLE, VA
APRIL 30–MAY 6, 1863
MAY 1 FIGHTING
Presented by the American Battlefield Trust

© American Battlefield Trust. Map prepared by Steven Stanley.

The historic battlefield is shown alongside modern efforts to preserve this land.

Maps are available for download for personal use only at www.battlefields.org/maps.

49

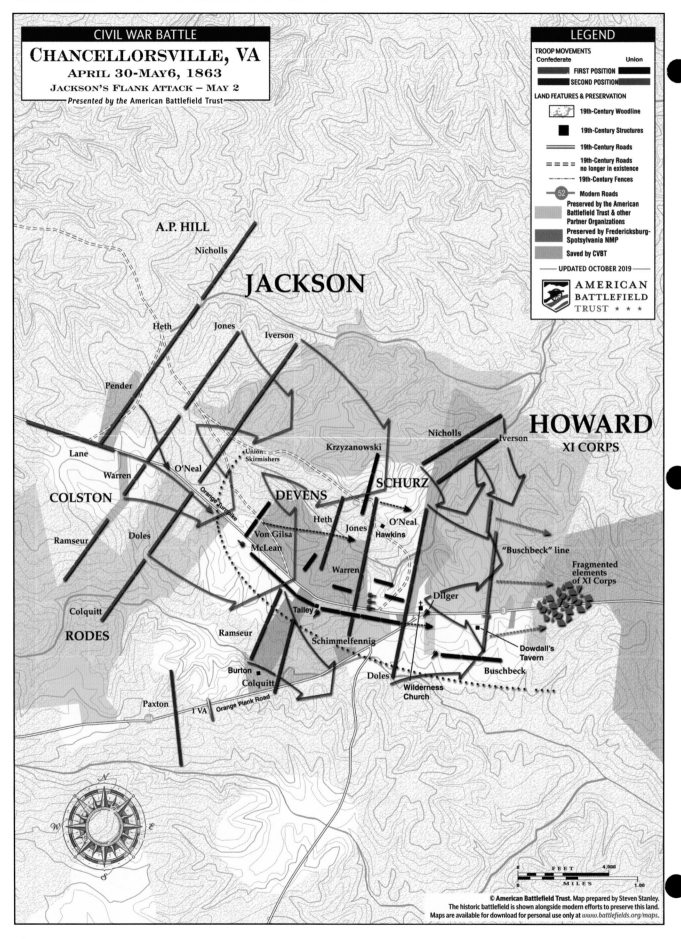

CIVIL WAR BATTLE

CHANCELLORSVILLE, VA

APRIL 30–MAY 6, 1863

JACKSON'S FLANK ATTACK – MAY 2

Presented by the American Battlefield Trust

LEGEND

TROOP MOVEMENTS

Confederate   Union

FIRST POSITION

SECOND POSITION

LAND FEATURES & PRESERVATION

19th-Century Woodline

19th-Century Structures

19th-Century Roads

19th-Century Roads no longer in existence

19th-Century Fences

52 Modern Roads

Preserved by the American Battlefield Trust & other Partner Organizations

Preserved by Fredericksburg-Spotsylvania NMP

Saved by CVBT

— UPDATED OCTOBER 2019 —

AMERICAN BATTLEFIELD TRUST ★ ★ ★

A.P. HILL

Nicholls

JACKSON

Heth

Jones

Iverson

Pender

HOWARD

XI CORPS

Nicholls

Iverson

Lane

Union Skirmishers

O'Neal

Krzyzanowski

SCHURZ

Warren

COLSTON

DEVENS

Orange Turnpike

Heth

Jones

O'Neal

Hawkins

"Buschbeck" line

Ramseur

Doles

Von Gilsa

McLean

Warren

Fragmented elements of XI Corps

Colquitt

Dilger

RODES

Ramseur

Talley

Dowdall's Tavern

Schimmelfennig

Buschbeck

Burton

Colquitt

Doles

Wilderness Church

Paxton

1 VA

Orange Plank Road

N

FEET   4,000

MILES   1.00

© **American Battlefield Trust.** Map prepared by Steven Stanley.
The historic battlefield is shown alongside modern efforts to preserve this land.
Maps are available for download for personal use only at *www.battlefields.org/maps*.

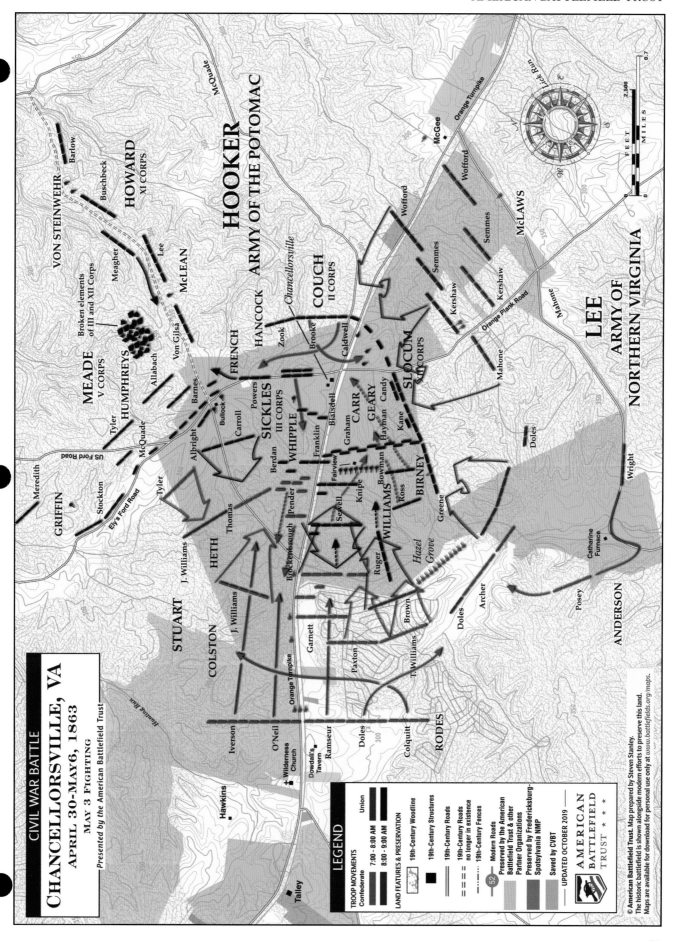

CIVIL WAR BATTLE

CHANCELLORSVILLE, VA

APRIL 30–MAY 6, 1863

MAY 3 FIGHTING

Presented by the American Battlefield Trust

LEGEND

TROOP MOVEMENTS

Confederate   Union

7:00 - 8:00 AM

8:00 - 9:00 AM

LAND FEATURES & PRESERVATION

19th-Century Woodline

19th-Century Structures

19th-Century Roads

19th-Century Roads no longer in existence

19th-Century Fences

Modern Roads

52 Preserved by the American Battlefield Trust & other Partner Organizations

Preserved by Fredericksburg-Spotsylvania NMP

Saved by CVBT

UPDATED OCTOBER 2019

AMERICAN BATTLEFIELD TRUST ★ ★ ★

© American Battlefield Trust. Map prepared by Steven Stanley.
The historic battlefield is shown alongside modern efforts to preserve this land.
Maps are available for download for personal use only at *www.battlefields.org/maps*.

HOOKER

ARMY OF THE POTOMAC

LEE

ARMY OF NORTHERN VIRGINIA

51

BATTLE *of* BRANDY STATION

JUNE 9, 1863

WITH THE STRATEGIC INITIATIVE ONCE AGAIN SQUARELY in his hands, Lee pressed the Confederate high command to allow his army to move north and carry the war to enemy soil. On June 3, Lee set his army into motion for what would become the most famous campaign of the American Civil War.

Lee amassed much of his army near Culpeper, Virginia, including his cavalry force, which would screen his force's northward movements. Jeb Stuart was set to undertake this mission on June 9.

Word reached Federal commander Joseph Hooker that something was amiss with the enemy. Hooker, in turn, dispatched a force of cavalry and infantry to the Culpeper area. On the morning of June 9, Union troopers initiated the largest cavalry engagement of the Civil War. Maj. Gen. Alfred Pleasonton's Federal horsemen struck Stuart's men in camp at Brandy Station, with orders to "disperse or destroy" Stuart's entire command.

At 4:30 a.m., Brig. Gen. John Buford's men splashed across Beverly's Ford, four and a half miles northeast of Brandy Station, and quickly scattered surprised Confederate pickets. The pickets scrambled back toward the main camp near St. James Church, along the direct road to Brandy Station from Beverly's Ford. Confederates at St. James Church hurled themselves into the fray and managed to stall Buford's advance, claiming the life of Buford's lead subordinate, Col. Benjamin "Grimes" Davis.

Stuart's horsemen suffered heavily, but bought enough time for Rebel artillery to deploy and open a murderous fire on the congested Union column from the high ground around the church. His position in peril, Buford ordered a desperate charge on the Confederate battery. Union horsemen overran the guns before Brig. Gen. "Grumble" Jones's Confederates repulsed them.

With the Confederate guns back in action, Buford now sought to reach them by moving around the Confederate left flank on Yew Ridge. Dismounted Confederate troopers repulsed repeated attacks from behind a stone wall before being dislodged around noon.

Meanwhile, at 11:30 a.m. Brig. Gen. David Gregg's troopers reached Brandy Station, and were now firmly in the Confederate rear. Gregg found the path to St. James Church blocked by Fleetwood Hill, a broad elevation where Jeb Stuart had established his headquarters. Union artillery opened on the hill, giving a considerable shock to Stuart, whose main force was entirely committed to the battle at his front. Gregg's preparatory barrage, however, gave Stuart time to pull troops back to Fleetwood Hill to meet the first Union charge. The opposing lines crashed into one another again and again for almost five hours. Finally, hearing reports of incoming Confederate reinforcements, the Federal cavalry leader, Pleasanton, decided to withdraw around 5 p.m. Stuart did not pursue.

Although Pleasanton's troopers failed to destroy Stuart's command, the hard fighting at Brandy Station proved the fighting prowess of the Northern horsemen. Stuart was harshly criticized for his unpreparedness, spurred by vanity and foreshadowing graver future failures.

✳ ✳ PRESERVATION ✳ ✳

To date, the **American Battlefield Trust** has saved **2,158 acres** at Brandy Station Battlefield.

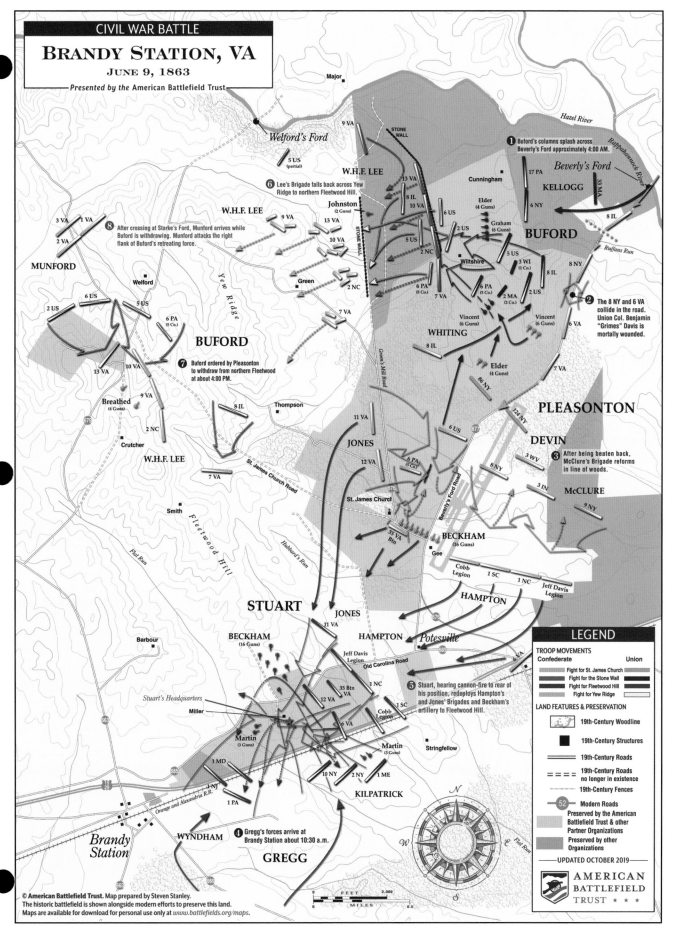

CIVIL WAR BATTLE
BRANDY STATION, VA
JUNE 9, 1863
Presented by the American Battlefield Trust

Major

Welford's Ford

9 VA

5 US
(partial)

STONE WALL

W.H.F. LEE

Hazel River

1 Buford's columns splash across
Beverly's Ford approximately 4:00 AM.

17 PA

Beverly's Ford

Cunningham

13 VA

KELLOGG

6 Lee's Brigade falls back across Yew
Ridge to northern Fleetwood Hill.

W.H.F. LEE

8 IL
10 VA

Elder
(4 Guns)

6 US

6 NY

33 MA

8 IL

BUFORD

Ruffans Run

Johnston
(2 Guns)

2 US

Graham
(6 Guns)

3 VA 1 VA
2 VA

8 After crossing at Starke's Ford, Munford arrives while
Buford is withdrawing. Munford attacks the right
flank of Buford's retreating force.

9 VA

13 VA

5 US

2 NC

5 US
5 US

Wiltshire

5 US
3 WI
(1 Co.)

8 IL

8 NY

MUNFORD

10 VA

6 PA
(5 Co.)

6 PA
(5 Co.)

7 VA

2 MA
(2 Co.)

2 US

2 The 8 NY and 6 VA
collide in the road.
Union Col. Benjamin
"Grimes" Davis is
mortally wounded.

Welford

Green

2 NC

Vincent
(6 Guns)

Vincent
(6 Guns)

6 VA

6 US
2 US
5 US

6 PA
(5 Co.)

WHITING

8 IL

7 VA

7 Buford ordered by Pleasonton
to withdraw from northern Fleetwood
at about 4:00 PM.

7 VA

Elder
(4 Guns)

Thompson

Breathed
(4 Guns)

9 VA

8 IL

11 VA

86 NY

12 VA

PLEASONTON

124 NY

DEVIN

2 NC

Crutcher

W.H.F. LEE

7 VA

St. James Church Road

JONES

6 US

8 NY

3 WV

3 After being beaten back,
McClure's Brigade reforms
in line of woods.

Smith

6 PA
(5 Co.)

St. James Church

3 IN

McCLURE

9 NY

Fleetwood Hill

Flat Run

Hubard's Run

35 VA
Btn

Gee

BECKHAM
(16 Guns)

Barbour

STUART

BECKHAM
(16 Guns)

JONES
11 VA

Cobb
Legion

1 SC

1 NC

Jeff Davis
Legion

HAMPTON

Potesville

HAMPTON

Jeff Davis
Legion

Old Carolina Road

LEGEND

Stuart's Headquarters

Miller

35 Btn
VA

12 VA

Cobb
Legion

1 SC

5 Stuart, hearing cannon-fire to rear of
his position, redeploys Hampton's
and Jones' Brigades and Beckham's
artillery to Fleetwood Hill.

6 VA

1 NC

Martin
(3 Guns)

Martin
(3 Guns)

Stringfellow

TROOP MOVEMENTS
Confederate   Union

Fight for St. James Church
Fight for the Stone Wall
Fight for Fleetwood Hill
Fight for Yew Ridge

LAND FEATURES & PRESERVATION

19th-Century Woodline

19th-Century Structures

19th-Century Roads

19th-Century Roads
no longer in existence

19th-Century Fences

52 Modern Roads

Preserved by the American
Battlefield Trust & other
Partner Organizations

Preserved by other
Organizations

1 MD

10 NY

2 NY

1 ME

1 NJ

KILPATRICK

1 PA

Orange and Alexandria R.R.

WYNDHAM

4 Gregg's forces arrive at
Brandy Station about 10:30 a.m.

*Brandy
Station*

GREGG

N

W   E

S

—UPDATED OCTOBER 2019—

**AMERICAN
BATTLEFIELD
TRUST ★ ★ ★**

FEET   2,000

MILES   0.5

© **American Battlefield Trust**. Map prepared by Steven Stanley.
The historic battlefield is shown alongside modern efforts to preserve this land.
Maps are available for download for personal use only at *www.battlefields.org/maps*.

BATTLE *of* GETTYSBURG

JULY 1 -3, 1863

BY JUNE 30, 1863, FEDERAL AND CONFEDERATE FORCES WERE making their way toward the crossroads town of Gettysburg, Pennsylvania. Confederates visited the town on June 26, as they cut a swath across south-central Pennsylvania. Rebel forces reached the banks of the Susquehanna River across from the state capital of Harrisburg before being recalled to the Gettysburg area.

On the morning of July 1, an engagement between Union cavalry commanded by John Buford and Confederate infantry and artillery commanded by Lt. Gen. A. P. Hill set into motion one of the most famous battles in military history.

By 10 a.m., Hill's men had Buford's troopers on their heels. Timely Union infantry reinforcements poured onto the field, overseen by "Left Wing" Cdr. John Reynolds. Shortly after entering the battle, Reynolds was killed, and after an hour and a half of stout resistance, the Federals held their own as a lull came across the field.

Tens of thousands of Confederate soldiers approached the field from the west and the north, as tens of thousands of Federals approached from the south. Late in the afternoon, outnumbered and in a poor tactical position, the Federals were driven from the north and west sides of the town. The Yankees rallied on Cemetery Hill and bolstered their line, incorporating the dominating Culp's Hill on their right flank into their defensive position. Meanwhile, on their left, the Federals extended their line south along Cemetery Ridge, to the base of Little Round Top.

Late on the afternoon of July 2, the Rebel army renewed its assaults, striking the Federals at Devil's Den, Little Round Top, the Peach Orchard and the Wheatfield. The next three hours witnessed some of the most intense fighting of the war. The Rebels were able to secure Devil's Den, the Peach Orchard and the Wheatfield, and they dislodged much of the Federal line. Yet, the Federals still held tenaciously to Little Round Top and Cemetery Ridge.

An ill-coordinated Confederate assault struck the right of the Union line at Culp's Hill and East Cemetery Hill. At the end of the day, the Federal army was determined to stay and fight it out.

The battle renewed at 4:30 a.m. on July 3 at Culp's Hill. For seven hours—the longest sustained fighting of the battle—the two sides grappled. In the end, the Federal position proved too strong to dislodge.

After striking each Union flank, Lee set his sights on the Federal center. Amassing some 120 cannon, Lee bombarded that Union position. Union cannon roared to life, responding in kind. At the conclusion of the bombardment, 12,000 Confederate soldiers launched the most infamous assault of Lee's career. In less than an hour, the Confederates were repulsed, and the next day, Lee started the long march back to Virginia. The last great Confederate offensive in the Eastern Theater was over.

Four months after the battle, President Lincoln used the dedication ceremony for Gettysburg's Soldiers National Cemetery to honor the fallen Union soldiers and define the purpose of the war in his historic Gettysburg Address.

✳ ✳ PRESERVATION ✳ ✳

To date, the **American Battlefield Trust** has saved **1,183 acres** at Gettysburg\ Battlefield.

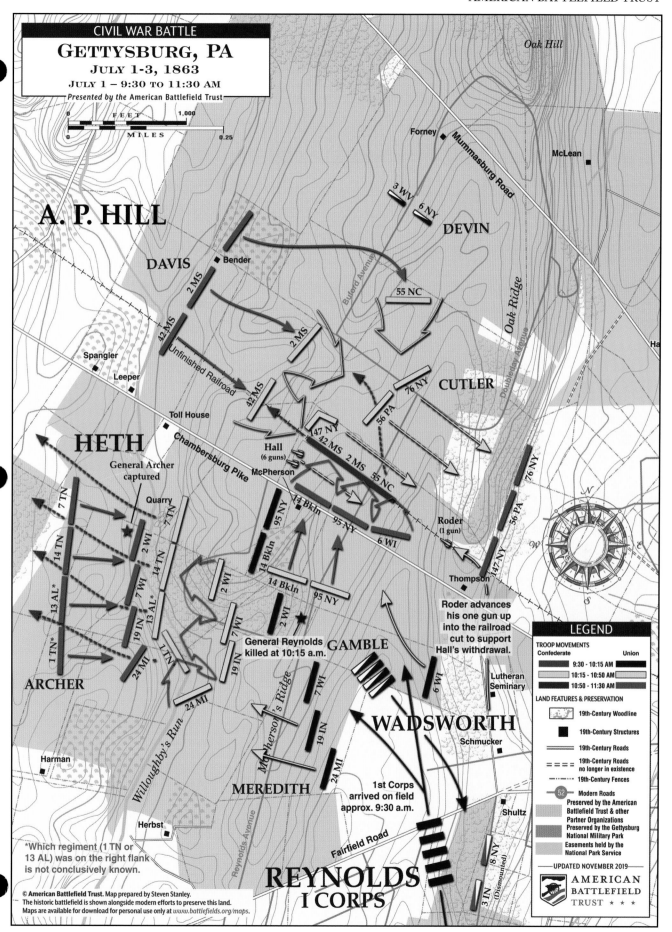

CIVIL WAR BATTLE
GETTYSBURG, PA
JULY 1-3, 1863
JULY 1 – 9:30 TO 11:30 AM
Presented by the American Battlefield Trust

FEET 1,000
MILES 0.25

Oak Hill

A. P. HILL

Forney

McLean

3 WV   6 NY

DEVIN

DAVIS   Bender

55 NC

2 MS

42 MS

Spangler

Leeper

Unfinished Railroad

Toll House

42 MS

CUTLER

76 NY

56 PA

HETH

Chambersburg Pike

Hall
(6 guns)

47 NY   42 MS   2 MS

McPherson   55 NC

General Archer
captured

Quarry

7 TN

14 Bkln   95 NY

95 NY   6 WI

Roder
(1 gun)

76 NY

56 PA

147 NY

General Reynolds
killed at 10:15 a.m.

GAMBLE

Thompson

Roder advances
his one gun up
into the railroad
cut to support
Hall's withdrawal.

7 TN

2 WI

14 TN

7 WI   14 TN

13 AL*

19 IN   7 WI   13 AL*

1 TN

1 TN*

24 MI   1 TN

ARCHER

Harman

Willoughby's Run

24 MI

2 WI

14 Bkln

14 Bkln   95 NY

2 WI

2 WI

19 IN   7 WI

6 WI

WADSWORTH

Lutheran
Seminary

Schmucker

1st Corps
arrived on field
approx. 9:30 a.m.

MEREDITH

7 WI

19 IN

24 MI

Herbst

Shultz

Fairfield Road

*Which regiment (1 TN or
13 AL) was on the right flank
is not conclusively known.

3 IN   (8 NY)
(Dismounted)

REYNOLDS
I CORPS

© **American Battlefield Trust.** Map prepared by Steven Stanley.
The historic battlefield is shown alongside modern efforts to preserve this land.
Maps are available for download for personal use only at *www.battlefields.org/maps.*

LEGEND
TROOP MOVEMENTS
Confederate   Union
9:30 - 10:15 AM
10:15 - 10:50 AM
10:50 - 11:30 AM

LAND FEATURES & PRESERVATION
19th-Century Woodline
19th-Century Structures
19th-Century Roads
19th-Century Roads
no longer in existence
19th-Century Fences
52 Modern Roads
Preserved by the American
Battlefield Trust & other
Partner Organizations
Preserved by the Gettysburg
National Military Park
Easements held by the
National Park Service

—UPDATED NOVEMBER 2019—
AMERICAN
BATTLEFIELD
TRUST ★ ★ ★

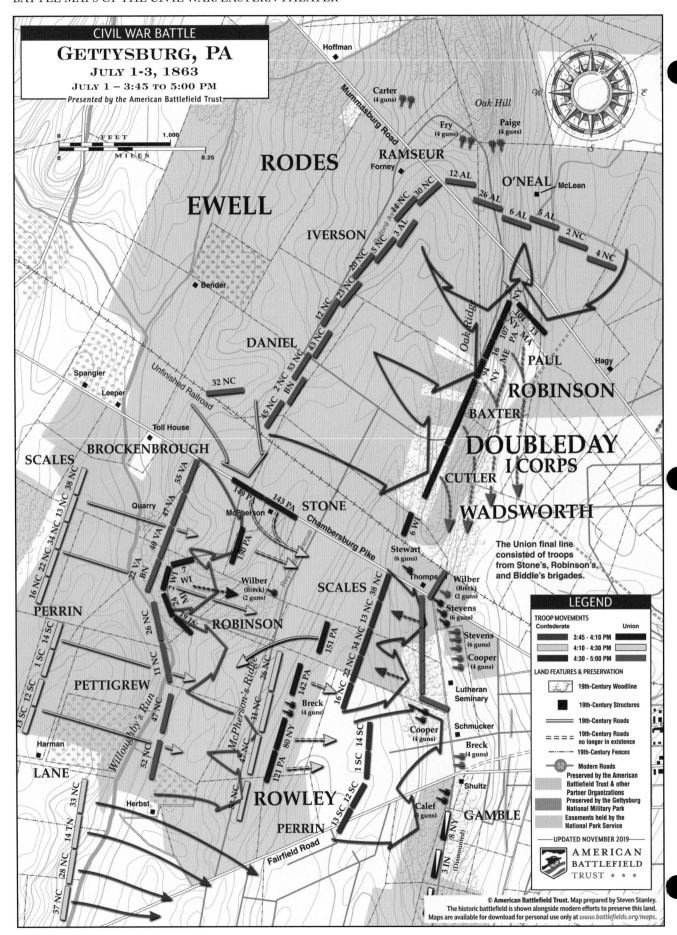

CIVIL WAR BATTLE
GETTYSBURG, PA
JULY 1-3, 1863
JULY 1 – 3:45 TO 5:00 PM
Presented by the American Battlefield Trust

FEET 1,000
MILES 0.25

The Union final line consisted of troops from Stone's, Robinson's, and Biddle's brigades.

LEGEND

TROOP MOVEMENTS
Confederate	Union
	3:45 - 4:10 PM
	4:10 - 4:30 PM
	4:30 - 5:00 PM

LAND FEATURES & PRESERVATION
- 19th-Century Woodline
- 19th-Century Structures
- 19th-Century Roads
- 19th-Century Roads no longer in existence
- 19th-Century Fences
- 52 Modern Roads
- Preserved by the American Battlefield Trust & other Partner Organizations
- Preserved by the Gettysburg National Military Park
- Easements held by the National Park Service

— UPDATED NOVEMBER 2019 —

AMERICAN BATTLEFIELD TRUST ★ ★ ★

© American Battlefield Trust. Map prepared by Steven Stanley.
The historic battlefield is shown alongside modern efforts to preserve this land.
Maps are available for download for personal use only at www.battlefields.org/maps.

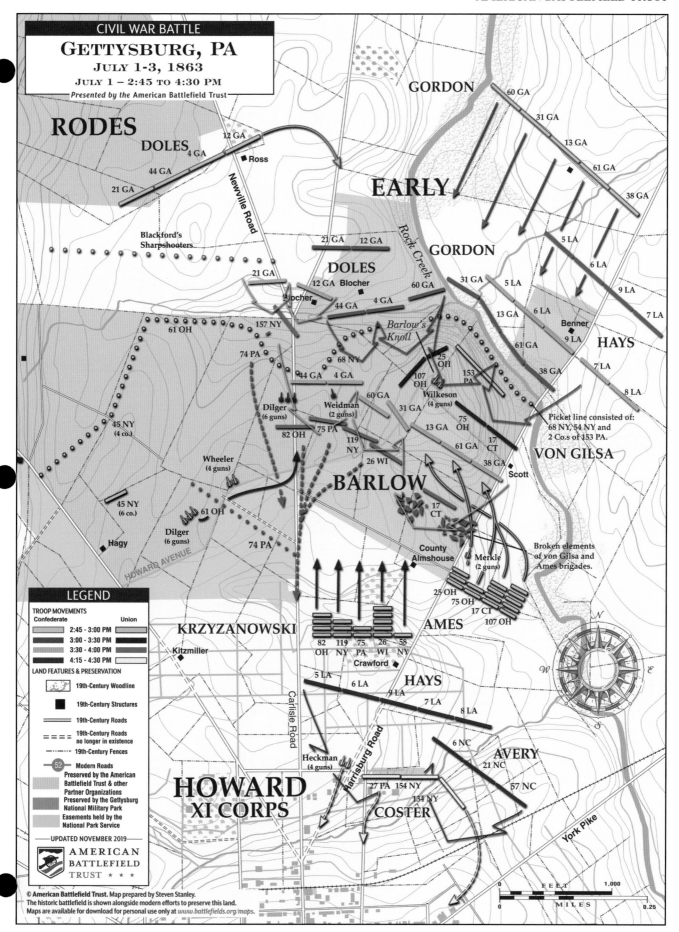

CIVIL WAR BATTLE
GETTYSBURG, PA
JULY 1-3, 1863
JULY 1 – 2:45 TO 4:30 PM
Presented by the American Battlefield Trust

RODES

DOLES

12 GA
4 GA
Ross
44 GA
21 GA

Newville Road

Blackford's
Sharpshooters

EARLY

60 GA
31 GA
13 GA
61 GA
38 GA

5 LA
6 LA
9 LA
7 LA

GORDON

21 GA   12 GA

DOLES

12 GA   Blocher
60 GA
44 GA   4 GA

31 GA
5 LA
13 GA   6 LA

Benner
9 LA

HAYS

7 LA

8 LA

Barlow's Knoll

61 OH
157 NY

74 PA

68 NY

44 GA   4 GA

60 GA

31 GA

13 GA

25 OH
107 OH   153 PA
Wilkeson
(4 guns)

75 OH
61 GA   17 CT

38 GA

Scott

Picket line consisted of:
68 NY, 54 NY and
2 Co.s of 153 PA.

VON GILSA

45 NY
(4 co.)

Dilger
(6 guns)

82 OH

Weidman
(2 guns)

75 PA

119 NY

26 WI

BARLOW

17 CT

Broken elements
of von Gilsa and
Ames brigades.

45 NY
(6 co.)

Wheeler
(4 guns)

61 OH

Dilger
(6 guns)

74 PA

County
Almshouse

Merkle
(2 guns)

25 OH
75 OH
17 CT
107 OH

Hagy

HOWARD AVENUE

LEGEND
TROOP MOVEMENTS

Confederate		Union	
	2:45 - 3:00 PM		
	3:00 - 3:30 PM		
	3:30 - 4:00 PM		
	4:15 - 4:30 PM		

LAND FEATURES & PRESERVATION

19th-Century Woodline

19th-Century Structures

19th-Century Roads

19th-Century Roads
no longer in existence

19th-Century Fences

52   Modern Roads

Preserved by the American
Battlefield Trust & other
Partner Organizations

Preserved by the Gettysburg
National Military Park

Easements held by the
National Park Service

—— UPDATED NOVEMBER 2019 ——

**AMERICAN
BATTLEFIELD
TRUST ★ ★ ★**

KRZYZANOWSKI

Kitzmiller

82   119   75   26   58
OH   NY   PA   WI   NY
Crawford

AMES

HAYS

5 LA
6 LA
9 LA
7 LA
8 LA

6 NC

21 NC

AVERY

57 NC

Heckman
(4 guns)

27 PA   154 NY

134 NY

**HOWARD
XI CORPS**

COSTER

York Pike

Carlisle Road

Harrisburg Road

© American Battlefield Trust. Map prepared by Steven Stanley.
The historic battlefield is shown alongside modern efforts to preserve this land.
Maps are available for download for personal use only at www.battlefields.org/maps.

FEET   1,000

MILES   0.25

57

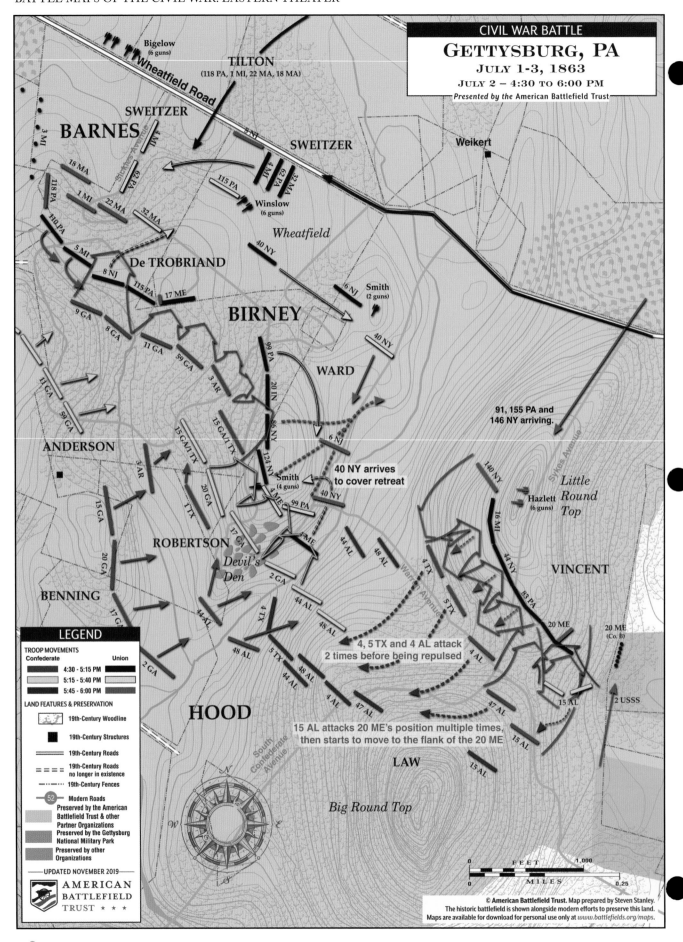

CIVIL WAR BATTLE
GETTYSBURG, PA
JULY 1-3, 1863
JULY 2 – 4:30 TO 6:00 PM
Presented by the American Battlefield Trust

Bigelow
(6 guns)

TILTON
(118 PA, 1 MI, 22 MA, 18 MA)

Wheatfield Road

SWEITZER

BARNES

SWEITZER

Weikert

3 MI

18 MA

62 PA

4 INF

8 NJ

4 MI

20 PA

32 MA

115 PA

118 PA

1 MI

22 MA

32 MA

Winslow
(6 guns)

HO.PA

5 MI

De TROBRIAND

Wheatfield

40 NY

8 NJ

115 PA

17 ME

Smith
(2 guns)

9 GA

BIRNEY

6 NJ

8 GA

11 GA

59 GA

3 AR

99 PA

WARD

40 NY

11 GA

59 GA

20 IN

86 NY

91, 155 PA and
146 NY arriving.

ANDERSON

15 GA/1 TX

15 GA/1 TX

124 NY

6 NJ

3 AR

20 GA

1 TX

Smith
(4 guns)

4 ME

40 NY

**40 NY arrives
to cover retreat**

140 NY

*Little
Round
Top*

Hazlett
(6 guns)

15 GA

99 PA

16 MI

20 GA

ROBERTSON

17 GA

4 ME

44 AL

48 AL

4 TX

5 TX

44 NY

VINCENT

*Devil's
Den*

2 GA

83 PA

BENNING

17 GA

44 AL

4 TX

44 AL

48 AL

4 AL

20 ME

20 ME
(Co. B)

2 GA

48 AL

5 TX

48 AL

44 AL

**4, 5 TX and 4 AL attack
2 times before being repulsed**

4 AL

15 AL

2 USSS

HOOD

4 AL

47 AL

47 AL

15 AL

**15 AL attacks 20 ME's position multiple times,
then starts to move to the flank of the 20 ME**

LAW

15 AL

Big Round Top

LEGEND
TROOP MOVEMENTS
Confederate   Union

4:30 - 5:15 PM

5:15 - 5:40 PM

5:45 - 6:00 PM

LAND FEATURES & PRESERVATION

19th-Century Woodline

19th-Century Structures

19th-Century Roads

19th-Century Roads
no longer in existence

19th-Century Fences

52 Modern Roads

Preserved by the American
Battlefield Trust & other
Partner Organizations

Preserved by the Gettysburg
National Military Park

Preserved by other
Organizations

— UPDATED NOVEMBER 2019 —

**AMERICAN
BATTLEFIELD
TRUST ★ ★ ★**

FEET   1,000

MILES   0.25

© American Battlefield Trust. Map prepared by Steven Stanley.
The historic battlefield is shown alongside modern efforts to preserve this land.
Maps are available for download for personal use only at *www.battlefields.org/maps*.

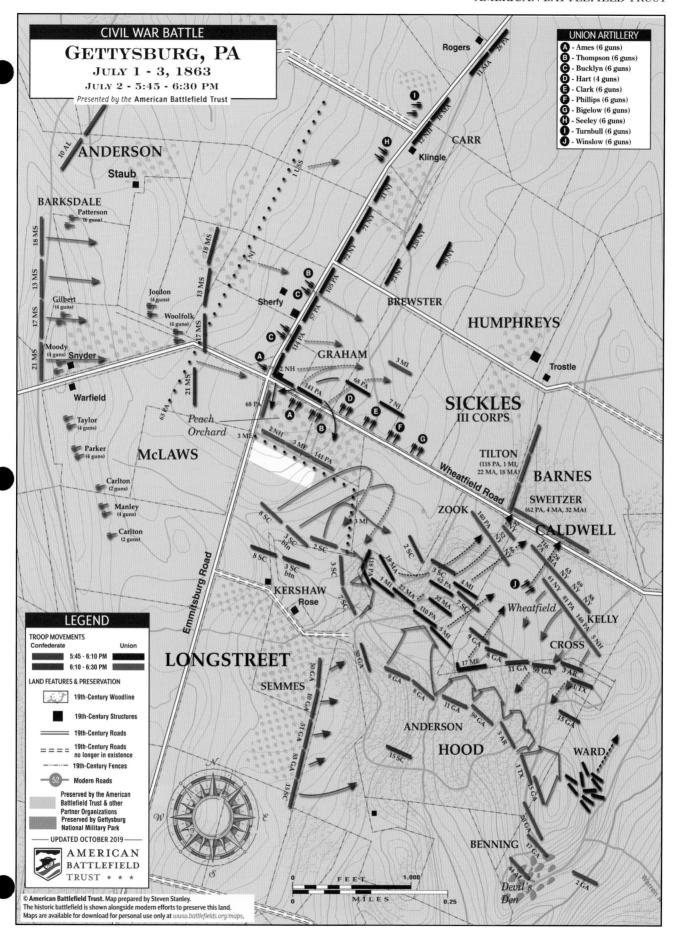

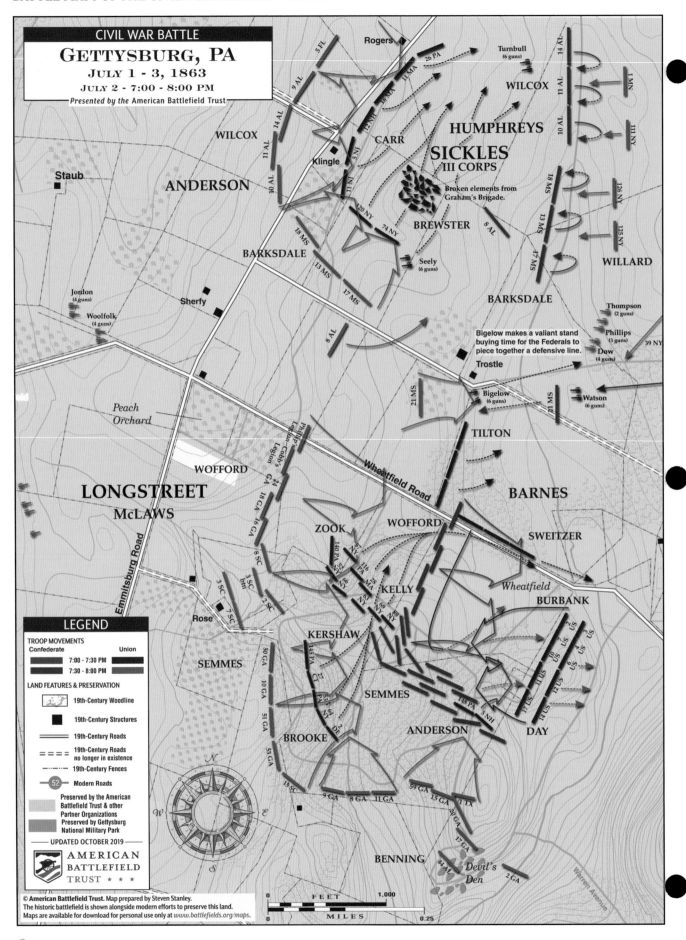

CIVIL WAR BATTLE
GETTYSBURG, PA
JULY 1 - 3, 1863
JULY 2 · 7:00 - 8:00 PM
Presented by the American Battlefield Trust

LEGEND

TROOP MOVEMENTS
Confederate   Union

7:00 - 7:30 PM

7:30 - 8:00 PM

LAND FEATURES & PRESERVATION

19th-Century Woodline

19th-Century Structures

19th-Century Roads

19th-Century Roads no longer in existence

19th-Century Fences

52 Modern Roads

Preserved by the American Battlefield Trust & other Partner Organizations

Preserved by Gettysburg National Military Park

— UPDATED OCTOBER 2019 —

AMERICAN BATTLEFIELD TRUST ★ ★ ★

© American Battlefield Trust. Map prepared by Steven Stanley.
The historic battlefield is shown alongside modern efforts to preserve this land.
Maps are available for download for personal use only at www.battlefields.org/maps.

Bigelow makes a valiant stand buying time for the Federals to piece together a defensive line.

Broken elements from Graham's Brigade.

FEET   1,000

MILES   0.25

60

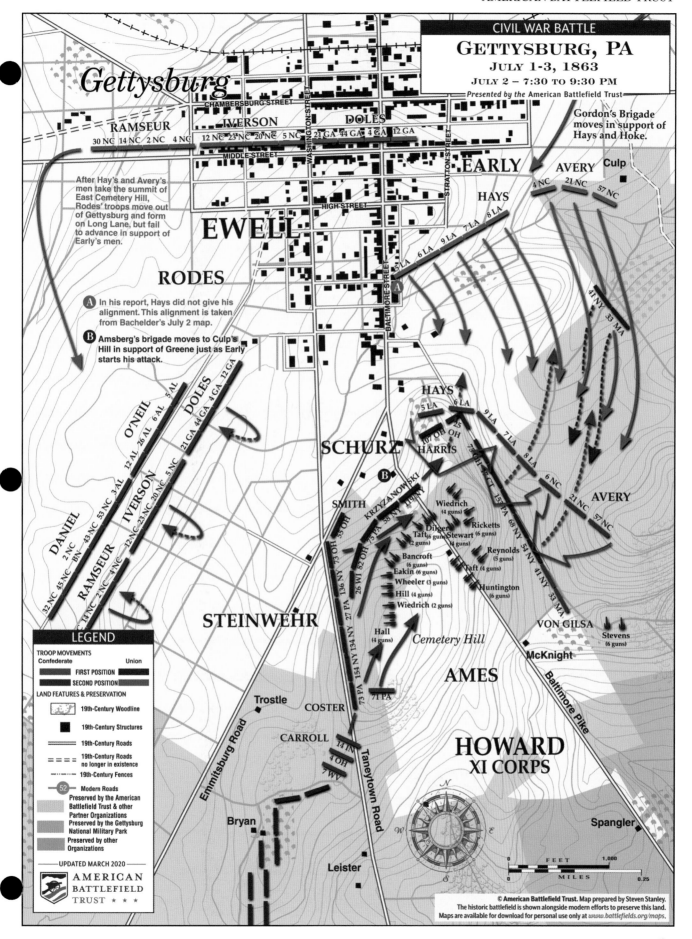

CIVIL WAR BATTLE

GETTYSBURG, PA

JULY 1-3, 1863

JULY 2 – 7:30 TO 9:30 PM

Presented by the American Battlefield Trust

Gordon's Brigade moves in support of Hays and Hoke.

Gettysburg

CHAMBERSBURG STREET

RAMSEUR
30 NC 14 NC 2 NC 4 NC

IVERSON
12 NC 23 NC 20 NC 5 NC

DOLES
21 GA 44 GA 4 GA 12 GA

EARLY

AVERY
4 NC 21 NC 57 NC Culp

MIDDLE STREET

HAYS
5 LA 8 LA
7 LA
9 LA
6 LA
5 LA

EWELL

HIGH STREET

After Hay's and Avery's men take the summit of East Cemetery Hill, Rodes' troops move out of Gettysburg and form on Long Lane, but fail to advance in support of Early's men.

RODES

41 NY 33 MA

Ⓐ In his report, Hays did not give his alignment. This alignment is taken from Bachelder's July 2 map.

Ⓑ Amsberg's brigade moves to Culp's Hill in support of Greene just as Early starts his attack.

O'NEIL
3 AL 6 AL 5 AL
12 AL 26 AL 5 AL

DOLES
21 GA 44 GA 4 GA 12 GA

HAYS
5 LA 6 LA
9 LA 7 LA
107 OH 25 OH 8 LA
HARRIS 6 NC
21 NC AVERY
57 NC

IVERSON
23 NC 20 NC 5 NC

DANIEL
2 NC

RAMSEUR

SCHURZ

Ⓑ

SMITH
55 OH
KRZYZANOWSKI
73 OH 58 NY 119 NY
82 OH 75 PA
26 WI 136 NY
27 PA
154 NY 134 NY
73 PA

Wiedrich (4 guns)
Dilger
Taft (6 guns) Stewart (2 guns) (4 guns)
Ricketts (6 guns)
Bancroft (6 guns)
Eakin (6 guns)
Wheeler (3 guns)
Hill (4 guns)
Wiedrich (2 guns)
Reynolds (5 guns)
Taft (4 guns)
Huntington (6 guns)

32 NC 45 NC BN 43 NC 53 NC 3 AL
14 NC 2 NC 4 NC 32 NC 23 NC

STEINWEHR

Hall (4 guns)

Cemetery Hill

VON GILSA

Stevens (6 guns)

McKnight

AMES

71 PA

HOWARD
XI CORPS

Trostle

COSTER

CARROLL
14 IN
4 OH
7 WV

Bryan

Leister

Spangler

LEGEND

TROOP MOVEMENTS
Confederate   Union

FIRST POSITION

SECOND POSITION

LAND FEATURES & PRESERVATION

19th-Century Woodline

19th-Century Structures

19th-Century Roads

19th-Century Roads no longer in existence

19th-Century Fences

52 Modern Roads

Preserved by the American Battlefield Trust & other Partner Organizations

Preserved by the Gettysburg National Military Park

Preserved by other Organizations

UPDATED MARCH 2020

AMERICAN BATTLEFIELD TRUST ★★★

Emmitsburg Road

Taneytown Road

Baltimore Pike

FEET 1,000

MILES 0.25

© American Battlefield Trust. Map prepared by Steven Stanley.
The historic battlefield is shown alongside modern efforts to preserve this land.
Maps are available for download for personal use only at *www.battlefields.org/maps*.

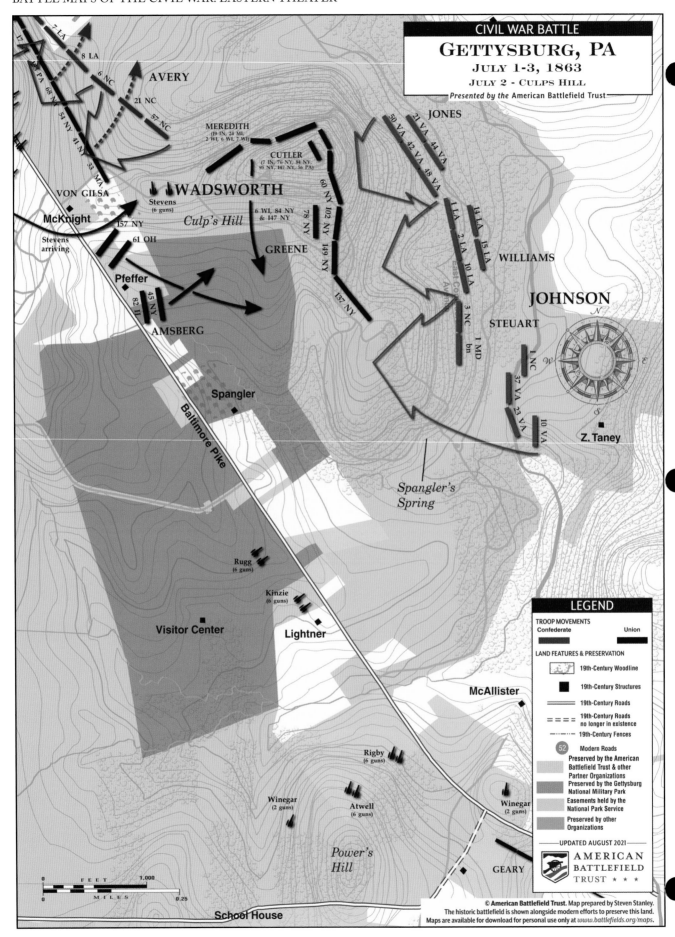

CIVIL WAR BATTLE

GETTYSBURG, PA

JULY 1-3, 1863
JULY 2 - CULPS HILL

Presented by the American Battlefield Trust

7 LA

8 LA

6 NC

AVERY

21 NC

57 NC

153 PA 68 NC 54 NY 41 NY 33 MA

VON GILSA

McKnight

Stevens arriving

157 NY

61 OH

Pfeffer

82 IL

45 NY

AMSBERG

Stevens
(6 guns)

WADSWORTH

Culp's Hill

MEREDITH
(19 IN, 24 MI,
2 WI, 6 WI, 7 WI)

CUTLER
(7 IN, 76 NY, 84 NY,
95 NY, 147 NY, 56 PA)

6 WI, 84 NY
& 147 NY

78 NY

60 NY

102 NY

149 NY

GREENE

137 NY

50 VA

21 VA

42 VA

44 VA

48 VA

JONES

1 LA

2 LA

10 LA

14 LA

15 LA

WILLIAMS

3 NC

1 MD
bn

JOHNSON

STEUART

1 NC

37 VA

23 VA

10 VA

Z. Taney

Spangler

Baltimore Pike

*Spangler's
Spring*

Rugg
(6 guns)

Kinzie
(6 guns)

Visitor Center

Lightner

McAllister

Rigby
(6 guns)

Winegar
(2 guns)

Atwell
(6 guns)

Winegar
(2 guns)

*Power's
Hill*

GEARY

LEGEND

TROOP MOVEMENTS
Confederate   Union

LAND FEATURES & PRESERVATION

19th-Century Woodline

19th-Century Structures

19th-Century Roads

19th-Century Roads
no longer in existence

19th-Century Fences

52   Modern Roads

Preserved by the American
Battlefield Trust & other
Partner Organizations

Preserved by the Gettysburg
National Military Park

Easements held by the
National Park Service

Preserved by other
Organizations

—UPDATED AUGUST 2021—

AMERICAN
BATTLEFIELD
TRUST ★ ★ ★

FEET   1,000

MILES   0.25

School House

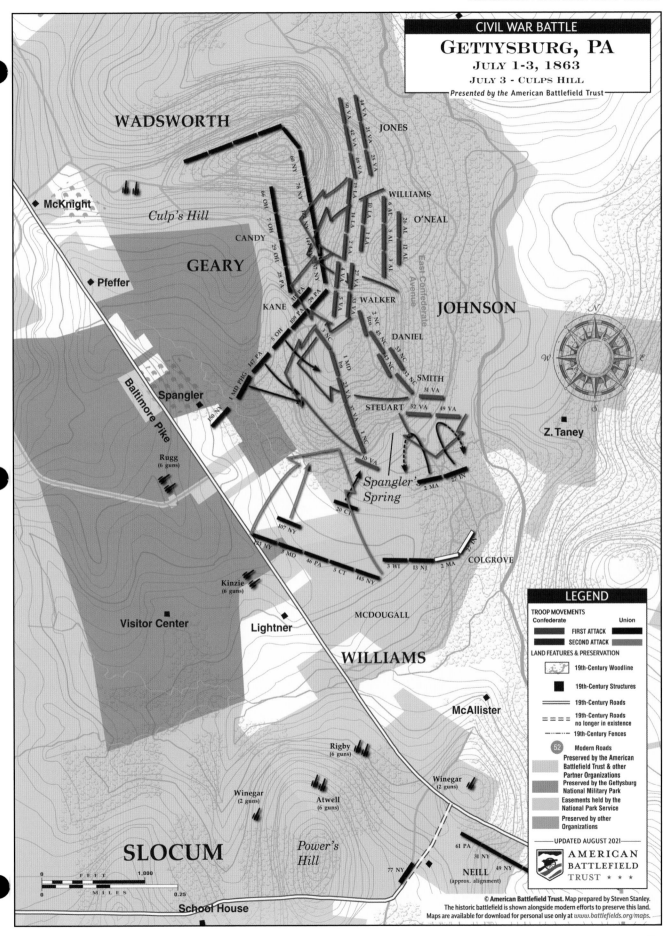

AMERICAN BATTLEFIELD TRUST

CIVIL WAR BATTLE
GETTYSBURG, PA
JULY 1-3, 1863
JULY 3 - CULPS HILL
Presented by the American Battlefield Trust

WADSWORTH

JONES

Culp's Hill

◆ McKnight

CANDY

WILLIAMS

GEARY

O'NEAL

◆ Pfeffer

KANE

WALKER

JOHNSON

DANIEL

Baltimore Pike

Spangler

SMITH

STEUART

◼ Z. Taney

Rugg
(6 guns)

Spangler's Spring

COLGROVE

Kinzie
(6 guns)

Visitor Center

Lightner

MCDOUGALL

WILLIAMS

◼ McAllister

Rigby
(6 guns)

Winegar
(2 guns)

Winegar
(2 guns)

Atwell
(6 guns)

SLOCUM

Power's Hill

NEILL
(approx. alignment)

FEET 1,000
MILES 0.25

School House

LEGEND

TROOP MOVEMENTS
Confederate   Union
FIRST ATTACK
SECOND ATTACK

LAND FEATURES & PRESERVATION

19th-Century Woodline
19th-Century Structures
19th-Century Roads
19th-Century Roads no longer in existence
19th-Century Fences
52 Modern Roads
Preserved by the American Battlefield Trust & other Partner Organizations
Preserved by the Gettysburg National Military Park
Easements held by the National Park Service
Preserved by other Organizations

— UPDATED AUGUST 2021 —

AMERICAN BATTLEFIELD TRUST ★ ★ ★

© American Battlefield Trust. Map prepared by Steven Stanley.
The historic battlefield is shown alongside modern efforts to preserve this land.
Maps are available for download for personal use only at www.battlefields.org/maps.

63

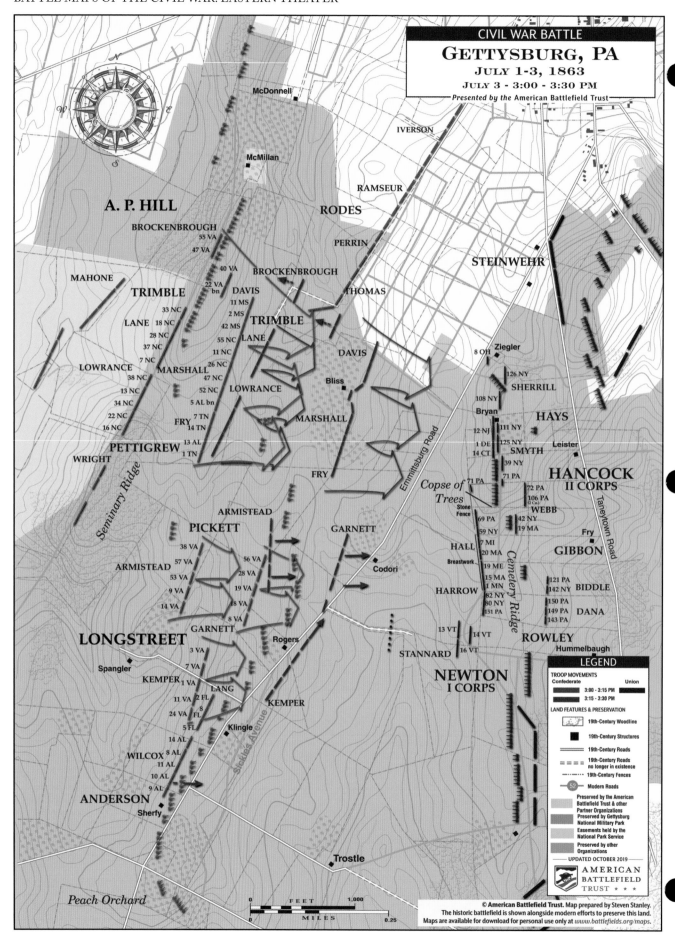

CIVIL WAR BATTLE
GETTYSBURG, PA
JULY 1-3, 1863
JULY 3 - 3:00 - 3:30 PM
Presented by the American Battlefield Trust

McDonnell

IVERSON

McMillan

RAMSEUR

A. P. HILL

RODES

BROCKENBROUGH

55 VA

47 VA

PERRIN

STEINWEHR

MAHONE

40 VA

BROCKENBROUGH

22 VA bn

DAVIS

THOMAS

TRIMBLE

11 MS

33 NC

2 MS

LANE   18 NC

42 MS

TRIMBLE

28 NC

55 NC

37 NC

LANE

DAVIS

Ziegler

8 OH

7 NC

11 NC

126 NY

26 NC

SHERRILL

LOWRANCE

MARSHALL

47 NC

38 NC

Bliss

108 NY

13 NC

52 NC

LOWRANCE

Bryan

HAYS

34 NC

5 AL bn

12 NJ

111 NY

22 NC

7 TN

MARSHALL

1 DE

125 NY

16 NC

FRY

14 TN

14 CT

SMYTH

Leister

13 AL

39 NY

PETTIGREW

1 TN

71 PA   71 PA

HANCOCK

WRIGHT

Seminary Ridge

FRY

Copse of Trees

72 PA

II CORPS

106 PA (2 Co.)

Stone Fence

WEBB

69 PA

42 NY

59 NY

19 MA

Fry

ARMISTEAD

PICKETT

GARNETT

HALL

7 MI

20 MA

GIBBON

38 VA

Breastwork

19 ME

ARMISTEAD

57 VA

56 VA

Codori

15 MA   121 PA

53 VA

28 VA

1 MN   142 NY   **BIDDLE**

9 VA

19 VA

HARROW

82 NY

150 PA

14 VA

18 VA

80 NY   149 PA   **DANA**

151 PA   143 PA

8 VA

GARNETT

Rogers

13 VT

14 VT

ROWLEY

LONGSTREET

3 VA

16 VT

Hummelbaugh

Spangler

7 VA

STANNARD

KEMPER   1 VA

NEWTON

KEMPER   11 VA   2 FL

LANG

I CORPS

24 VA   8 FL

KEMPER

5 FL

Klingle

14 AL

WILCOX   8 AL

11 AL

10 AL

9 AL

ANDERSON

Sherfy

Trostle

Peach Orchard

0   FEET   1,000

0   MILES   0.25

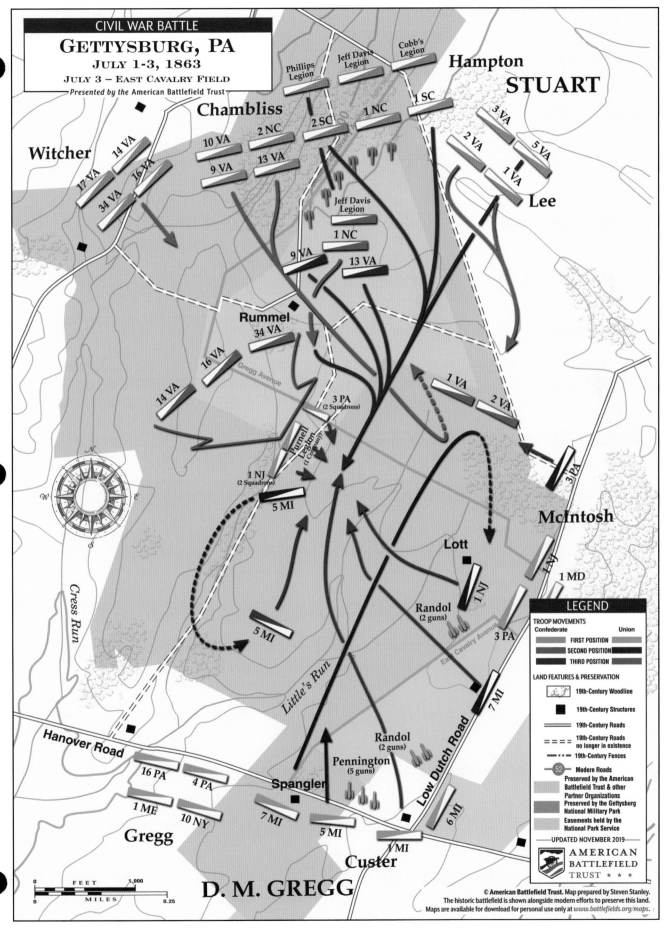

CIVIL WAR BATTLE
GETTYSBURG, PA
JULY 1-3, 1863
JULY 3 – EAST CAVALRY FIELD
Presented by the American Battlefield Trust

Phillips Legion
Jeff Davis Legion
Cobb's Legion
Hampton
STUART
Chambliss
1 SC
3 VA
5 VA
2 VA
10 VA
2 NC
2 SC
1 NC
Witcher
14 VA
9 VA
13 VA
1 VA
17 VA
16 VA
Lee
34 VA
Jeff Davis Legion
1 NC
9 VA
13 VA
Rummel
34 VA
16 VA
1 VA
2 VA
Gregg Avenue
14 VA
3 PA
(2 Squadrons)
Purnell Legion
(1 Company)
1 NJ
(2 Squadrons)
5 MI
3 PA
McIntosh
1 NJ
1 MD
Lott
Randol
(2 guns)
1 NJ
5 MI
East Cavalry Avenue
3 PA
Little's Run
Cress Run
7 MI
Hanover Road
16 PA
4 PA
Randol
(2 guns)
Spangler
Pennington
(5 guns)
Low Dutch Road
1 ME
10 NY
7 MI
6 MI
Gregg
5 MI
1 MI
Custer
D. M. GREGG

LEGEND
TROOP MOVEMENTS
Confederate   Union
FIRST POSITION
SECOND POSITION
THIRD POSITION

LAND FEATURES & PRESERVATION
19th-Century Woodline
19th-Century Structures
19th-Century Roads
19th-Century Roads no longer in existence
19th-Century Fences
52 Modern Roads
Preserved by the American Battlefield Trust & other Partner Organizations
Preserved by the Gettysburg National Military Park
Easements held by the National Park Service
—UPDATED NOVEMBER 2019—
AMERICAN BATTLEFIELD TRUST ★ ★ ★

FEET 1,000
MILES 0.25

© American Battlefield Trust. Map prepared by Steven Stanley.
The historic battlefield is shown alongside modern efforts to preserve this land.
Maps are available for download for personal use only at *www.battlefields.org/maps*.

BATTLE *of* THE WILDERNESS

MAY 5 - 6, 1864

IN THE MONTHS FOLLOWING THE BATTLE OF GETTYSBURG, much maneuvering, but little decisive action, took place across northern Virginia. The Battles of Bristoe Station, Rappahannock Station and Mine Run kept Lee and the victor of Gettysburg, George G. Meade, on their toes, but accomplished little else.

In March of 1864, President Lincoln turned to the winningest general in his stable, Ulysses S. Grant. After meeting with Lincoln and chief of staff, Henry Halleck, Grant settled on a strategy to apply simultaneous pressure across the entire expanse of the Confederacy. At the urging of Lincoln, he also settled on a strategy of annihilation. With 1864 an election year in the North, swift and decisive action had to be taken to end the Southern Confederacy. In April, Grant established his headquarters in the East and attached himself to Meade's Army of the Potomac. In May, Union armies moved into Louisiana, Georgia and Virginia. The Federal objective in 1864 was the destruction of the Confederate armies, as well as the South's capacity for making war.

Grant clashed with Robert E. Lee and his Army of Northern Virginia for the first time in May of 1864. In what was to become known as the Overland Campaign, Lee, with a force half the size of Grant's, utilized the terrain to nullify the large numbers of Federal infantry and artillery. The dense 70-square-mile second-growth forest had an oppressive, ominous feel about it—an apt setting for the bloodletting to follow.

Fighting erupted late in the morning of May 5, 1864, as along the the Orange Turnpike. Although the Federal infantry managed to break through at several points, the Confederate line held. The battle then shifted to the south, as both sides vied for control of the vital Orange Plank Road and Brock Road intersection. Darkness brought an end to the fighting, with the Federals in firm control of the junction.

Before daylight on May 6, a combined Federal force under Maj. Gen. Winfield S.Hancock rolled west along the Orange Plank Road and smashed through the Confederate line. Fortunately for Lee, Confederate reinforcements arrived under Lt. Gen. James Longstreet in time to stabilize the position.

Late on the morning of the 6th, Longstreet launched an audacious flank attack on the Federals, but just over one year removed and less than 3.5 miles from where Jackson had been felled by friendly fire, Longstreet, too, was wounded in the midst of a flank attack by his own men.

Lee took personal command and led a frontal assault against the Orange Plank Road and Brock Road intersection. Localized breakthroughs penetrated the Federal line, but the Confederates were played out.

The next day, with fires raging in the Wilderness, Grant and Mead rode into the intersection. They turned their horses south, and pressed on toward Richmond. There would be "no turning back."

✳ ✳ PRESERVATION ✳ ✳

To date, the **American Battlefield Trust** has saved **259 acres** at The Wilderness Battlefield.

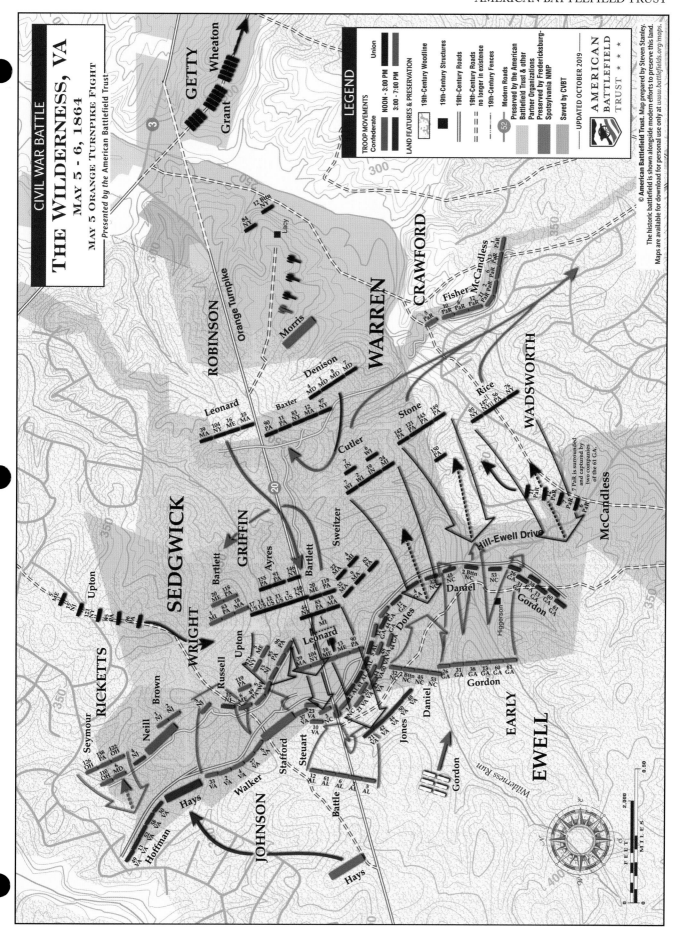

CIVIL WAR BATTLE

THE WILDERNESS, VA

MAY 5 - 6, 1864

MAY 5 ORANGE TURNPIKE FIGHT

Presented by the American Battlefield Trust

LEGEND

TROOP MOVEMENTS

Confederate | Union

LAND FEATURES & PRESERVATION

NOON - 3:00 PM
3:00 - 7:00 PM

19th-Century Woodline
19th-Century Structures
19th-Century Roads
19th-Century Roads no longer in existence
19th-Century Fences
Modern Roads
Preserved by the American Battlefield Trust & other Partner Organizations
Preserved by Fredericksburg-Spotsylvania NMP
Saved by CVBT

— UPDATED OCTOBER 2019

© American Battlefield Trust. Map prepared by Steven Stanley.
The historic battlefield is shown alongside modern efforts to preserve this land.
Maps are available for download for personal use only at *www.battlefields.org/maps*.

67

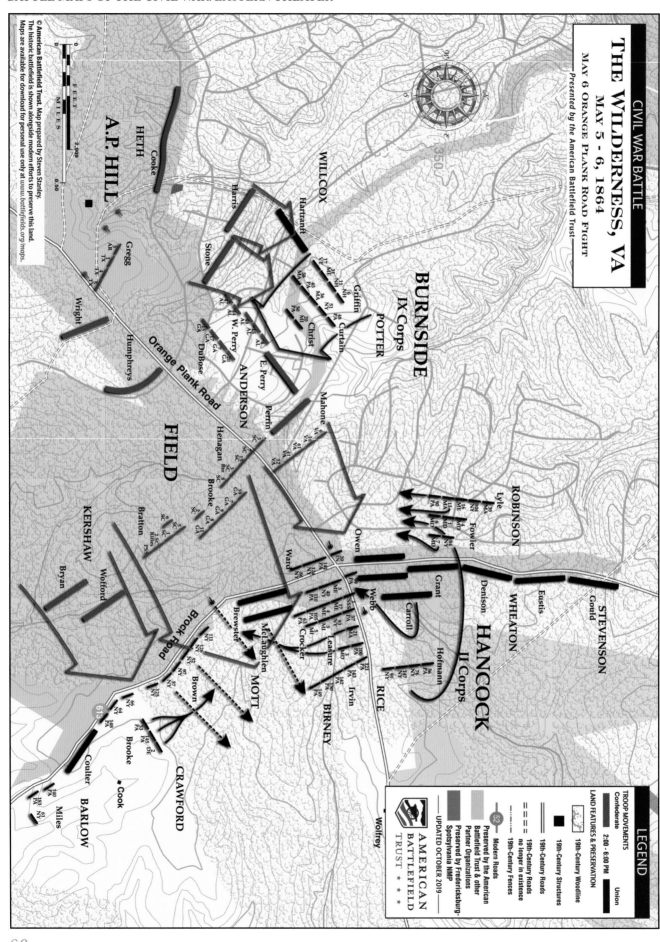

CIVIL WAR BATTLE

THE WILDERNESS, VA

MAY 5 - 6, 1864

MAY 6 ORANGE PLANK ROAD FIGHT

Presented by the American Battlefield Trust

LEGEND

TROOP MOVEMENTS
Confederate
Union

LAND FEATURES & PRESERVATION
2:00 - 6:00 PM
19th-Century Woodline

19th-Century Structures
19th-Century Roads
19th-Century Roads no longer in existence
19th-Century Fences

Modern Roads
Preserved by the American Battlefield Trust & other Partner Organizations
Preserved by Fredericksburg-Spotsylvania NMP

UPDATED OCTOBER 2019

AMERICAN
BATTLEFIELD
TRUST ★ ★ ★

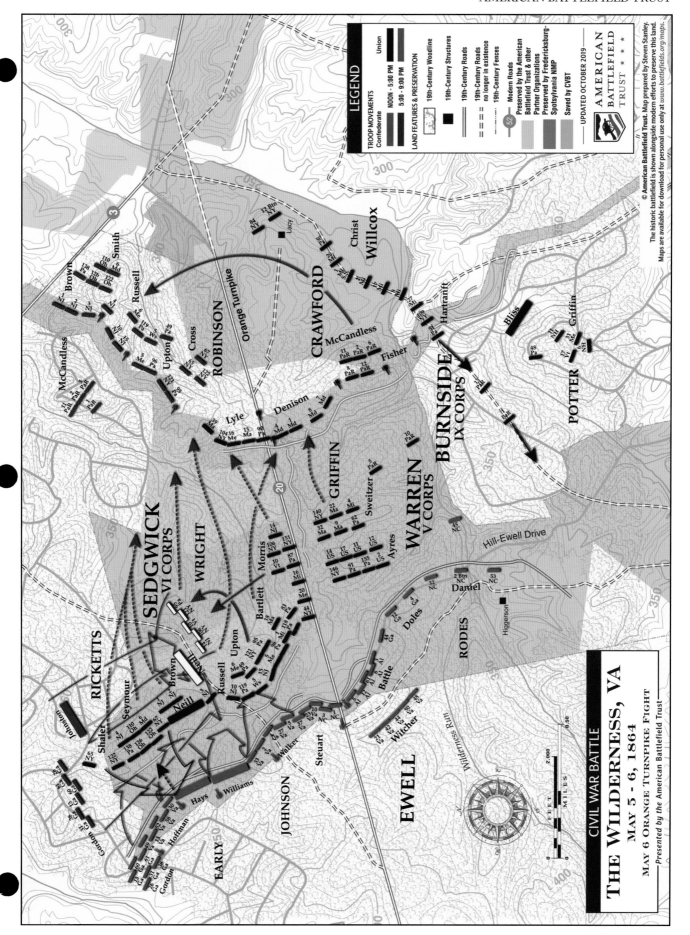

CIVIL WAR BATTLE
THE WILDERNESS, VA
MAY 5 - 6, 1864

May 6 Orange Turnpike Fight

Presented by the American Battlefield Trust

BATTLE *of* SPOTSYLVANIA COURTHOUSE

MAY 8 - 21, 1864

GRANT AND MEADE ENTERED THE ORANGE PLANK ROAD AND Brock Road intersection on the evening of May 7. Their destination was the crossroads hamlet of Spotsylvania Court House. Grant hoped to steal a march on Lee by interposing the Army of the Potomac between his foe and Richmond, thereby forcing Lee to attack Grant on ground of Grant's own choosing. Lee, on the other hand, was contending with the fires of the Wilderness, and even though Grant held the Brock Road, the inside track to Spotsylvania, Lee evened the odds by cutting a road of his own through the woods to Spotsylvania.

By mid-morning of May 8, the Federals were two miles from their objective, though they were hampered by Jeb Stuart's cavalry all morning. Atop the last defensible ridge, Stuart's dismounted troopers made a desperate stand. As the Federal infantry rushed up the north face of Laurel Hill, Confederate reinforcements appeared over the crest. The Confederates won the race to Spotsylvania.

Unlike the Wilderness, the area around Spotsylvania offered open farm fields. Lee ordered his men to dig in. The Federals attempted to dislodge the Rebels through a series of uncoordinated attacks. On May 9, the beloved VI Corps commander John Sedgwick was felled by a sharpshooter's bullet and killed instantly.

On the 10th, Grant launched assaults on the Confederate left at the Po River. Lee countered. Still undaunted, Grant launched assaults from the Federal left flank, in an area soldiers dubbed the "Mule Shoe"—a large salient position that protruded outward from the Confederate lines, which, to the men, resembled a Mule Shoe. A force of 4,500 Federals breached the salient, using a compact formation. Although the success was short-lived, Grant now had the tactics in place to penetrate Lee's lines, and he had found the weak point his army so desperately needed.

On May 12, Grant launched the largest Federal assault at Spotsylvania Court House. Men of the Union II Corps spearheaded a thrust into the apex of Lee's salient. More than 20,000 Federals struck Lee's lines from the north. To the east, the IX Corps struck the base of the salient. To the west, the V Corps was to hold Lee's men in place at Laurel Hill. The II and IX Corps struck, by the V Corps held fast. With his men in disarray, and having misjudged Grant's intentions, Lee caught a bit of luck. With V Corps not assaulting Laurel Hill, he was given a free hand to shift men from his left and into his center, to help seal the breach.

For nearly 22 hours, the fighting in the mud and rain raged in the Mule Shoe. Lee's men bought time with lives, as his engineers constructed a new and what would be impregnable line. The men in blue and gray fought tenaciously over a small portion of the line dubbed the "Bloody Angle." The small-arms fire was so intense, it felled trees and men alike. On the morning of May 13, the Confederates withdrew to their new line. Federals crept forward through the Confederate positions. They found Lee's new line of freshly churned dirt lined with infantry, cannon and impediments of all nature. For the next week, Grant tried to find a weak point in Lee's line. A weakness did not exist. Still undaunted, Grant disengaged the army and moved south once more toward Richmond.

✳ ✳ PRESERVATION ✳ ✳

To date, the **American Battlefield Trust** has saved **5 acres** at Spotsylvania Court House Battlefield.

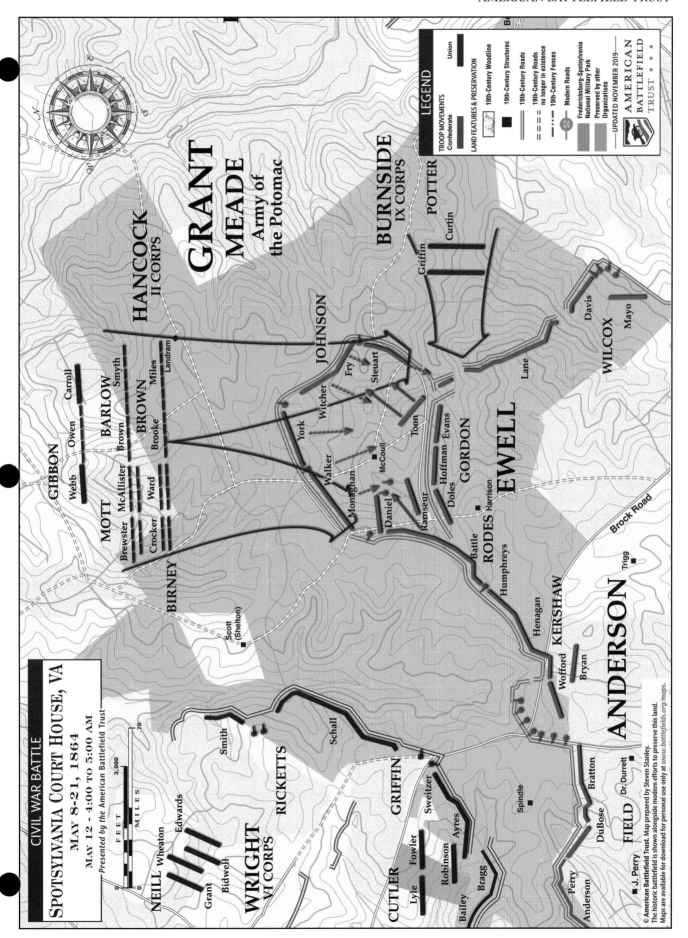

CIVIL WAR BATTLE

SPOTSYLVANIA COURT HOUSE, VA

MAY 8–21, 1864

MAY 12 – 4:00 TO 5:00 AM

Presented by the American Battlefield Trust

LEGEND

TROOP MOVEMENTS
Confederate   Union

LAND FEATURES & PRESERVATION
19th-Century Woodline
19th-Century Structures
19th-Century Roads
19th-Century Roads no longer in existence
19th-Century Fences
Modern Roads
Fredericksburg-Spotsylvania National Military Park
Preserved by other Organizations

UPDATED NOVEMBER 2019

AMERICAN BATTLEFIELD TRUST ★ ★ ★

© American Battlefield Trust. Map prepared by Steven Stanley.
The historic battlefield is shown alongside modern efforts to preserve this land.
Maps are available for download for personal use only at *www.battlefields.org/maps.*

71

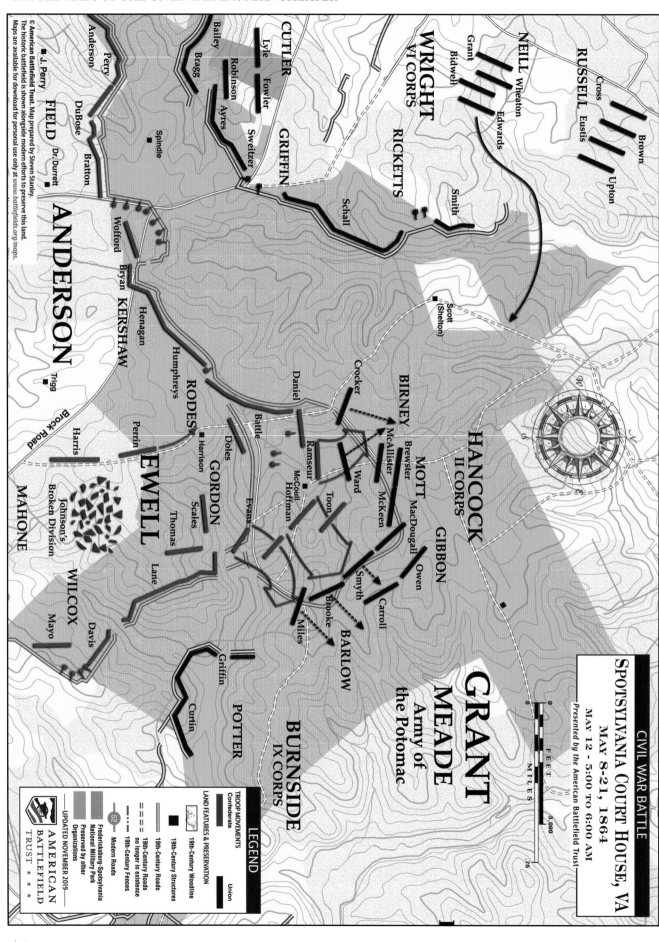

CIVIL WAR BATTLE

SPOTSYLVANIA COURT HOUSE, VA

MAY 8-21, 1864

MAY 12 - 5:00 TO 6:00 AM

Presented by the American Battlefield Trust

LEGEND

TROOP MOVEMENTS
- Confederate
- Union

LAND FEATURES & PRESERVATION
- 19th-Century Woodline
- 19th-Century Structures
- 19th-Century Fences
- 19th-Century Roads no longer in existence
- 19th-Century Roads
- Modern Roads
- 52 19th-Century Organizations
- Preserved by other Organizations
- Fredericksburg-Spotsylvania National Military Park

UPDATED NOVEMBER 2019

AMERICAN BATTLEFIELD TRUST ★ ★ ★

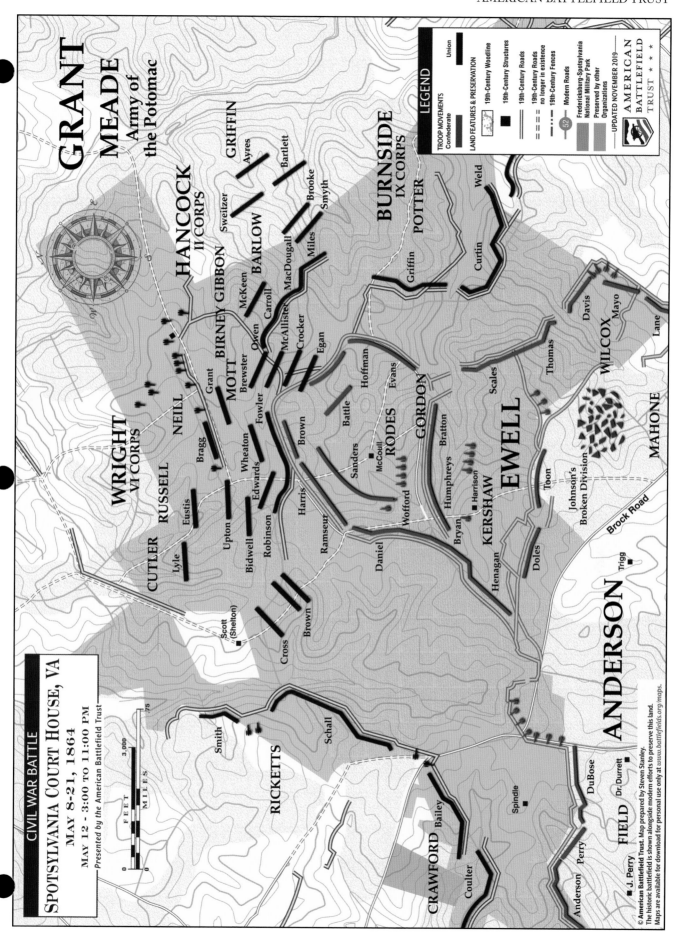

GRANT
MEADE
Army of
the Potomac

CIVIL WAR BATTLE
SPOTSYLVANIA COURT HOUSE, VA
MAY 8-21, 1864
MAY 12 - 3:00 TO 11:00 PM
Presented by the American Battlefield Trust

HANCOCK
II CORPS

GRIFFIN

BURNSIDE
IX CORPS

POTTER

WRIGHT
VI CORPS

RUSSELL

NEILL

CUTLER

BIRNEY

GIBBON

MOTT

BARLOW

RICKETTS

EWELL

KERSHAW

GORDON

RODES

WILCOX

MAHONE

ANDERSON

FIELD

CRAWFORD

LEGEND

TROOP MOVEMENTS
Confederate   Union

LAND FEATURES & PRESERVATION
19th-Century Woodline
19th-Century Structures
19th-Century Roads
19th-Century Roads
no longer in existence
19th-Century Fences
52   Modern Roads

Fredericksburg-Spotsylvania
National Military Park
Preserved by other
Organizations

AMERICAN
BATTLEFIELD
TRUST ★ ★ ★

——UPDATED NOVEMBER 2019——

© American Battlefield Trust. Map prepared by Steven Stanley.
The historic battlefield is shown alongside modern efforts to preserve this land.
Maps are available for download for personal use only at www.battlefields.org/maps.

FEET
0   3,000

MILES
0   .75

73

BATTLE *of* NORTH ANNA

MAY 23 - 26, 1864

JUST THREE WEEKS INTO THE NEW CAMPAIGN, THE MEN and leaders of the respective armies were on the verge of exhaustion. The combined casualties of the prior two battles had exceeded 60,000, and there was no end to the campaign in sight. Reinforcements arrived to bolster each army.

By the third week of May, Grant knew that Lee's line at Spotsylvania Court House was impregnable. In an effort to draw him out from behind his works, Grant sent his most trusted corps, the II, on a wide march of the east. The Federal commander hoped that Lee would take the bait and go after this lone corps. Once he pounced, Grant would sweep in and attack the Rebels with his other three corps.

Lee did not take the bait. Instead, he moved to block Grant's southward movements toward Richmond. His objective was the defensible North Anna River, 25 miles to the south of Spotsylvania.

Confederates reached the North Anna River and established a defensive line on the south bank of the waterway. Lee and his chief engineer Martin Luther Smith set a trap for Grant's army. Using terrain and Grant's own aggressive spirit against him, Lee hoped to draw the Union army into a trap. A strong salient—in the form of an inverted V—anchored on the dominant bluffs at Ox Ford became the centerpiece of Lee's defensive position, which was almost impregnable. Should Grant advance, he would need to break his army into three parts—one on the Telegraph Road, another at Ox Ford and a third at Jericho Mills. Each flank would have to cross the river twice to reinforce the other.

On May 23, one of A. P. Hill's divisions assaulted the isolated V Corps on the Union right, which had crossed the river at Jericho Mill. After a bloody seesaw fight, the Federal bridgehead remained intact. On the Union left flank, Winfield Hancock's II Corps seized Henagan's Redoubt and the Chesterfield Bridge over the North Anna.

Troubled by the lack of movement in his center, Grant ordered his only available unit, Ambrose Burnside's IX Corps, to move toward Ox Ford on May 24. Finding the Confederate defenses there too strong, Burnside sent a division to cross above Ox Ford to come in from behind, while another division approached over the Chesterfield Bridge. With two divisions converging on Ox Ford, Burnside hoped the Confederates would withdraw. Once across, however, the Federals discovered exceptionally strong enemy trench lines. Unfortunately, a rash order from a drunk officer, Brig. Gen. James H. Ledlie, sent a brigade of Federals to within 100 yards of the Rebel works, where they were swept from the field.

On May 25, Grant evaluated Lee's position and admitted, "To make a direct attack from either wing would cause a slaughter of our men that even success would not justify." As he had done at Wilderness and Spotsylvania, Grant gave up the field and moved south in an attempt to draw Lee into the open.

✳ ✳ PRESERVATION ✳ ✳

To date, the **American Battlefield Trust** has saved **874 acres** at North Anna Battlefield.

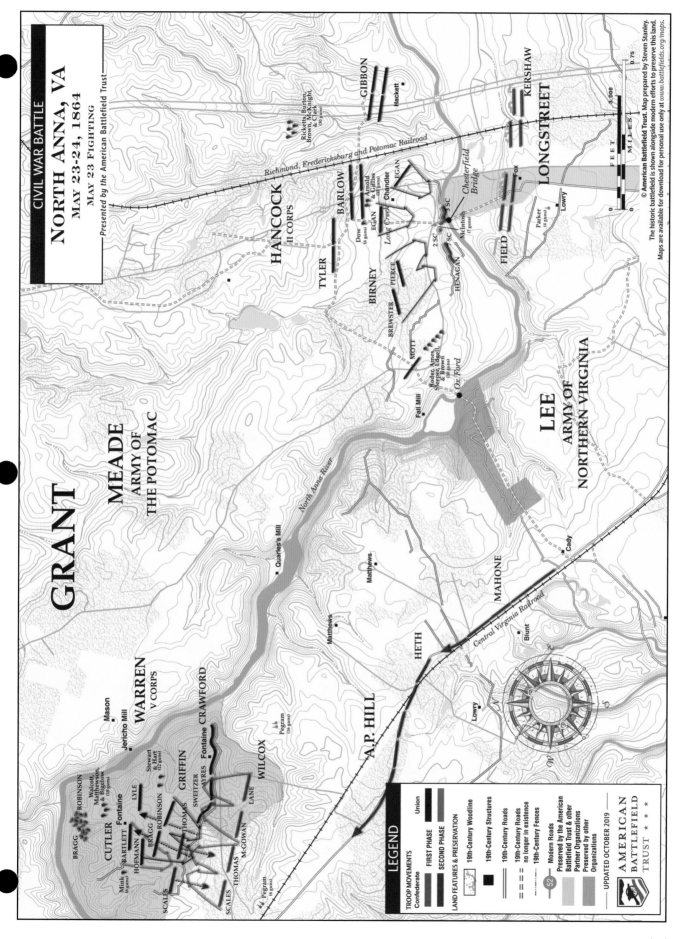

CIVIL WAR BATTLE
NORTH ANNA, VA
MAY 23-24, 1864
— MAY 23 FIGHTING —
— Presented by the American Battlefield Trust —

GRANT

MEADE
ARMY OF
THE POTOMAC

WARREN
V CORPS

CRAWFORD

GRIFFIN

WILCOX

BRAGG
ROBINSON
CUTLER
Mason
Jericho Mill
Walcott,
Matthewson,
& Bigelow
(13 guns)
Fontaine
Bartlett
LYLE
HOFMANN
Mink
(6 guns)
BRAGG
ROBINSON
THOMAS
SWEITZER
AYRES
Fontaine
Stewart
& Hart
(12 guns)
SCALES
SCALES
THOMAS
McGOWAN
LANE
Pegram
(6 guns)
Pegram
(16 guns)

A.P. HILL

Quarles's Mill

Matthews
Matthews

HANCOCK
II CORPS

TYLER

BARLOW

BIRNEY

Dow
(6 guns)
EGAN
EGAN
PIERCE
BREWSTER
MOTT
Meader, Ames,
Sleeper, Edgell,
& Brown
(30 guns)
Fall Mill
Ox. Ford

GIBBON
Hackett

Ricketts, Burton,
Brown, McKnight,
& Clark
(30 guns)

Arnold
& Giffis
(4 guns)
Chandler

Richmond, Fredericksburg and Potomac Railroad

North Anna River

Long Creek

1 SC
2 SC
McIntosh
(7 guns)
HENAGAN
2 SC

Chesterfield
Bridge

Fox

Parker
(4 guns)
Lowry

KERSHAW

LONGSTREET

FIELD

LEE
ARMY OF
NORTHERN VIRGINIA

MAHONE

HETH

Central Virginia Railroad

Blunt
Cady
Lowry

LEGEND

TROOP MOVEMENTS
Confederate   Union

FIRST PHASE
SECOND PHASE

LAND FEATURES & PRESERVATION
19th-Century Woodline
19th-Century Structures
19th-Century Roads
19th-Century Roads
no longer in existence
19th-Century Fences
52   Modern Roads
Preserved by the American
Battlefield Trust & other
Partner Organizations
Preserved by other
Organizations
— UPDATED OCTOBER 2019

**AMERICAN
BATTLEFIELD**
TRUST ★ ★ ★

© American Battlefield Trust. Map prepared by Steven Stanley.
The historic battlefield is shown alongside modern efforts to preserve this land.
Maps are available for download for personal use only at www.battlefields.org/maps.

FEET   3,000
MILES   0.75

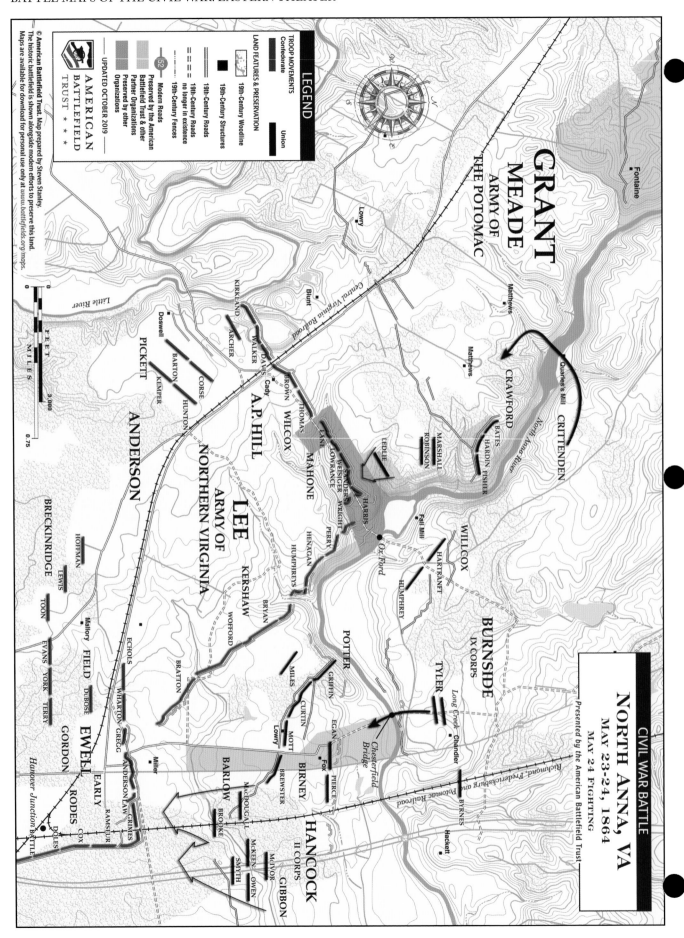

AMERICAN BATTLEFIELD TRUST ★ ★ ★

UPDATED OCTOBER 2019

LEGEND

TROOP MOVEMENTS
Confederate
Union

LAND FEATURES & PRESERVATION
19th-Century Woodline
19th-Century Structures
52 19th-Century Roads
Modern Roads
19th-Century Roads
Preserved by the American Battlefield Trust & other Partner Organizations
Preserved by other Organizations
19th-Century Roads no longer in existence
19th-Century Fences

Preserved by the American Battlefield Trust & other Partner Organizations

CIVIL WAR BATTLE

NORTH ANNA, VA

MAY 23-24, 1864

MAY 24 FIGHTING

Presented by the American Battlefield Trust

GRANT
MEADE
ARMY OF THE POTOMAC

LEE
ARMY OF NORTHERN VIRGINIA

A.P. HILL

ANDERSON

EWELL

BURNSIDE
IX CORPS

HANCOCK
II CORPS

GIBBON

Little River

Central Virginia Railroad

North Anna River

Richmond, Fredericksburg and Potomac Railroad

Hanover Junction

0
FEET
MILES
0
3,000
0.75

76

BATTLE *of* COLD HARBOR

MAY 31 - JUNE 12, 1864

THE NEXT FEDERAL THRUST PULLED THE ARMY OF THE POTOMAC away from the North Anna River in a sweeping movement to the east, south across the Pamunkey River and to within a dozen miles of Richmond. Ultimately though, Lee's army and not Richmond was Grant's objective.

Union and Confederate cavalry flooded the roads to the north and east of the Rebel capital in an attempt to secure vital crossroads and screen the movements of their respective armies.

The Army of the Potomac inched ever closer to Richmond. By May 31, the combatants vied over the Old Cold Harbor Crossroads, situated on the old Gaines' Mill Battlefield of 1862. Lee feared that possession of the crossroads by the Federals would enable them to turn his right flank, which would endanger Richmond. Confederate cavalry and infantry secured the crossroads, but were dislodged by the Union VI Corps and the newly arrived XVIII Corps from the Army of the James.

With reinforcements from both sides pouring onto the field, Grant launched an assault on the evening of June 1. The Federals briefly broke through the Confederate line, only to be pushed back by a strong counterattack. The Union infantry managed to gain some ground during the attack, which emboldened Grant to launch another assault two days later.

George Meade ordered an early morning attack for June 2, but miscommunications, an ill fated night march, and boarderline insubordination plagued the Federals. Meade postponed the attack until 5 p.m. that day, but Grant, advised Meade to wait until June 3. By then, Lee's men had created and bolstered some of the most formidable field works ever seen in the Eastern Theater.

At 4:30 a.m. on the morning of June 3, the II, VI and XVIII Corps launched the main attack through the darkness and fog. As the attack began, the corps became caught in the swamps, ravines and heavy vegetation, losing contact with each other. Angles in the Confederate works allowed Lee's men to easily enfilade the Federal ranks as they advanced. An estimated 7,000 men were killed or wounded within the first hour of the assault. In the II Corps sector, elements of the unit managed to seize a portion of the Rebel works, only to be bombarded by Confederate artillery that turned the trenches into a deathtrap. Other Federals were funneled into two ravines and subsequently mowed down when they reached the Confederates' position. Pinned down by the tremendous volume of Confederate fire, the remaining Federals dug trenches of their own, sometimes including bodies of dead comrades as part of their improvised earthworks. At 12:30 p.m., after riding the beleaguered Union lines himself, Grant suspended his attack.

From June 4 to June 12, the days were filled with minor attacks, artillery duels and sniping. On June 7, Lee and Grant agreed to a two-hour truce to allow the Federals a chance to retrieve their wounded. Thwarted once again, Grant looked to renew the offensive. He sent Maj. Gen. Philip Sheridan's cavalry west to destroy the Virginia Central Railroad. On June 12, Grant ordered Meade to evacuate Cold Harbor, cross the James River and proceed toward the "Cockade City"— Petersburg.

✳ ✳ PRESERVATION ✳ ✳

To date, the **American Battlefield Trust** has saved **232 acres** at Cold Harbor Battlefield.

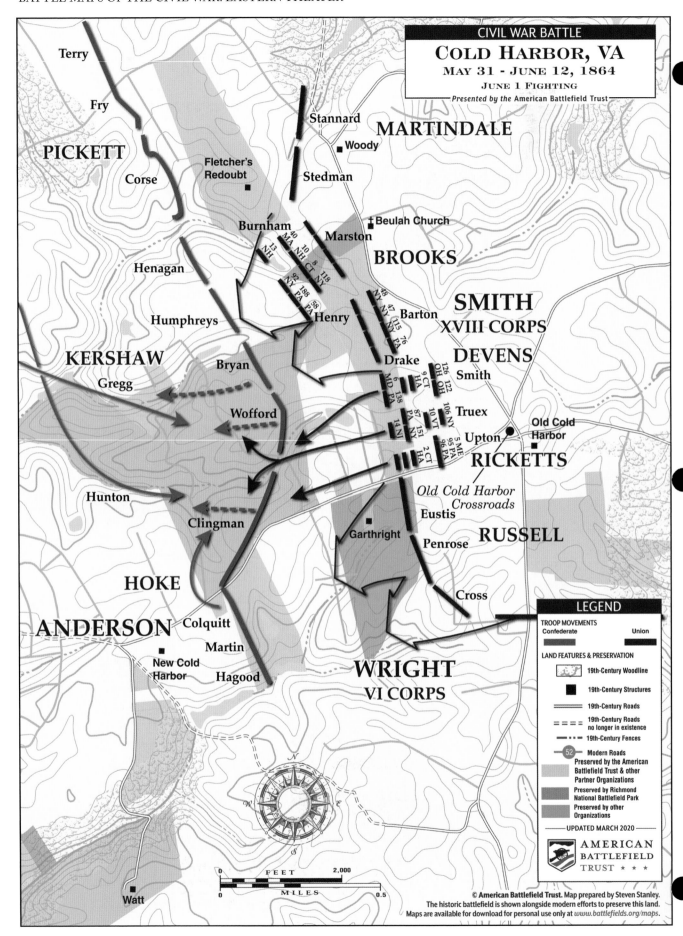

CIVIL WAR BATTLE
COLD HARBOR, VA
MAY 31 - JUNE 12, 1864
JUNE 1 FIGHTING
Presented by the American Battlefield Trust

Terry

Fry

PICKETT

Corse

Stannard

Woody

MARTINDALE

Fletcher's Redoubt

Stedman

Burnham

Beulah Church

Marston

13 NH

40 MA

10 NH

8 CT

118 NY

BROOKS

Henagan

92 PA

188 PA

58 PA

Henry

48 NY

47 NY

115 NY

76

Barton

SMITH
XVIII CORPS

Humphreys

KERSHAW

Bryan

Drake

DEVENS

Smith

Gregg

6 MD

138 PA

9 CT

126 OH

122 OH

Wofford

87 PA

151 NY

10 VT

106 NY

Truex

14 NY

5 ME

2 CT HA

96 PA

95 PA

Upton

Old Cold Harbor

Hunton

RICKETTS

Clingman

Garthright

Old Cold Harbor Crossroads

Eustis

RUSSELL

Penrose

HOKE

Colquitt

Cross

ANDERSON

Martin

New Cold Harbor

Hagood

WRIGHT
VI CORPS

Watt

LEGEND
TROOP MOVEMENTS
Confederate | Union

LAND FEATURES & PRESERVATION
- 19th-Century Woodline
- 19th-Century Structures
- 19th-Century Roads
- 19th-Century Roads no longer in existence
- 19th-Century Fences
- 52 Modern Roads
- Preserved by the American Battlefield Trust & other Partner Organizations
- Preserved by Richmond National Battlefield Park
- Preserved by other Organizations

— UPDATED MARCH 2020 —

AMERICAN BATTLEFIELD TRUST ★ ★ ★

FEET 2,000

MILES 0.5

© American Battlefield Trust. Map prepared by Steven Stanley.
The historic battlefield is shown alongside modern efforts to preserve this land.
Maps are available for download for personal use only at *www.battlefields.org/maps*.

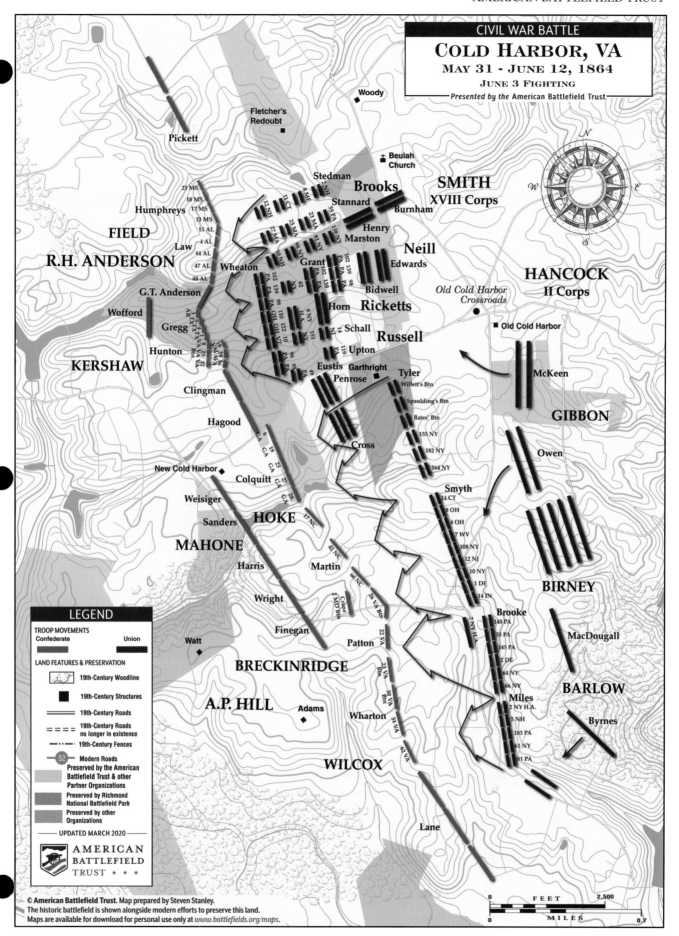

CIVIL WAR BATTLE

COLD HARBOR, VA
MAY 31 - JUNE 12, 1864
JUNE 3 FIGHTING
Presented by the American Battlefield Trust

LEGEND

TROOP MOVEMENTS
Confederate   Union

LAND FEATURES & PRESERVATION

19th-Century Woodline

19th-Century Structures

19th-Century Roads

19th-Century Roads no longer in existence

19th-Century Fences

52 Modern Roads

Preserved by the American Battlefield Trust & other Partner Organizations

Preserved by Richmond National Battlefield Park

Preserved by other Organizations

UPDATED MARCH 2020

AMERICAN BATTLEFIELD TRUST ★★★

© American Battlefield Trust. Map prepared by Steven Stanley.
The historic battlefield is shown alongside modern efforts to preserve this land.
Maps are available for download for personal use only at www.battlefields.org/maps.

FEET   2,500
MILES   0.7

79

BATTLE *of* TREVILIAN STATION

JUNE 11 - 12, 1864

WITH THE FEDERAL OFFENSIVE TEMPORARILY STALLED NORTHEAST of Richmond, at Cold Harbor, Ulysses S. Grant devised his plan. The renewed offensive called for the Army of the Potomac and the attached units from the Army of the James to move southeast to the James River. The Federals would cross the river and bypass Richmond altogether. The line of march would take the blue masses to the city of Petersburg, 23 miles below the Rebel capital. Petersburg contained vital road and railroad junctions that carried supplies from the Deep South, north to Richmond and beyond.

Grant also employed his powerful mounted wing of 10,000 troopers, commanded by Maj. Gen. Philip H. Sheridan. Sheridan's role was twofold and vital. Rather than screening the troops now destined for Petersburg, his horsemen would ride west with orders to destroy the Virginia Central Railroad—cutting off Southern supplies from the Shenandoah Valley—and link up with Maj. Gen. David Hunter's Union army in Charlottesville. This massive raiding party was also designed to draw Lee's cavalry to the west, depriving the Army of Northern Virginia of its intelligence-gathering force. With Lee's troopers distracted by Sheridan's raid, Grant would quietly disengage from Cold Harbor and cross the James River.

When Robert E. Lee became aware of this Union movement, he sent the cavalry divisions of Gens. Wade Hampton and Fitzhugh Lee to attack the Federals near Trevilian Station, Virginia. What resulted was the largest and bloodiest all-cavalry battle of the Civil War.

On June 11, the two Confederate divisions approached the Union position along separate roads, with Hampton's men coming from Trevilian Station and Lee's men from nearby Louisa Court House. Hampton's division clashed with the Union troopers, and vicious dismounted fighting raged. When Fitz Lee's force encountered Union general George A. Custer's men on the road, the Rebels fell back after a brief fight, a dangerous decision that created an opening for Custer to take Hampton's supply train.

The impulsive Custer immediately took advantage of this gap, driving a wedge between the two Confederate divisions. However, in its haste to claim the spoils of its momentary victory, Custer's cavalry allowed itself to be cut off from the rest of Sheridan's force. When Confederate reinforcements arrived, Custer's forces were quickly surrounded. This clash has become known as "Custer's First Last Stand." Only Sheridan's arrival saved the "Boy General" and his men from capture or death.

The next morning, Sheridan advanced on Hampton's position to the west. Hampton's men had spent the night establishing a strong position. Time and time again, Sheridan ordered his cavalry to attack this line, and time and time again, they were driven back. Ultimately, Sheridan was forced to abandon his attempts to break Hampton's line, and he withdrew that night, returning to the Army of the Potomac.

Sheridan succeeded in drawing Confederate attention away from Grant's movements near the James River, but he failed to link with Hunter or provoke any long-term disruption of the Confederate supply line.

✳ ✳ PRESERVATION ✳ ✳

To date, the **American Battlefield Trust** has saved **2,238 acres** at Trevilian Station Battlefield.

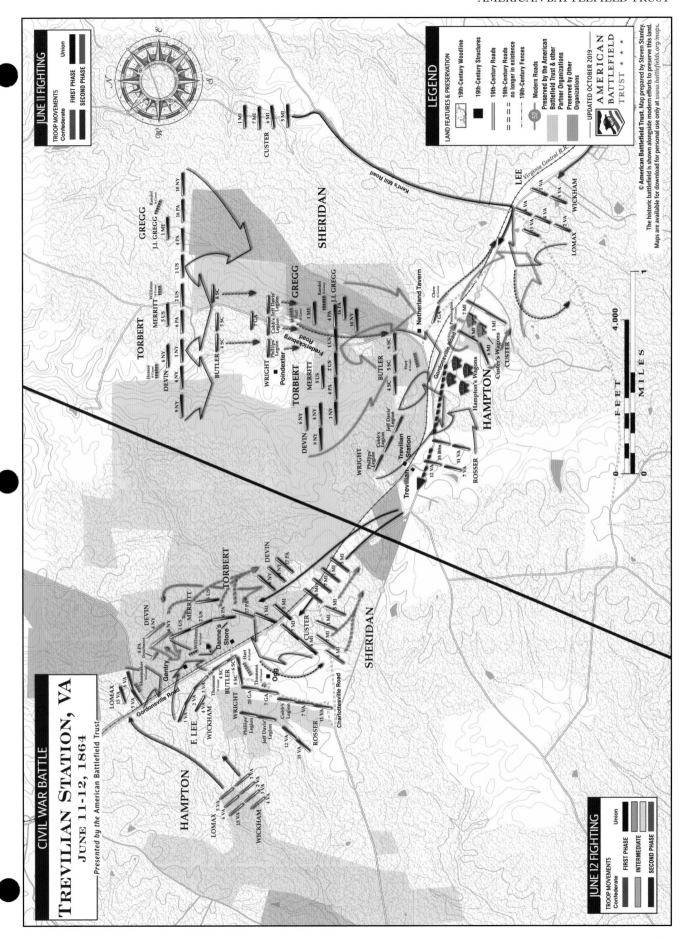

CIVIL WAR BATTLE

TREVILIAN STATION, VA

JUNE 11-12, 1864

Presented by the American Battlefield Trust

JUNE 11 FIGHTING

TROOP MOVEMENTS	
Confederate	Union
	FIRST PHASE
	SECOND PHASE

LEGEND

LAND FEATURES & PRESERVATION

- 19th-Century Woodline
- 19th-Century Structures
- 19th-Century Roads
- 19th-Century Roads no longer in existence
- 19th-Century Fences
- Modern Roads
- Preserved by the American Battlefield Trust & other Partner Organizations
- Preserved by Other Organizations

UPDATED OCTOBER 2019

AMERICAN BATTLEFIELD TRUST ★ ★ ★

© American Battlefield Trust. Map prepared by Steven Stanley.

The historic battlefield is shown alongside modern efforts to preserve this land. Maps are available for download for personal use only at *www.battlefields.org/maps*.

JUNE 12 FIGHTING

TROOP MOVEMENTS	
Confederate	Union
	FIRST PHASE
	INTERMEDIATE
	SECOND PHASE

SIEGE *of* PETERSBURG
(OPENING ASSAULTS)

JUNE 15 - 18, 1864

ROBERT E. LEE WAS CAUGHT OFF GUARD WHEN THE NEWS FIRST reached him that the Federals had arrived in force outside Petersburg, Virginia. Throughout early May, Gens. P. G. T. Beauregard and George Pickett worked feverously to prepare the city for an assault by Maj. Gen. Ben Butler's Union Army of the James. Butler's army crept along a peninsula of land called Bermuda Hundred, which lay between Richmond and Petersburg. Although outnumbered, the Confederates were able to "bottle up" Butler at a line of fortifications dubbed the Howlett Line, north of Petersburg.

While Lee may have been caught off guard, the city of Petersburg was not wholly unprepared for war. In the summer of 1862, a fortified defensive line 10 miles in length, with emplacements for 55 batteries, was laid out by Capt. Charles Dimmock. The "Dimmock Line," as it became known, formed the backbone of the Confederate position at Petersburg that would eventually stretch for 35 miles.

Through stealth and deception, George G. Meade's army withdrew from its Cold Harbor trenches and was marching once again to the southeast. By June 14, the Army of the Potomac began crossing the James River on transports and a 2,200-foot-long pontoon bridge at Windmill Point. The next day, Butler's army, too, was on the move—crossing the Appomattox River and forming to attack the Petersburg defenses.

Union Gen. William F. "Baldy" Smith cautiously led his XVIII Corps—the vanguard of Grant's legions—west from City Point on June 15, impressed by the intimidating works that confronted him here east of Petersburg. Expecting the momentary arrival of Winfield S. Hancock's delayed II Corps, Smith deferred his assault until 7:00 p.m. With daylight waning, the best chance to capture Petersburg with relatively little fighting was gone.

Once finally underway, the Union attack proved anticlimactic. Federal troops utilized a ravine to gain the rear of Battery Five, throwing the defenders into a panic. Shortly thereafter, Batteries 3 through 8 also fell. The 5,400 Confederate defenders were driven from their first line of entrenchments back to Harrison Creek. By then, darkness had enveloped the battlefield, and Smith, joined at last by Hancock, decided to postpone further offensive action until dawn.

On June 16, the Union II Corps captured Redans No. 4, 12, 13 and 14, but these gains came at a frightful cost in casualties. Also on the 16th, Beauregard stripped the Howlett Line around Bermuda Hundred to defend the city. Lee subsequently rushed reinforcements from other elements of the Army of Northern Virginia to man the Howlett Line.

On June 18, the Federals made a strong effort to take Petersburg, but the time and opportunities wasted by the Yankees over the last few days finally caught up with them. By 2 p.m., the Federals attacked in full force, but were unable to secure a major breakthrough, and the assault was repulsed with heavy casualties. At this point, the Confederate works were heavily manned, and the greatest opportunity to capture Petersburg without a siege was lost. Grant now settled in for the next phase of his campaign—tying Lee down in a prolonged siege.

✳ ✳ PRESERVATION ✳ ✳

To date, the **American Battlefield Trust** has saved **88 acres** at Petersburg Battlefield.

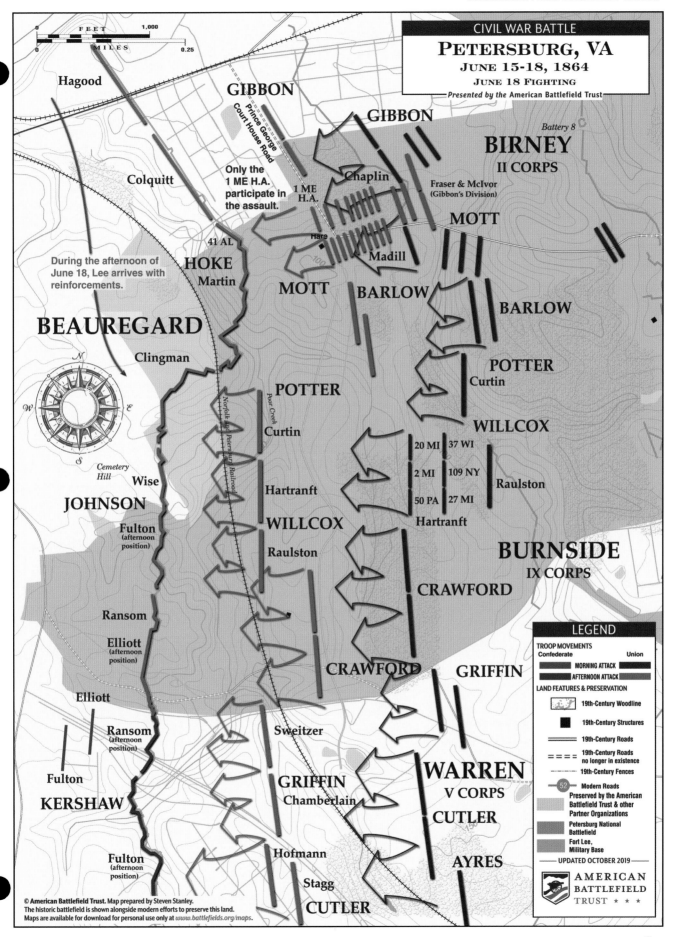

AMERICAN BATTLEFIELD TRUST

CIVIL WAR BATTLE
PETERSBURG, VA
JUNE 15-18, 1864
JUNE 18 FIGHTING
Presented by the American Battlefield Trust

FEET 1,000
MILES 0.25

Hagood

GIBBON

GIBBON

Battery 8

BIRNEY
II CORPS

Prince George Court House Road

Chaplin

Fraser & McIvor
(Gibbon's Division)

Colquitt

Only the
1 ME H.A.
participate in
the assault.

1 ME
H.A.

MOTT

41 AL

During the afternoon of
June 18, Lee arrives with
reinforcements.

HOKE
Martin

Hare

Madill

MOTT

BARLOW

BARLOW

BEAUREGARD

Clingman

POTTER
Curtin

POTTER
Curtin

WILLCOX

Poor Creek

20 MI	37 WI
2 MI	109 NY
50 PA	27 MI

Raulston

Cemetery Hill

Wise

JOHNSON

Fulton
(afternoon
position)

Hartranft

WILLCOX

Raulston

Hartranft

BURNSIDE
IX CORPS

Ransom

Elliott
(afternoon
position)

CRAWFORD

Elliott

Ransom
(afternoon
position)

Sweitzer

CRAWFORD

GRIFFIN

Fulton

KERSHAW

GRIFFIN
Chamberlain

WARREN
V CORPS

CUTLER

Fulton
(afternoon
position)

Hofmann

AYRES

Stagg

CUTLER

LEGEND
TROOP MOVEMENTS
Confederate — Union
MORNING ATTACK
AFTERNOON ATTACK
LAND FEATURES & PRESERVATION
19th-Century Woodline
19th-Century Structures
19th-Century Roads
19th-Century Roads
no longer in existence
19th-Century Fences
52 — Modern Roads
Preserved by the American
Battlefield Trust & other
Partner Organizations
Petersburg National
Battlefield
Fort Lee,
Military Base
— UPDATED OCTOBER 2019 —

AMERICAN
BATTLEFIELD
TRUST ★ ★ ★

© American Battlefield Trust. Map prepared by Steven Stanley.
The historic battlefield is shown alongside modern efforts to preserve this land.
Maps are available for download for personal use only at *www.battlefields.org/maps.*

SIEGE *of* PETERSBURG

(BATTLE OF THE CRATER)

JULY 30, 1864

TWO WEEKS AFTER UNION FORCES ARRIVED TO PESTER THE CONFEDERATE defenders of Petersburg, the battle lines of both sides had settled into a stalemate. Since Cold Harbor and the opening assaults on Petersburg, Ulysses S. Grant was reluctant to mount a frontal attack against well-fortified Confederate positions. By late June, his lines covered most of the eastern approaches to Petersburg, but neither side seemed ready to risk an offensive move.

As the siege wore on, and Grant's men sought a way to break the impasse. Col. Henry Pleasants of the 48th Pennsylvania, a mining engineer by profession, saw a way to end the stalemate at Petersburg. Pleasants proposed to dig a mine running from the Federal lines and under Elliott's Salient on the high ground within the Confederate line. A large gallery would be excavated and packed with black powder and ignited. This would blow a huge hole in the enemy line, opening a clear path to Petersburg. Pleasants began digging on June 25, completing a 510-foot shaft within three weeks. By July 27, the mine was packed with 8,000 pounds of gunpowder and ready to ignite.

At the end of July, Grant authorized the explosion. Spearheading the Federal attack was Ambrose Burnside's IX Corps. Burnside planned to pass his leading division through the gap created by the explosion and then have his troops turn north and south, respectively, to widen the breach and clear the way. The IX Corps commander chose Brig. Gen. Edward Ferrero's division of United States Colored Troops (USCTs) to spearhead the assault. Though these troops had spent most of their service guarding wagon trains and building fortifications, Burnside believed their enthusiasm would compensate for their lack of combat experience. Each brigade in Ferrero's division trained for its role in Burnside's carefully choreographed scheme.

On the day before the assault, however, General Meade ordered Burnside to select a white unit instead, fearing the public image of sacrificing colored troops. Burnside had his division commanders draw lots for the job.

The mine exploded at 4:44 a.m. on July 30, 1864. The result stunned everyone who witnessed it. When the dust settled, a crater 130 feet long, 60 feet wide and 30 feet deep scarred the landscape where Elliott's Salient had stood a moment before. A total of 352 Confederates were killed by the blast.

The Federals, however, failed to widen the breach. Instead, many Yankee soldiers plunged into the Crater. The Confederate defenders on either side of the Crater recovered quickly after their initial shock and poured fire from both flanks into Burnside's men. Eventually, the U.S. Colored Troops were fed into the fray, only to receive "no quarter" from the enemy.

The Crater was a debacle. Burnside was treated as a scapegoat and relieved of command, and Grant would have to find another way into Petersburg.

✳ ✳ **PRESERVATION** ✳ ✳

To date, the **American Battlefield Trust** has saved **2 acres** at The Crater Battlefield.

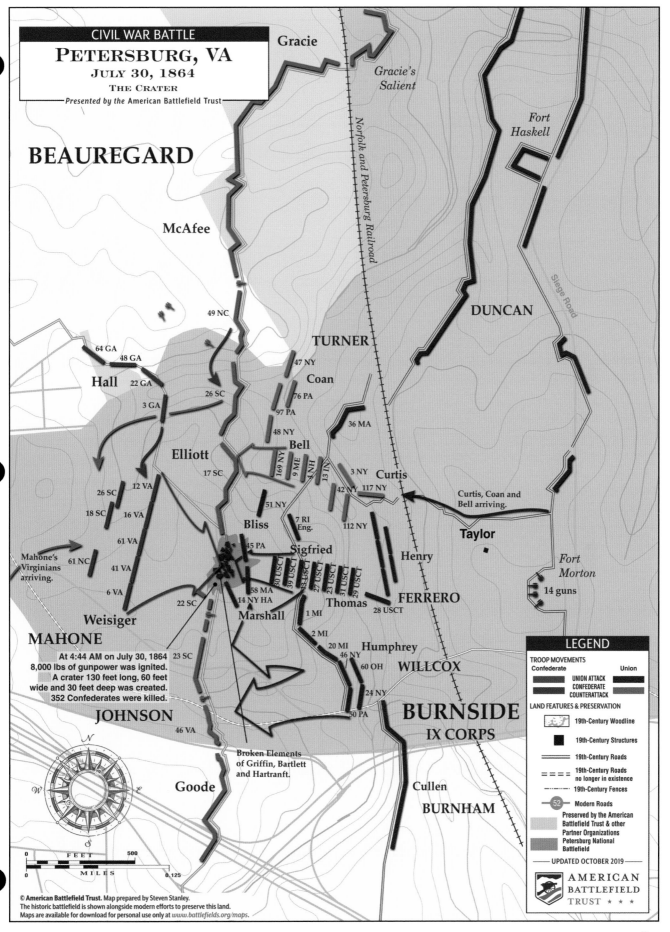

CIVIL WAR BATTLE
PETERSBURG, VA
JULY 30, 1864
THE CRATER
Presented by the American Battlefield Trust

BEAUREGARD

Gracie

Gracie's Salient

Fort Haskell

McAfee

Norfolk and Petersburg Railroad

DUNCAN

Siege Road

49 NC

64 GA
48 GA
Hall   22 GA
3 GA

26 SC

TURNER

47 NY
Coan
76 PA
97 PA
48 NY
Bell
169 NY
9 ME
4 NH
13 IN

36 MA

3 NY
Curtis
42 NY   117 NY

Curtis, Coan and Bell arriving.

Elliott

17 SC

26 SC   12 VA

18 SC   16 VA

61 VA

41 VA

6 VA

Bliss
51 NY
7 RI Eng.
45 PA
Sigfried
30 USCT
39 USCT
43 USCT
27 USCT
23 USCT
31 USCT
29 USCT
112 NY

Taylor

Fort Morton

Henry

14 guns

Mahone's Virginians arriving.
61 NC

58 MA
14 NY HA
Marshall
22 SC

1 MI

Thomas
28 USCT

FERRERO

Weisiger

MAHONE

At 4:44 AM on July 30, 1864 8,000 lbs of gunpower was ignited. A crater 130 feet long, 60 feet wide and 30 feet deep was created. 352 Confederates were killed.

23 SC

2 MI

20 MI
46 NY
60 OH

Humphrey

WILLCOX

24 NY

JOHNSON

46 VA

50 PA

BURNSIDE
IX CORPS

Broken Elements of Griffin, Bartlett and Hartranft.

Goode

Cullen

BURNHAM

LEGEND

TROOP MOVEMENTS
Confederate	Union

UNION ATTACK
CONFEDERATE COUNTERATTACK

LAND FEATURES & PRESERVATION

- 19th-Century Woodline
- 19th-Century Structures
- 19th-Century Roads
- 19th-Century Roads no longer in existence
- 19th-Century Fences
- 52 Modern Roads
- Preserved by the American Battlefield Trust & other Partner Organizations
- Petersburg National Battlefield

— UPDATED OCTOBER 2019 —

AMERICAN BATTLEFIELD TRUST ★ ★ ★

N
W — E
S

FEET 0 — 500
MILES 0 — 0.125

THIRD BATTLE *of* WINCHESTER

SEPTEMBER 19, 1864

WHILE SIEGE OPERATIONS DRAGGED ON AROUND PETERSBURG, Jubal Early and his men wreaked havoc on the Federals in the Shenandoah Valley. Early cleared David Hunter's men from the Valley, and then crossed the Potomac River to threaten Washington. Lee's gambit of dispatching Early had paid off, but ultimately, not in the way that he would have liked.

Grant did transfer troops from the Petersburg front to meet this new Confederate threat. These soldiers helped turn back Early's raid into Maryland, and now formed the nucleus of the new Federal Army of the Shenandoah. Hunter was replaced as the primary commander in the Valley, and Grant's protégé, Philip H. Sheridan, was given command of the new army. What Sheridan lacked in scruples and brains, he more than made up for in audacity and bravery.

With the 1864 presidential election looming, Early's force had to be dealt with and not allowed to threaten Washington again. To clear the Shenandoah Valley of Confederates, Sheridan moved on Winchester, Virginia, in mid-September 1864. Sheridan's force of more than 39,000 men was better than twice the size of Early's Confederate army defending the Valley.

After Brig. Gen. Joseph Kershaw's division left Winchester to rejoin Robert E. Lee's army at Petersburg, Early renewed his raids on the Baltimore & Ohio Railroad at Martinsburg in the lower Valley, dispersing his four remaining infantry divisions. He felt that Sheridan "possessed an excessive caution which amounted to timidity." Early could not have been more wrong about his opponent.

On September 19, Sheridan advanced toward Winchester from the north and east, his superior cavalry force flooding several of the major roads. Along the Berryville Pike two-thirds of Sheridan's infantry, the VI Corps and XIX Corps, crossed Opequon Creek east of town.

Early reacted quickly. The topography of the Berryville Canyon created a natural choke point for the Federals, and Maj. Gen. Stephen Ramseur's Confederate division fought a stubborn delaying action, giving the Confederates the time needed to concentrate their forces to meet the main assault.

Around noon, Sheridan launched an aggressive attack. Union soldiers pierced the Confederate lines, but strong artillery fire and a determined counterattack drove the Northerners back across the "Middle Field"— now the bloodiest ground in the Shenandoah Valley. The Federal VI Corps staunched the Confederate onslaught.

In the mid-afternoon, Brig. Gen. George Crook's VIII Corps and two Union cavalry divisions under Brig. Gen. Alfred Torbert turned the Confederate left flank. Early scrambled to maintain the position, but was steadily forced back. By early evening, Early was falling back through Winchester southward toward Fisher's Hill.

Third Winchester was the bloodiest battle of the Shenandoah Valley, resulting in more casualties than the entire 1862 Valley Campaign. By the end of October 1864, Sheridan had brought the Valley firmly under Union control, helping to secure the reelection of President Abraham Lincoln.

✳ ✳ PRESERVATION ✳ ✳

To date, the **American Battlefield Trust** has saved **473 acres** at Winchester Battlefield.

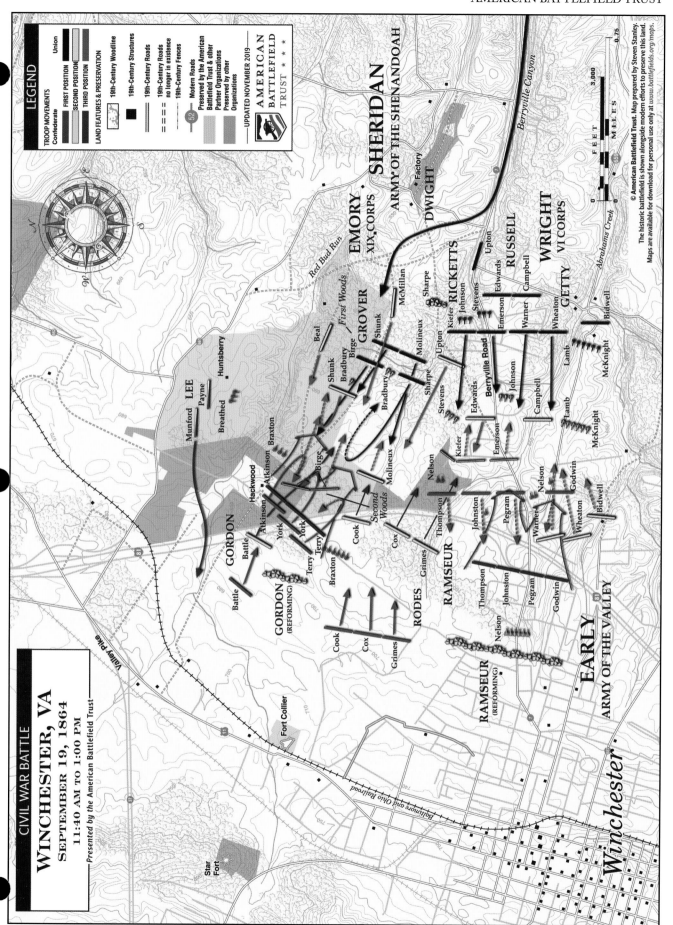

CIVIL WAR BATTLE

WINCHESTER, VA

SEPTEMBER 19, 1864
11:40 AM TO 1:00 PM

Presented by the American Battlefield Trust

LEGEND

TROOP MOVEMENTS
Confederate   Union

FIRST POSITION
SECOND POSITION
THIRD POSITION

LAND FEATURES & PRESERVATION

19th-Century Woodline
19th-Century Structures
19th-Century Roads
19th-Century Roads no longer in existence
19th-Century Fences

Modern Roads

52   Preserved by the American Battlefield Trust & other Partner Organizations

Preserved by other Organizations

—— UPDATED NOVEMBER 2019 ——

AMERICAN BATTLEFIELD TRUST ★ ★ ★

© American Battlefield Trust. Map prepared by Steven Stanley.
The historic battlefield is shown alongside modern efforts to preserve this land.
Maps are available for download for personal use only at *www.battlefields.org/maps*.

SHERIDAN
ARMY OF THE SHENANDOAH

EMORY
XIX CORPS

DWIGHT

Factory

WRIGHT
VI CORPS

RUSSELL

RICKETTS

GETTY

GROVER

McMillan

Sharpe

Kiefer

Johnson

Stevens

Upton

Edwards

Campbell

Warner

Wheaton

Bidwell

McKnight

Beal

First Woods

Shunk

Bradbury

Birge

Bradbury

Molineux

Upton

Sharpe

Stevens

Edwards

Johnson

Campbell

Lamb

Kiefer

Emerson

Nelson

Lamb

McKnight

Huntsberry

LEE

Munford

Payne

Breathed

Hackwood

Braxton

Atkinson

Birge

Second Woods

Molineux

Cox

Nelson

Thompson

Johnston

Pegram

Nelson

Godwin

Bidwell

McKnight

GORDON

Battle

Atkinson

York

York

Terry

Cook

Grimes

Braxton

RODES

RAMSEUR

Thompson

Johnston

Pegram

Warner

Wheaton

Godwin

GORDON
(REFORMING)

Cook

Cox

Grimes

RAMSEUR
(REFORMING)

Nelson

EARLY
ARMY OF THE VALLEY

Fort Collier

Star Fort

Valley Pike

Red Bud Run

Berryville Road

Berryville Canyon

Abrahams Creek

Baltimore and Ohio Railroad

Winchester

FEET
3,000
MILES
0.75

87

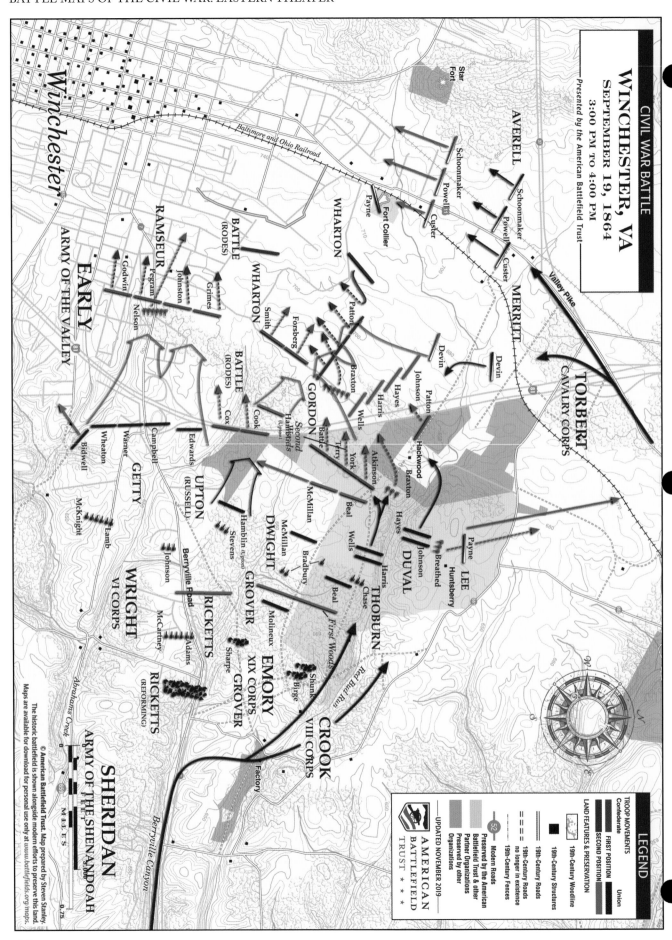

CIVIL WAR BATTLE

WINCHESTER, VA
SEPTEMBER 19, 1864
3:00 PM TO 4:00 PM

Presented by the American Battlefield Trust

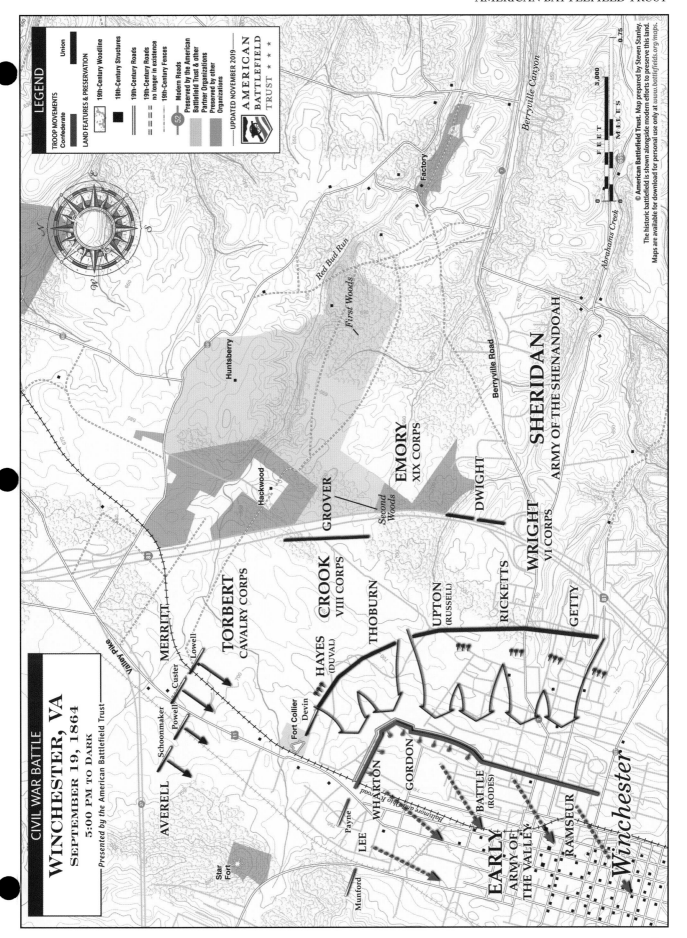

CIVIL WAR BATTLE

WINCHESTER, VA

SEPTEMBER 19, 1864

5:00 PM TO DARK

Presented by the American Battlefield Trust

LEGEND

TROOP MOVEMENTS
Confederate   Union

LAND FEATURES & PRESERVATION

19th-Century Woodline

19th-Century Structures

19th-Century Roads

19th-Century Roads
no longer in existence

19th-Century Fences

52   Modern Roads

Preserved by the American
Battlefield Trust & other
Partner Organizations

Preserved by other
Organizations

UPDATED NOVEMBER 2019

AMERICAN BATTLEFIELD TRUST ★ ★ ★

© American Battlefield Trust. Map prepared by Steven Stanley. The historic battlefield is shown alongside modern efforts to preserve this land. Maps are available for download for personal use only at www.battlefields.org/maps.

Factory

Red Bud Run

First Woods

Huntsberry

Berryville Canyon

Abrahams Creek

Berryville Road

EMORY
XIX CORPS

SHERIDAN
ARMY OF THE SHENANDOAH

DWIGHT

Hackwood

GROVER

Second Woods

WRIGHT
VI CORPS

Valley Pike

MERRITT

TORBERT
CAVALRY CORPS

Lowell

Custer

CROOK
VIII CORPS

THOBURN

HAYES
(DUVAL)

UPTON
(RUSSELL)

RICKETTS

GETTY

Schoonmaker

Powell

Fort Collier

Devin

AVERELL

Star Fort

Munford

Payne

LEE

WHARTON

GORDON

BATTLE
(RODES)

EARLY
ARMY OF
THE VALLEY

RAMSEUR

Baltimore and Ohio Railroad

Winchester

89

BATTLE *of* NEW MARKET HEIGHTS

SEPTEMBER 29, 1864

IN LATE SEPTEMBER OF 1864, THE SIEGE OF PETERSBURG was entering its third month, and there was no end in sight. Grant issued orders for his next offensive around Petersburg. It called for the disruption of the vital Southside Railroad. This action resulted in the Battle of Peeble's Farm. At the same time, Grant ordered an assault on the works outside Richmond, specifically against Forts Harrison and Gilmer. The attack against the Richmond works would serve a dual purpose. The first would be to draw Lee's attention away from the Federal strike force south of Petersburg. The second would be to hold the Confederates in the Richmond area so that they could not send reinforcements to Petersburg or west to the now threatened Shenandoah Valley.

During the night of September 28–29, Maj. Gen. Benjamin Butler's Army of the James crossed its namesake to assault the Richmond defenses. Butler's objective was the south end of the Confederate line anchored on the north bank of the James River in an open area near the Chaffin Family farm.

Butler's right column, the X Corps under Maj. Gen. David Birney, would attack the Confederate positions on the high ground above the New Market Road, while on his left, Maj. Gen. Edward O. C. Ord's XVIII Corps would attack nearby Fort Harrison on the Richmond defensive perimeter. Both columns attacked at dawn on the 29th.

Ord's men attacked across the open, fire-swept ground toward Fort Harrison. The Federals quickly captured the fort, although the brief battle cost the brigade commander Hiram Burnham, after whom the fort was later renamed, his life.

Farther down the line, Birney's attack column met with stiffer resistance along the New Market Road. The Federals came up against the remnants of the famed Texas Brigade. Colonel Samuel Duncan launched the first attack against New Market Heights. The men quickly became mired in a swamp and entangled in Confederate obstacles. Severe Confederate fire threw back the Colored Troops with grievous losses.

Undaunted, a second group of Colored Troops stepped into the fray. They, too, were slowed by the swamp and thwarted by Confederate fire. The Federals stood to it though, and after 30 minutes surged forward, capturing the Confederate line of works.

Lee reinforced his lines north of the James and, on September 30, counterattacked unsuccessfully. The Federals entrenched, and the Confederates erected a new line of works. As Grant had anticipated, Lee shifted 10,000 troops to meet the new threat against Richmond, weakening his lines west of Petersburg.

Proud of his men's actions at New Market Heights, Ben Butler had a special medal created and issued to the USCTs for their bravery. The motto, written in Latin on the medal stated, "Freedom will be theirs by the sword." The U.S. government went one step further and awarded no less than 14 Medals of Honor to USCT troops for their heroism at New Market Heights.

NOTE: The Battle of New Market Heights should not be mistaken for the similarly named Battle of New Market, Virginia, which took place in the Shenandoah Valley on May 15, 1864.

✳ ✳ PRESERVATION ✳ ✳

To date, the **American Battlefield Trust** has saved **65 acres** at New Market Heights Battlefield.

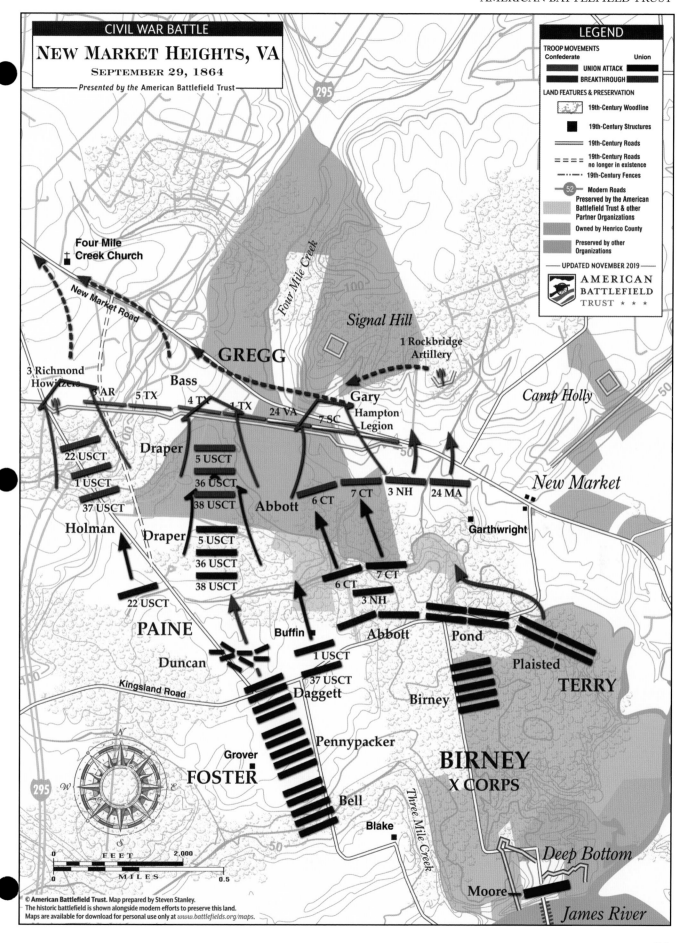

CIVIL WAR BATTLE
NEW MARKET HEIGHTS, VA
SEPTEMBER 29, 1864
Presented by the American Battlefield Trust

LEGEND
TROOP MOVEMENTS
Confederate　　　Union
UNION ATTACK
BREAKTHROUGH

LAND FEATURES & PRESERVATION
19th-Century Woodline
19th-Century Structures
19th-Century Roads
19th-Century Roads no longer in existence
19th-Century Fences
52　Modern Roads
Preserved by the American Battlefield Trust & other Partner Organizations
Owned by Henrico County
Preserved by other Organizations

— UPDATED NOVEMBER 2019 —
AMERICAN BATTLEFIELD TRUST ★ ★ ★

Four Mile Creek Church

New Market Road

Four Mile Creek

Signal Hill

1 Rockbridge Artillery

GREGG

Camp Holly

3 Richmond Howitzers

3 AR
Bass
5 TX
4 TX
1 TX
24 VA
Gary
Hampton Legion
7 SC

22 USCT
Draper
5 USCT
36 USCT
38 USCT
Abbott
6 CT
7 CT
3 NH
24 MA

New Market

1 USCT
37 USCT
Holman

Draper
5 USCT
36 USCT
38 USCT

Garthwright

7 CT
6 CT
3 NH

22 USCT
PAINE

Buffin
1 USCT
37 USCT
Daggett

Abbott

Pond
Plaisted
TERRY

Duncan
Kingsland Road

Birney

Grover
FOSTER

Pennypacker

BIRNEY
X CORPS

Bell

Blake

Three Mile Creek

Deep Bottom

Moore

James River

N
W　E
S
FEET
0　　2,000
MILES
0　　0.5

BATTLE *of* CEDAR CREEK

OCTOBER 19, 1864

THE 1864 SHENANDOAH VALLEY CAMPAIGN HAD BEEN A wild success by late October 1864. Union Gen. Philip H. Sheridan stole the initiative from his opponent, Jubal A. Early. Sheridan strung together a series of victories at Third Winchester, Fisher's Hill and Tom's Brook. All the while, his men were driving Early's troops up the Valley. They were also at work burning barns and mills and destroying crops in the Loudon and Shenandoah Valleys. Grant and Sheridan looked to deprive Lee's army of the vital supplies provided by these lush valleys.

Early and his exhausted Army of the Valley were on the verge of breaking. Battlefield losses, coupled with the loss of key leaders and the relentless Union cavalry, wore down the Confederates, mentally and physically. Nevertheless, though outnumbered two to one, Early sought to even the odds against him by launching a daring attack intended to drive the Federals into the lower Valley and reverse Southern fortunes in 1864.

With his army camped around Cedar Creek, just north of Strasburg and the Shenandoah River, Sheridan was confident that he had broken his enemy. Little Phil went to Washington to confer with the War Department.

Early split his army, sending one part down the Valley Turnpike. The other part made an audacious night march, following a "pig path" on the north face of Massanutten Mountain. Confederate troops forded the North Fork of the Shenandoah River and attacked the Federals near Cedar Creek on the morning of October 19, 1864. The thick morning fog did much to aid the smaller Confederate force, concealing their numbers and causing confusion in the Union ranks. The Rebels caught them completely by surprise.

The Southerners drove first one, then another, then a third Union corps from their camps near Cedar Creek. As the sun came up, it looked as if the Confederates had won an astounding victory.

This success, however, brought problems of its own. The very fog that had shielded their advance had also caused Confederate units to become jumbled in the aftermath of their morning assault. Furthermore, many soldiers and officers in Early's army looted the abandoned Union camps, where food and supplies were abundant. Untold numbers of Confederates fell out of ranks to pilfer the enemy's stores. Thus, by midday, Early required considerable time to reorganize his force for a final, crushing blow.

Meanwhile, word of the battle reached Sheridan, who was 20 miles away at Winchester. The diminutive Union chief saddled his prized horse, Rienzi, and rode furiously to the battlefield, rallying stragglers along the way. His arrival restored the spirits of his beleaguered troops who, Sheridan said, would be back in their camps by nightfall. Around 4:00 p.m., the reorganized Federal host launched a savage counterattack for which Early's men were ill-prepared and from which they could not recover. In the course of an afternoon, the Confederates were forced to yield the very ground they had captured scarcely 12 hours before. As the sun set over the Alleghenies, the Federals had not only regained the ground they lost, they had also extinguished any hope of further Confederate offensives in the Shenandoah Valley.

✳ ✳ PRESERVATION ✳ ✳

To date, the **American Battlefield Trust** has saved **728 acres** at Cedar Creek Battlefield.

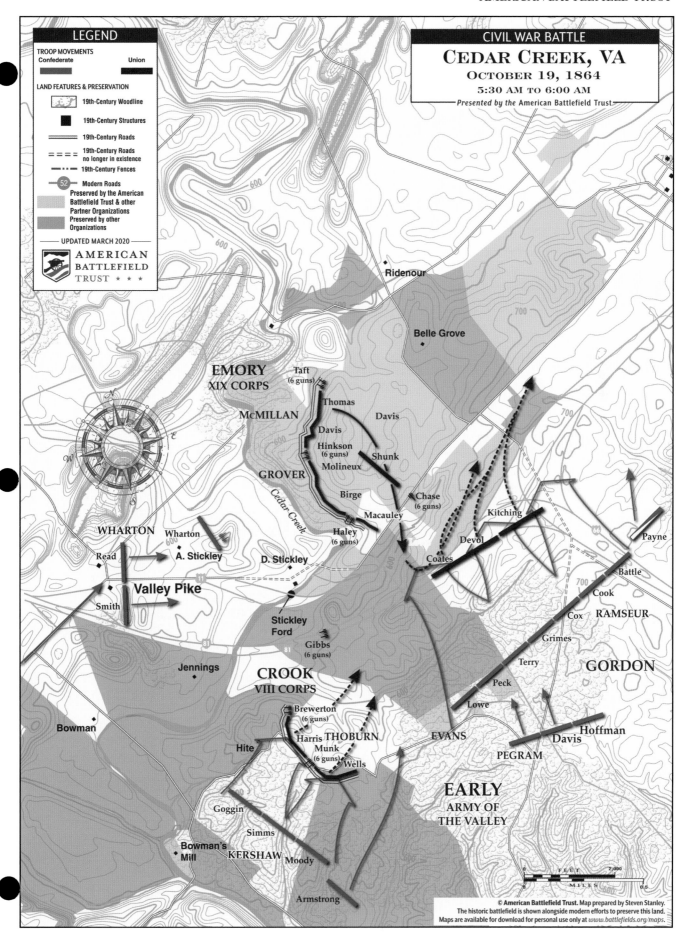

LEGEND

TROOP MOVEMENTS
Confederate   Union

LAND FEATURES & PRESERVATION

- 19th-Century Woodline
- 19th-Century Structures
- 19th-Century Roads
- 19th-Century Roads no longer in existence
- 19th-Century Fences
- 52   Modern Roads
- Preserved by the American Battlefield Trust & other Partner Organizations
- Preserved by other Organizations

— UPDATED MARCH 2020 —

AMERICAN BATTLEFIELD TRUST ★ ★ ★

CIVIL WAR BATTLE
CEDAR CREEK, VA
OCTOBER 19, 1864
5:30 AM TO 6:00 AM
Presented by the American Battlefield Trust

Ridenour

Belle Grove

EMORY
XIX CORPS

McMILLAN

Taft (6 guns)

Thomas

Davis

Davis

Hinkson (6 guns)

Shunk

Molineux

GROVER

Birge

Chase (6 guns)

Kitching

Macauley

Devol

Payne

Haley (6 guns)

Coates

Battle

WHARTON

Wharton

Cook

Read

A. Stickley

Cox

RAMSEUR

Cedar Creek

D. Stickley

Grimes

Valley Pike

GORDON

Smith

Terry

Stickley Ford

Peck

Gibbs (6 guns)

Lowe

Jennings

CROOK
VIII CORPS

Evans

Hoffman

Brewerton (6 guns)

Davis

Harris **THOBURN**

Hite

Munk (6 guns)

PEGRAM

Wells

EARLY
ARMY OF THE VALLEY

Goggin

Bowman

Simms

Bowman's Mill

KERSHAW

Moody

Armstrong

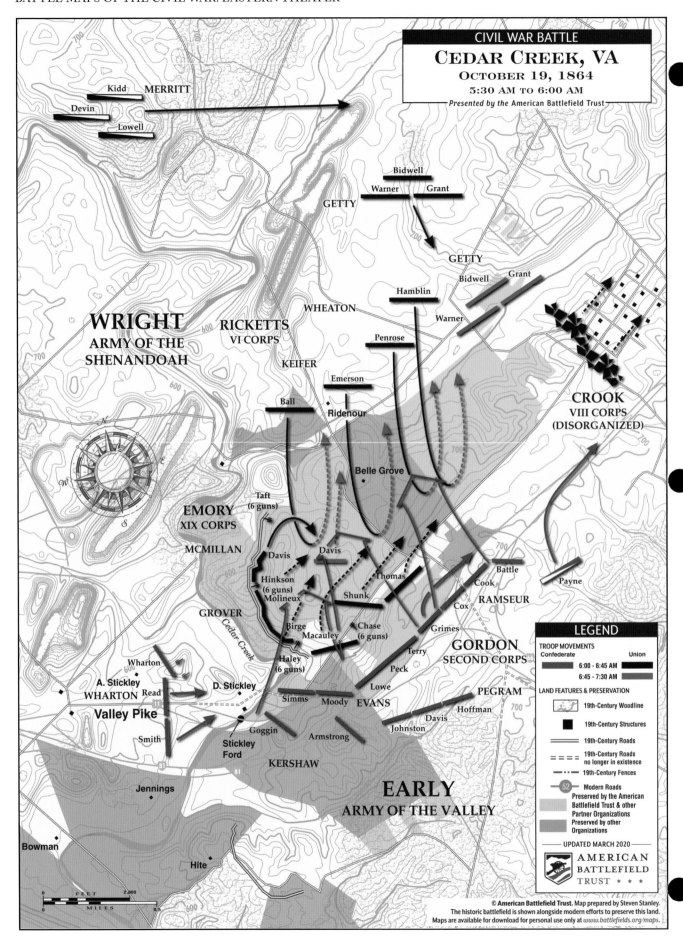

CIVIL WAR BATTLE
CEDAR CREEK, VA
OCTOBER 19, 1864
5:30 AM TO 6:00 AM
Presented by the American Battlefield Trust

Kidd
MERRITT
Devin
Lowell

Bidwell
Warner
Grant
GETTY

GETTY
Bidwell
Grant
Warner

Hamblin
WHEATON
Penrose

WRIGHT
ARMY OF THE
SHENANDOAH

RICKETTS
VI CORPS

KEIFER

Emerson

Ball
Ridenour

CROOK
VIII CORPS
(DISORGANIZED)

Belle Grove

Taft
(6 guns)

EMORY
XIX CORPS

MCMILLAN

Davis
Davis

Battle

Payne

Hinkson
(6 guns)
Molineux

Thomas
Cook
Cox
RAMSEUR

GROVER

Shunk

Grimes

Birge
Macauley

Chase
(6 guns)

Terry

GORDON
SECOND CORPS

Haley
(6 guns)

Peck

Wharton
A. Stickley
WHARTON Read
Valley Pike

D. Stickley

Simms
Moody

Lowe
EVANS

PEGRAM

Hoffman
Davis
Johnston

Smith

Goggin
Stickley
Ford

Armstrong

KERSHAW

Jennings

EARLY
ARMY OF THE VALLEY

Bowman

Hite

LEGEND
TROOP MOVEMENTS
Confederate   Union
6:00 - 6:45 AM
6:45 - 7:30 AM

LAND FEATURES & PRESERVATION
19th-Century Woodline
19th-Century Structures
19th-Century Roads
19th-Century Roads
no longer in existence
19th-Century Fences
52   Modern Roads
Preserved by the American
Battlefield Trust & other
Partner Organizations
Preserved by other
Organizations

— UPDATED MARCH 2020 —

**AMERICAN
BATTLEFIELD
TRUST ★ ★ ★**

FEET   2,800
MILES   0.5

© **American Battlefield Trust.** Map prepared by Steven Stanley.
The historic battlefield is shown alongside modern efforts to preserve this land.
Maps are available for download for personal use only at *www.battlefields.org/maps.*

94

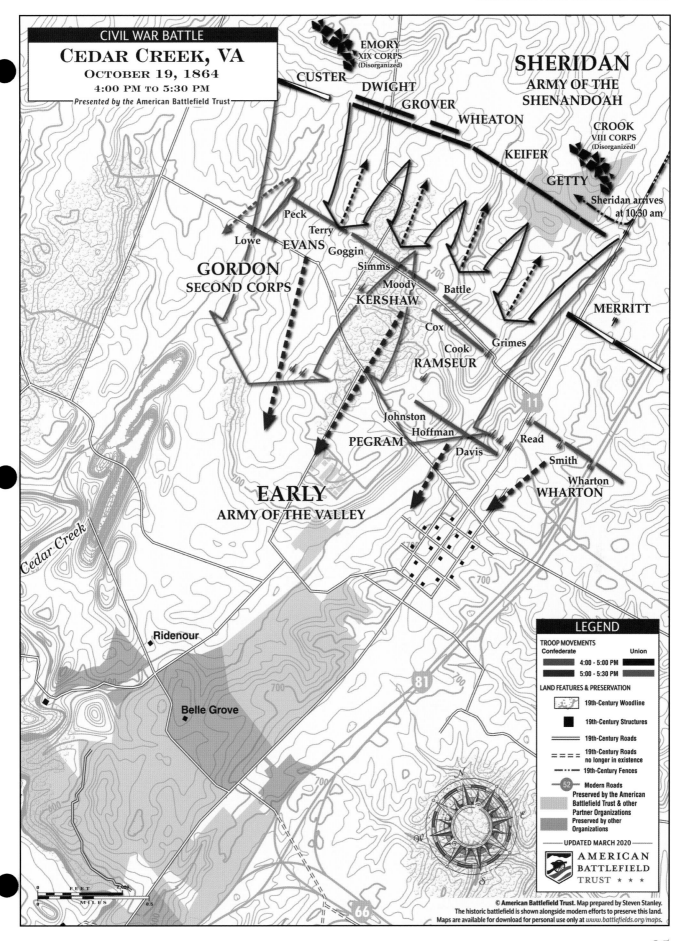

CIVIL WAR BATTLE
CEDAR CREEK, VA
OCTOBER 19, 1864
4:00 PM TO 5:30 PM
Presented by the American Battlefield Trust

SHERIDAN
ARMY OF THE
SHENANDOAH

EMORY
XIX CORPS
(Disorganized)

CUSTER

DWIGHT

GROVER

WHEATON

KEIFER

CROOK
VIII CORPS
(Disorganized)

GETTY

Sheridan arrives
at 10:30 am

Peck

Terry

Lowe

EVANS

Goggin

Simms

GORDON
SECOND CORPS

Moody

KERSHAW

Battle

MERRITT

Cox

Grimes

Cook

RAMSEUR

Johnston

Hoffman

Read

PEGRAM

Davis

Smith

EARLY
ARMY OF THE VALLEY

Wharton
WHARTON

Cedar Creek

Ridenour

Belle Grove

LEGEND

TROOP MOVEMENTS
Confederate | Union
4:00 - 5:00 PM
5:00 - 5:30 PM

LAND FEATURES & PRESERVATION

19th-Century Woodline

19th-Century Structures

19th-Century Roads

19th-Century Roads
no longer in existence

19th-Century Fences

52 Modern Roads

Preserved by the American
Battlefield Trust & other
Partner Organizations

Preserved by other
Organizations

— UPDATED MARCH 2020 —

AMERICAN
BATTLEFIELD
TRUST ★ ★ ★

FEET
MILES

© **American Battlefield Trust.** Map prepared by Steven Stanley.
The historic battlefield is shown alongside modern efforts to preserve this land.
Maps are available for download for personal use only at *www.battlefields.org/maps.*

95

BATTLE *of* WHITE OAK ROAD

MARCH 31, 1865

THE SIEGE OF PETERSBURG HAD DRAGGED ON FOR A GRUELING NINE months as April 1865 approached. With siege lines now running for nearly 35 miles, Ulysses S. Grant knew that victory was inevitable around Petersburg, as the Confederate lines were stretched to their max. On March 25, Lee launched his last offensive of the war at Fort Steadman. Initial success gave way to Federal counterattacks. In the end, Lee's last gambit was for naught.

Before Lee's offensive, Grant had been planning one of his own. Recently, Philip H. Sheridan had arrived back at the Union siege lines with the bulk of the Army of the Potomac's cavalry, after his successful Shenandoah Valley Campaign. This aggressive commander and mobile strike force gave Grant the tools with which he could potentially end the siege.

Grant eyed the Southside Railroad and the Boydton Plank Road, the last two arteries of supply into the Cockade City. In an effort to cut these vital links to the outside world, the Federal commander shifted the Union II and V Corps westward, supported by Sheridan's troopers.

On March 29, the V Corps advanced up the Quaker Road. Taking the bait, Confederates moved out of their trenches in force, desperately trying to stop the westward movement around their right flank. A small, but fierce battle raged back and forth across the Lewis Farm, but ultimately, the Rebels fell back to their works.

The next day, Lee dispatched George Pickett's infantry division and Fitzhugh Lee's Cavalry Corps to the vicinity of Five Forks, a crossroads just north of Dinwiddie Court House. Sheridan's Federal troopers were reported to be operating in this area beyond the flank of the two armies.

On the morning of March 31, word reached the Rebels that Union soldiers had advanced to within less than a mile of the Confederate front line on White Oak Road. The lone, poorly positioned Federal division of Romeyn Ayres was isolated north of rain-choked Gravelly Run. Lee ordered Maj. Gen. Bushrod Johnson to attack the Union left, and Ayres' isolated men. While Johnson's men prepared to attack, Pickett and Fitzhugh Lee's men engaged with Sheridan's troopers north of Dinwiddie Court House.

As Lee was preparing for offensive action, the Federals were doing the same. Ayres received reinforcements from Brig. Gen. Samuel W. Crawford's division of the V Corps. The bolstered Union line lurched forward as the Confederates mirrored their enemy. A fierce battle broke out.

Johnson's men grappled with the Federals, while Brig. Gen. Samuel McGowan swung his North Carolina brigade out of the Confederate trenches and into the Union left flank. Crawford's and Ayres' men tumbled pell-mell back to Gravelly Run, where grizzled veteran Charles Griffin deployed the last division of the V Corps. Rallying on Griffin's men, and with reinforcements from the Union II Corps, the men of the V Corps counterattacked the Rebels, driving them back to their starting position.

While the Federals were not able to unseat the Rebels along the White Oak Road, they were able to secure a lodgment west of the Confederate line along the thoroughfare. More importantly, Grant was made aware of another prize, Pickett's and Fitzhugh Lee's men, who were isolated from the rest of Lee's army, in the open and out from behind their earthworks.

✳ ✳ PRESERVATION ✳ ✳

To date, the **American Battlefield Trust** has saved **903 acres** at White Oak Road Battlefield.

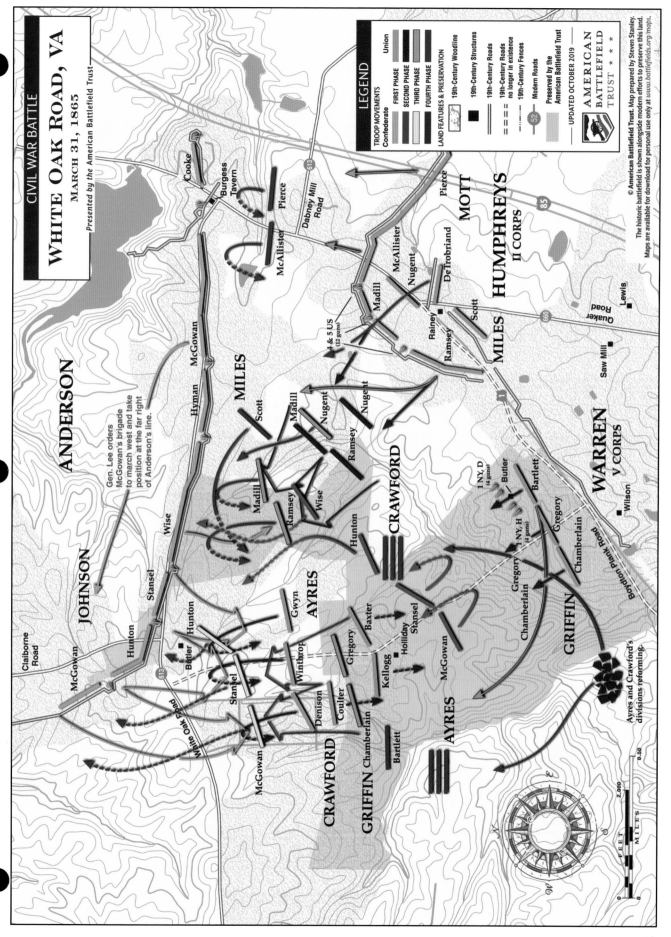

CIVIL WAR BATTLE

WHITE OAK ROAD, VA

MARCH 31, 1865

Presented by the American Battlefield Trust

LEGEND

TROOP MOVEMENTS
Confederate   Union

FIRST PHASE
SECOND PHASE
THIRD PHASE
FOURTH PHASE

LAND FEATURES & PRESERVATION

19th-Century Woodline
19th-Century Structures
19th-Century Roads
19th-Century Roads no longer in existence
19th-Century Fences
Modern Roads
Preserved by the American Battlefield Trust

UPDATED OCTOBER 2019

© American Battlefield Trust. Map prepared by Steven Stanley. The historic battlefield is shown alongside modern efforts to preserve this land. Maps are available for download for personal use only at *www.battlefields.org/maps.*

AMERICAN BATTLEFIELD TRUST ★ ★ ★

Gen. Lee orders McGowan's brigade to march west and take position at the far right of Anderson's line.

Ayres and Crawford's divisions reforming.

ANDERSON

JOHNSON

MILES

CRAWFORD

AYRES

GRIFFIN

CRAWFORD

GRIFFIN

AYRES

WARREN
V CORPS

HUMPHREYS
II CORPS

MOTT

MILES

Burgess Tavern

Cooke

Pierce

McAllister

Dabney Mill Road

Pierce

McAllister

Nugent

DeTrobriand

Madill

Rainey

Ramsey

Scott

4 & 5 US
(12 guns)

Scott

Madill

Nugent

Ramsey

Nugent

Madill

Ramsey

Wise

Hunton

Hyman

McGowan

Wise

Stansel

Hunton

McGowan

Butler

Hunton

Gwyn

Winthrop

Gregory

Baxter

Holliday

Stansel

McGowan

Denison

Coulter

Chamberlain

Kellogg

Stansel

Bartlett

Lewis

Saw Mill

Quaker Road

1 NY, D
(4 guns)

Butler

Bartlett

1 NY, H
(4 guns)

Gregory

Gregory

Chamberlain

Chamberlain

Wilson

Claiborne Road

McGowan

White Oak Road

Boydton Plank Road

BATTLE *of* FIVE FORKS

APRIL 1, 1865

THE UNION LODGMENT ALONG THE WHITE OAK ROAD SERVED TO isolate the infantry division of George Pickett and the cavalry corps of Fitzhugh Lee from the rest of the Confederate army. The 10,000 or so men who made up this mixed force were far too tempting a target for Grant to pass up.

Pickett took up a position at the country crossroads of Five Forks. There, he was ordered by Robert E. Lee to "hold Five Forks at all hazards." Directly north lay the Southside Railroad, a key supply line for Lee's army. Adding to the weight of the situation was the fact that the White Oak Road ran east to west through Five Forks. Should Pickett lose the position, Sheridan's troopers could hit Lee's flank and cut his supply line at the same time.

Roughly 10,000 Confederate soldiers were out of their main works and isolated from the rest of their army. Sheridan called for reinforcements, and Grant dispatched the closest Union infantry at hand, the V Corps, which had just finished its battle at the White Oak Road. Maj. Gen. Gouverneur K. Warren, commander of the Union V Corps, did his best to disengage his men from the front lines and march to Sheridan's position about six miles to the west, but heavy rains over the previous few days had turned the roads into quagmire. A bridge was washed out, necessitating a countermarch. The first of Warren's men trudged up to Sheridan's men shortly after dawn.

Little Phil devised a simple plan of battle for April Fools' Day. With Pickett's force positioned parallel to and just north of the White Oak Road, huddled behind some makeshift earthworks, Sheridan planned to dismount the majority of his troopers and have them advance on foot until they were within carbine range of the enemy. As the dismounted horsemen kept Pickett's attention, the V Corps would drive north across the White Oak Road, isolate the enemy and then wheel to the west and roll up the Confederates.

That afternoon, Sheridan put his plan into action. His troopers held the Confederates' attention, but as Warren struck across the White Oak Road, he missed the Rebel lines by a few hundred yards. Poor scouting on Sheridan's part meant Warren thought the Southern line was much more extended than it actually was. The veteran Warren quickly wrangled his divisions and rolled up the Confederate flank nonetheless. In the meantime, Sheridan could not locate Warren on the field and accused him of shirking his duty, relieving him of command.

On the Confederate side, Pickett, his command staff and other generals were having a fish bake as the battle raged. By the time he realized what was happening, it was too late. His men were swept from the field, and he was relieved of command a few days later.

When Grant received the news of the victory at Five Forks, he ordered a general assault along all of the Petersburg lines for the next morning. The Federals finally had the opportunity they had so longed for—a chance to breach the Confederate defenses at Petersburg.

✳ ✳ PRESERVATION ✳ ✳

To date, the **American Battlefield Trust** has saved **419 acres** at Five Forks Battlefield.

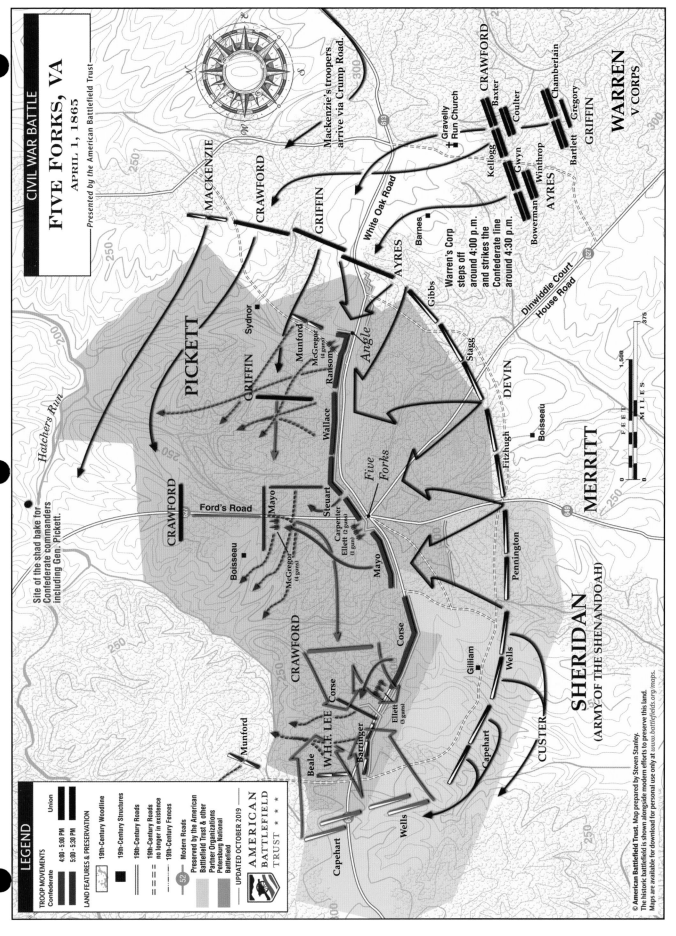

CIVIL WAR BATTLE

FIVE FORKS, VA
APRIL 1, 1865
Presented by the American Battlefield Trust

Mackenzie's troopers arrive via Crump Road.

Warren's Corp steps off around 4:00 p.m. and strikes the Confederate line around 4:30 p.m.

Site of the shad bake for Confederate commanders including Gen. Pickett.

Gravelly Run Church

WARREN
V CORPS

CRAWFORD
Baxter
Coulter
Chamberlain
Kellogg
Gwyn
Gregory
Bartlett
Winthrop
Bowerman
GRIFFIN
AYRES

MACKENZIE
CRAWFORD
GRIFFIN
AYRES

White Oak Road

Barnes
Gibbs
Stagg

Dinwiddie Court House Road

DEVIN

Fitzhugh
Boisseau

MERRITT

PICKETT
GRIFFIN
Sydnor
Munford
McGregor (4 guns)
Ransom
Wallace
Angle

Five Forks

CRAWFORD
Ford's Road
Mayo
Steuart
Carpenter (2 guns)
Ellett (1 gun)
Boisseau
McGregor (4 guns)

Pennington

CRAWFORD
Corse

Munford
Corse
Barringer
Ellett (3 guns)
Beale
W.H.F. LEE

Gilliam
Wells

SHERIDAN
(ARMY OF THE SHENANDOAH)

Capehart
Wells
CUSTER

Capehart
Wells

Hatchers Run

LEGEND
TROOP MOVEMENTS
Confederate   Union
4:00 - 5:00 PM
5:00 - 5:30 PM

LAND FEATURES & PRESERVATION
19th-Century Woodline
19th-Century Structures
19th-Century Roads
19th-Century Roads no longer in existence
19th-Century Fences
52 Modern Roads
Preserved by the American Battlefield Trust & other Partner Organizations
Petersburg National Battlefield

UPDATED OCTOBER 2019

AMERICAN
BATTLEFIELD
TRUST ★ ★ ★

© American Battlefield Trust. Map prepared by Steven Stanley.
The historic battlefield is shown alongside modern efforts to preserve this land.
Maps are available for download for personal use only at www.battlefields.org/maps.

MILES
FEET
1,500
375

SIEGE *of* PETERSBURG
(THE BREAKTHROUGH)

APRIL 2, 1865

WITH THE CONFEDERATE DEFEAT AT FIVE FORKS ON APRIL 1, Ulysses S. Grant ordered a general assault against the Petersburg lines to take place at dawn on April 2. Grant reasoned that by applying pressure along the entire front, the Confederates would not have a free hand to shift reinforcements along their interior lines.

Along the VI Corps front, Maj. Gen. Horatio Wright prepared his men for action. Rather than attack the Confederate position in a long line of men that stretched for a mile but was only two ranks deep, as most Civil War forces were wont to do, Wright's men utilized a compact formation, with some brigades offering only a single regiment front. The idea was to give weight to the attack and punch a hole through the Rebel lines. Once through, the compact formation would give the attackers many options, including advancing to the left or right in an effort to roll up the enemy line. This had also been a favorite formation and tactic of Napoleon Bonaparte.

Huddled behind their picket lines in the chilled night air of early spring, 14,000 Union soldiers waited impatiently for the signal gun that would launch their attack. Along a one-mile stretch of A. P. Hill's Third Corps sector of the Petersburg defenses, nearly 3,000 Confederates, well supported by nearly two dozen cannon, also waited, suspecting but unsure that a climactic battle would begin at dawn.

Wright delayed the assault until the first glimmer of daylight. The Federals quickly overran the enemy pickets, but for 10 or 15 minutes they endured a brutal fire of small arms and artillery in the open.

Undaunted, the blue wave crashed forward, as Federals ripped apart multiple lines of abatis, continued forward and scaled Hill's breastworks. Hand-to-hand fighting broke out all along the line. In the end, Wright's superior numbers held sway. Most of the North Carolinians and Georgians defending the line surrendered, although hundreds fled to fight elsewhere throughout the day, leaving scores of comrades on the ground who would never see another sunrise, including General Hill.

The crushing wave continued onward. A portion of the line wheeled to the southwest and cleared the Confederate line down to Hatcher's Run. Another portion wheeled to the northeast, driving north toward Forts Whitworth and Gregg. Approximately 400 or so men from Mississippi and Louisiana held the small earthen forts, buying time for other Confederates to withdraw with their lives. By now, the Union IX Corps had joined in the assault, adding its weight to the battle.

There was little that Robert E. Lee could do other than prepare to abandon the city. President Jefferson David urged him to defend Richmond, but Lee knew better. He wired Secretary of War James Seddon his intentions to evacuate the Confederate forces from Petersburg and Richmond and head west toward Amelia Court House.

At 3 a.m. on April 3 the rearguard pickets withdrew from Petersburg, and the Federals marched in to capture the Cockade City and the Rebel capital. After 292 days, the Siege of Petersburg was over, and the race to Appomattox Court House was on.

✳ ✳ PRESERVATION ✳ ✳

To date, the **American Battlefield Trust** has saved **407 acres** at the Breakthrough Battlefield.

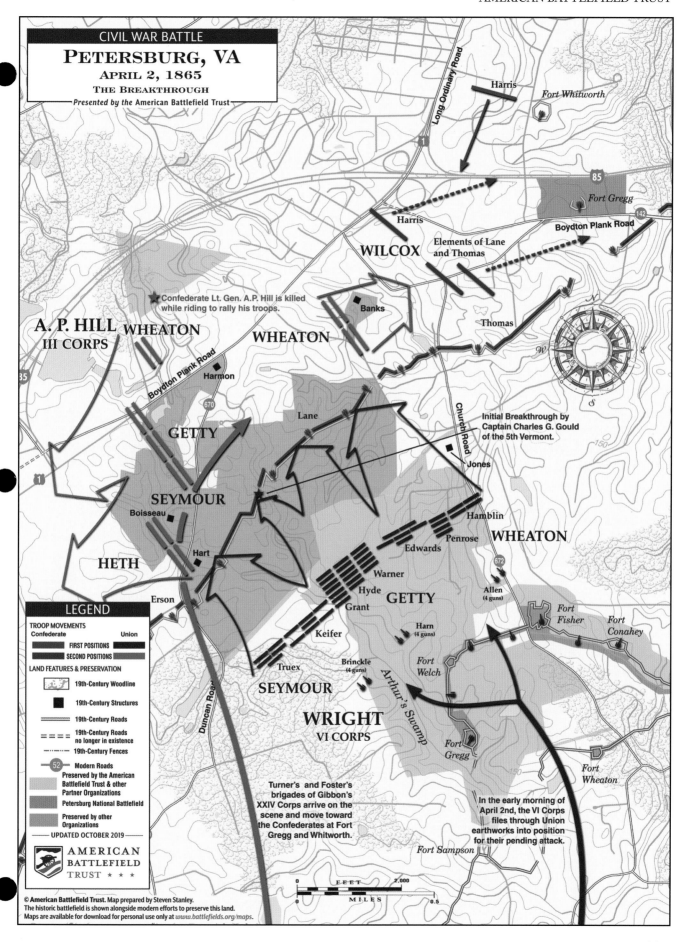

CIVIL WAR BATTLE

PETERSBURG, VA
APRIL 2, 1865
THE BREAKTHROUGH
Presented by the American Battlefield Trust

Harris

Fort Whitworth

Fort Gregg

Harris

Elements of Lane and Thomas

WILCOX

Boydton Plank Road

Banks

Thomas

★ Confederate Lt. Gen. A.P. Hill is killed while riding to rally his troops.

A. P. HILL
III CORPS

WHEATON

WHEATON

Initial Breakthrough by Captain Charles G. Gould of the 5th Vermont.

Boydton Plank Road

Harmon

GETTY

Lane

Jones

SEYMOUR

Boisseau

Hamblin

Penrose

WHEATON

Edwards

HETH

Hart

Warner

Hyde

Grant

GETTY

Allen
(4 guns)

Fort Fisher

Fort Conahey

Erson

Harn
(4 guns)

Keifer

Brinckle
(4 guns)

Fort Welch

Truex

SEYMOUR

Fort Gregg

WRIGHT
VI CORPS

Fort Wheaton

Turner's and Foster's brigades of Gibbon's XXIV Corps arrive on the scene and move toward the Confederates at Fort Gregg and Whitworth.

In the early morning of April 2nd, the VI Corps files through Union earthworks into position for their pending attack.

Fort Sampson

LEGEND
TROOP MOVEMENTS
Confederate   Union

FIRST POSITIONS

SECOND POSITIONS

LAND FEATURES & PRESERVATION

19th-Century Woodline

19th-Century Structures

19th-Century Roads

19th-Century Roads no longer in existence

19th-Century Fences

52 Modern Roads

Preserved by the American Battlefield Trust & other Partner Organizations

Petersburg National Battlefield

Preserved by other Organizations

— UPDATED OCTOBER 2019 —

AMERICAN BATTLEFIELD TRUST ★ ★ ★

FEET   2,000

MILES   0.5

© American Battlefield Trust. Map prepared by Steven Stanley.
The historic battlefield is shown alongside modern efforts to preserve this land.
Maps are available for download for personal use only at *www.battlefields.org/maps.*

101

BATTLE *of* SAILOR'S CREEK

APRIL 6, 1865

BY THE FIRST WEEK OF APRIL 1865, THE CONFEDERACY WAS falling in upon itself. In the Deep South, Maj. Gen. William T. Sherman's army marched through the Carolinas, and his troops engaged with Confederate Gen. Joseph E. Johnston's bedraggled army—composed of the remnants of Rebel armies and departments from across the Deep South. Sherman's goal was to link with Grant's armies around Petersburg. Johnston could slow Sherman, but not stop him.

In Virginia, Richmond and Petersburg fell to the Federals on April 3. Jefferson Davis and his cabinet fled the city, heading south toward Johnston's army. Abraham Lincoln arrived in Richmond shortly thereafter and toured the fallen Rebel capital.

In the meantime, Robert E. Lee and what remained of his army and the garrison troops of Richmond and Petersburg fled to the west. Lee hoped that he could supply his army and then turn his attention to making contact with Johnston's army. With the last two Confederate armies combined, Lee and others hoped that they could take to the offensive once more and pull victory from the jaws of defeat. It was not to be.

After finding ordnance—but no food—at Amelia Court House, and discovering the road to Danville blocked by Federal entrenchments, Lee directed his army toward the supply depot at Farmville. Heading Lee's column was the First and Third Corps, under the command of Gen. James Longstreet, followed by Gen. Richard Anderson's corps and the Reserve Corps under Gen. Richard Ewell, which was composed primarily of garrison units from the Confederate capital. The army's supply train followed, with Maj. Gen. John Gordon's Second Corps bringing up the rear. To evade the Union roadblock, Lee ordered a night march on April 5.

Union cavalry under Phil Sheridan effectively cut off Lee's army near Sailor's Creek, a tributary of the Appomattox River, while the Union II and VI Corps approached from the east. On April 6, two brigades of the II Corps overwhelmed two brigades of Gordon's division as the Confederates struggled to move their supply and artillery trains across the creek. Gordon's men were forced to make a stand at the Lockett Farm on the west bank. In a separate action, Anderson's Confederate infantry was attacked by Union cavalry at Marshall's Crossroads. In a third fight, two divisions of the Union VI Corps took up position on the Hillsman Farm north of Sailor's Creek opposite Ewell's corps. Union cavalry engaged Ewell's right, cutting his men off from retreating west to Farmville and forcing the Confederate commander to surrender.

That evening, Phil Sheridan reported his success to Grant saying, "If the thing is pressed I think that Lee will surrender." When word of this reached Abraham Lincoln, the president responded, "Let the thing be pressed."

April 6, 1865, came to be known as "Black Thursday" among the Confederates. In the three engagements along Sailor's Creek, Lee lost roughly one-fourth of his army, many of them captured. The Federals claimed 7,700 prisoners that day, including six generals. Among these were Ewell and Kershaw and Robert E. Lee's eldest son, Custis. Lee wrote to President Jefferson Davis, "[A] few more Sailor's Creeks and it will all be over."

✳ ✳ PRESERVATION ✳ ✳

To date, the **American Battlefield Trust** has saved **1,318 acres** at Sailor's Creek Battlefield.

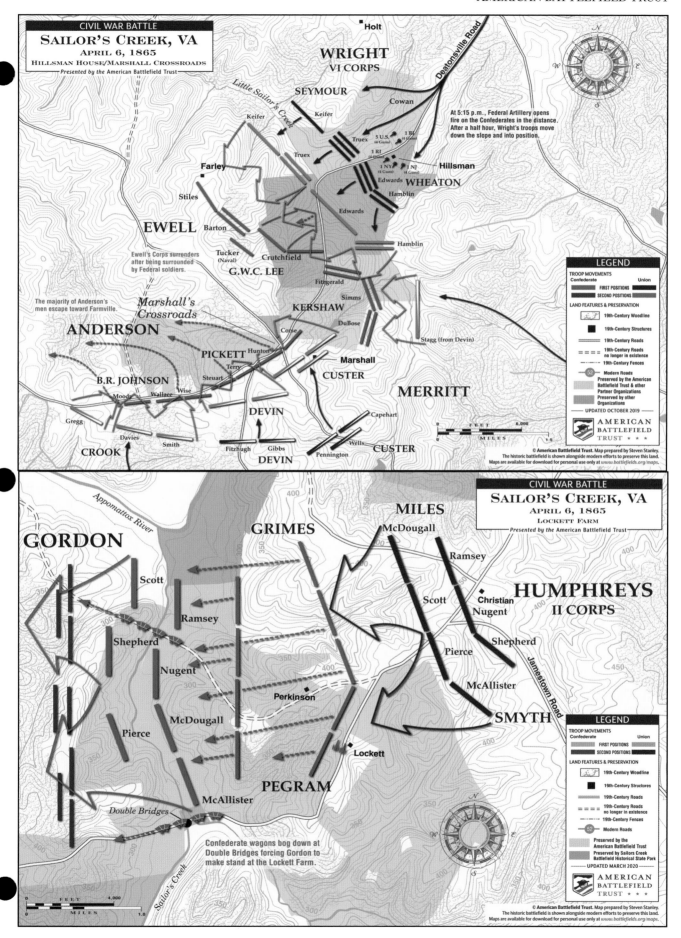

CIVIL WAR BATTLE
SAILOR'S CREEK, VA
APRIL 6, 1865
HILLSMAN HOUSE/MARSHALL CROSSROADS
Presented by the American Battlefield Trust

At 5:15 p.m., Federal Artillery opens fire on the Confederates in the distance. After a half hour, Wright's troops move down the slope and into position.

WRIGHT
VI CORPS

SEYMOUR

Ewell's Corps surrenders after being surrounded by Federal soldiers.

The majority of Anderson's men escape toward Farmville.

ANDERSON

Marshall's Crossroads

CIVIL WAR BATTLE
SAILOR'S CREEK, VA
APRIL 6, 1865
LOCKETT FARM
Presented by the American Battlefield Trust

Confederate wagons bog down at Double Bridges forcing Gordon to make stand at the Lockett Farm.

HUMPHREYS
II CORPS

GORDON

Double Bridges

103

SURRENDER *at* APPOMATTOX COURTHOUSE

APRIL 9, 1865

IN THE AFTERMATH OF SAILOR'S CREEK, ROBERT E. LEE FACED an ever-worsening situation. Lashing out at his own generals, he relieved a number of them of command, including George Pickett—the man who failed the commanding general at Five Forks.

Pressing ever farther westward, the Army of Northern Virginia searched for supplies and a way to turn south into North Carolina to link up with Joe Johnston's army. Federal cavalry bested Lee's hard-marching men at every turn.

Skirting along the Appomattox River, the Rebel army entered Appomattox County, Virginia, on April 8. Lee's objective was the Southside Railroad at Appomattox Station, where supplies awaited his beleaguered troops. Union cavalry under Brig. Gen. George A. Custer reached the supplies first, capturing then burning three supply trains.

The writing was on the wall. Grant offered peace terms, but Lee initially refused to surrender his army. More supplies lay to the west in Lynchburg, Virginia, now the Army of Northern Virginia's next objective.

On the morning of April 9, Maj. Gen. John B. Gordon's Confederate Second Corps attempted to break out from the Union stranglehold. Gordon's men attacked Union cavalry under Maj. Gen. Phil Sheridan not far from the county courthouse. Realizing the cavalry was supported by two Union infantry corps, and unable to link up with James Longstreet's corps, Gordon called off the assault. Lee's army was trapped.

Lee and Grant exchanged messages and agreed to meet at the home of Wilmer McLean at Appomattox Court House that afternoon.

Lee, in dapper dress, met with Grant, who sported muddy boots and a field uniform, for the first time, face-to-face, since the Mexican War. Grant followed Lincoln's guidance to "let 'em up easy": The surrendering Confederates were to stack their arms and roll their colors for the last time, but officers were allowed to keep their sidearms and personal baggage. Men could also keep their horses. The men were paroled, and their parole pass allowed them to draw rations from Federal depots and ride Federal trains free of charge home.

The surrender of the Army of Northern Virginia was signed on April 9. Three days later, a formal ceremony marked the disbanding of Lee's army, or what was left of it, and the parole of his 28,356 officers and men, ending the war in the Eastern Theater.

Yet for many Civil War buffs and historians, the surrender at Appomattox unofficially marks the end of the Civil War. Robert E. Lee surrendered only the troops under his direct command. And the war lingered on. On April 15, Abraham Lincoln died in Washington, DC, shot by assassin John Wilkes Booth in Ford's Theater. General Joseph E. Johnston's army was still a threat in North Carolina, and pockets of Confederate soldiers existed throughout the Deep South.

On April 26, 1865, Johnston surrendered to William T. Sherman at Bennett Place, which proved to be the largest surrender of Confederate forces—89,270 men scattered from North Carolina to Florida. Other Confederate commands soon followed suit, with the last surrender being that of the CSS Shenandoah, in November 1865.

✳ ✳ PRESERVATION ✳ ✳

To date, the **American Battlefield Trust** has saved **512 acres** at Appomattox Courthouse Battlefield.

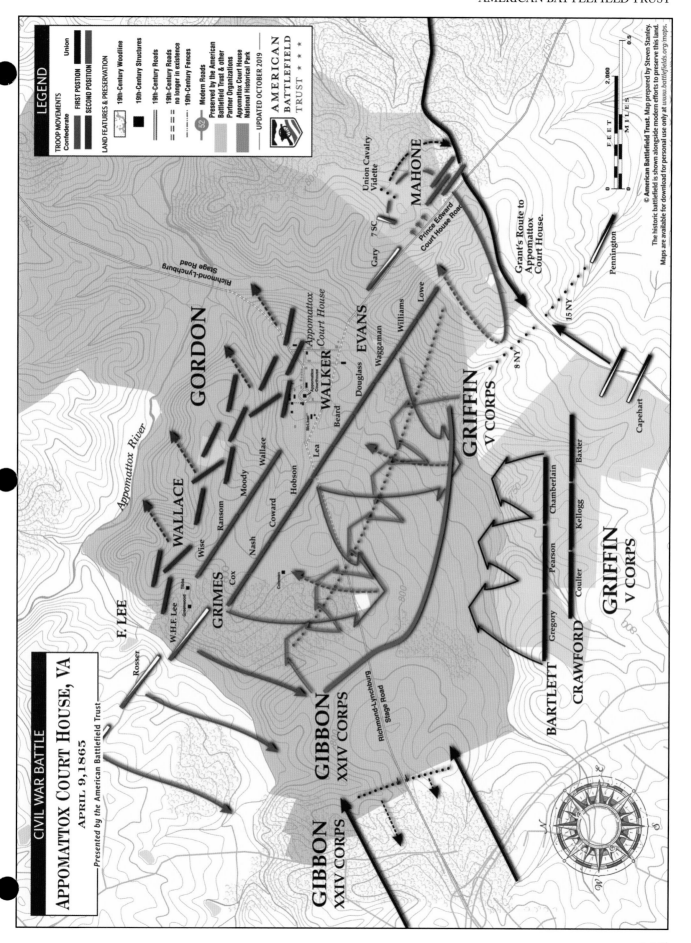

CIVIL WAR BATTLE
APPOMATTOX COURT HOUSE, VA
APRIL 9, 1865
Presented by the American Battlefield Trust

TROOP MOVEMENTS
Confederate   Union

FIRST POSITION
SECOND POSITION

LAND FEATURES & PRESERVATION

19th-Century Woodline
19th-Century Structures
19th-Century Roads
19th-Century Roads no longer in existence
19th-Century Fences
Modern Roads
Preserved by the American Battlefield Trust & other Partner Organizations
Appomattox Court House National Historical Park

— UPDATED OCTOBER 2019

AMERICAN BATTLEFIELD TRUST ★ ★ ★

© American Battlefield Trust. Map prepared by Steven Stanley.
The historic battlefield is shown alongside modern efforts to preserve this land.
Maps are available for download for personal use only at *www.battlefields.org/maps.*

MAHONE

Union Cavalry Vidette

7 SC

Gary

Prince Edward Court House Road

Grant's Route to Appomattox Court House.

Pennington

15 NY

8 NY

Capehart

Richmond-Lynchburg Stage Road

GORDON

Appomattox Court House

WALKER

EVANS

Lowe

Williams

Waggaman

Douglass

Beard

Lea

McLean

WALLACE

Wise

Ransom

Moody

Wallace

Nash

Coward

Hobson

Cox

Coleman

GRIMES

Tibbs

Greenwood

W.H.F. Lee

Appomattox River

F. LEE

Rosser

GRIFFIN
V CORPS

Chamberlain

Baxter

Pearson

Kellogg

Coulter

GRIFFIN
V CORPS

Gregory

BARTLETT

CRAWFORD

GIBBON
XXIV CORPS

Richmond-Lynchburg Stage Road

GIBBON
XXIV CORPS

GIBBON
XXIV CORPS

APPENDIX A
A SHORT HISTORY OF THE BATTLEFIELD PRESERVATION MOVEMENT

THE IDEA OF PROTECTING AMERICA'S BATTLEFIELDS IS NOT NEW. In the mid-19th century, portions of the Revolutionary War battlefields at places like Bunker Hill and Yorktown were set aside as a means of remembrance. Civil War veterans began erecting memorials to their units, actions, and fallen comrades almost as soon as the guns fell silent. Veterans reunions catalyzed battlefield preservation, as, at these gatherings, the men of the blue and the gray discussed creating open-air classrooms where the military could visit and learn the lessons from battles of the past.

By 1900, five national military parks — at Antietam, Chickamauga and Chattanooga, Gettysburg, Shiloh and Vicksburg — had been established under the auspices of the War Department. Gradually, additional parks were created at places like Cowpens, Guilford Court House, Fort McHenry, Fort Donelson and Petersburg, all of which were transferred to the control of the National Park Service in 1933. The so-called "cannonball circuit" continued to grow through the Civil War centennial commemoration in the 1960s, but federal battlefield preservation efforts then began to stall.

In the years following the Second World War, the pace of urban and suburban development in America dramatically escalated, leading to the destruction of battlefield land virtually across the map. The destruction was particularly devastating at battlefields adjacent to major cities. Witnessing commercial and residential construction destroying these historic sites, local preservation and park friends groups began to take shape and advocate for their protection. But there was no unified voice and success was both scattered and limited; entire battlefields like Chantilly and Salem Church, both Civil War sites in central Virginia, were all but swallowed by sprawl.

In July 1987, twenty or so stalwart souls met in Fredericksburg, Va., to discuss what could be done to protect the rapidly disappearing battlefields around them. Calling themselves the Association for the Preservation of Civil War Sites (APCWS), they decided the only way to save these sites for posterity was to buy the physical landscapes themselves.

In 1999, seeking to increase the scope of preservation opportunities that could be pursued, that first group merged with another organization sharing its vision to form the Civil War Preservation Trust. On the eve of the war's sesquicentennial commemoration in 2011, the group shortened its name to the Civil War Trust.

By mastering the art of seeking out public-private partnerships to maximize efficiency, and by working with developers to find win-win solutions, the Civil War Trust became the number one entity saving battlefield land in America, protecting land at a rate four times that of the National Park Service.

In 2014, responding to a clear need from the National Park Service, the Civil War Trust launched Campaign 1776, a limited scope project to lend its considerable expertise and clout to the protection of battlefields associated with the Revolutionary War and the War of 1812.

In May 2018, having concluded its 30th anniversary year, the group unveiled a new organizational structure, in which the Civil War Trust and the Revolutionary War Trust would operate as land preservation divisions under the banner of a broader American Battlefield Trust. With the mission to — Preserve. Educate. Inspire. — The American Battlefield Trust continues to be the leader in the land preservation community.

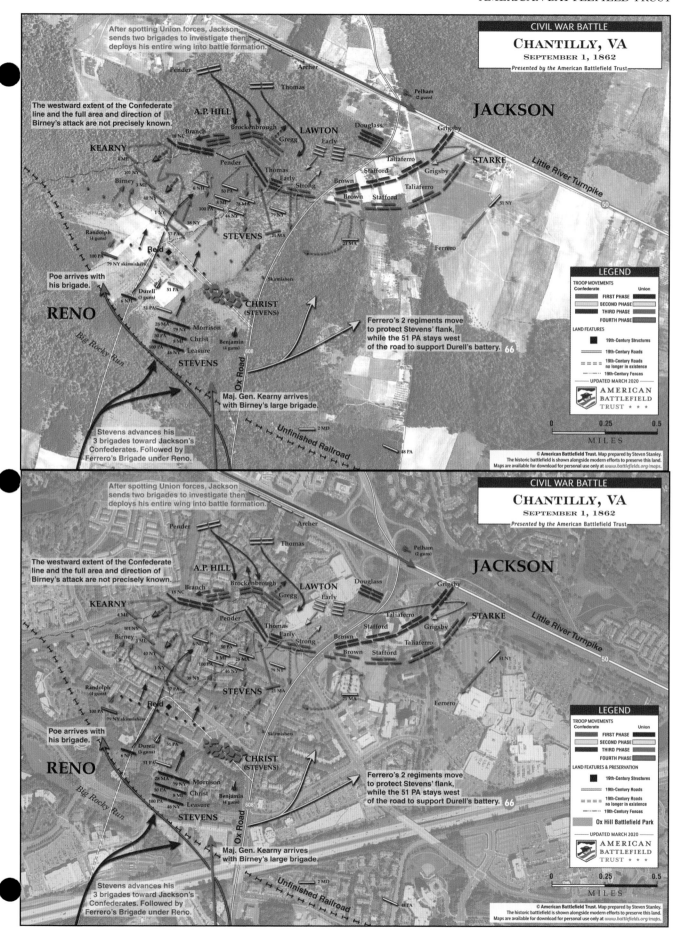

CIVIL WAR BATTLE

CHANTILLY, VA

SEPTEMBER 1, 1862

Presented by the American Battlefield Trust

After spotting Union forces, Jackson sends two brigades to investigate then deploys his entire wing into battle formation.

The westward extent of the Confederate line and the full area and direction of Birney's attack are not precisely known.

Poe arrives with his brigade.

Ferrero's 2 regiments move to protect Stevens' flank, while the 51 PA stays west of the road to support Durell's battery.

Maj. Gen. Kearny arrives with Birney's large brigade.

Stevens advances his 3 brigades toward Jackson's Confederates. Followed by Ferrero's Brigade under Reno.

LEGEND

TROOP MOVEMENTS
Confederate / Union
FIRST PHASE
SECOND PHASE
THIRD PHASE
FOURTH PHASE

LAND FEATURES
19th-Century Structures
19th-Century Roads
19th-Century Roads no longer in existence
19th-Century Fences

UPDATED MARCH 2020

AMERICAN BATTLEFIELD TRUST ★★★

0   0.25   0.5
MILES

© American Battlefield Trust. Map prepared by Steven Stanley.
The historic battlefield is shown alongside modern efforts to preserve this land.
Maps are available for download for personal use only at www.battlefields.org/maps.

107

APPENDIX B
DETERMINING THE LAND THAT WE SAVE

FOR MORE THAN 30 YEARS, THE AMERICAN BATTLEFIELD TRUST has been working to save hallowed battlefield land associated with the Revolutionary War, War of 1812 and American Civil War. To date, the American Battlefield Trust has preserved more than 52,000 acres of battlefield land in 24 states associated with 143 battles spanning the first 100 years of our nation's history.

The American Battlefield Trust preserves significant battlefield land in perpetuity by only working with willing sellers and utilizing well-established conservation strategies, chiefly, through fee simple transactions and conservation easements.

In order to determine the suitability of a particular property, we first consult the landmark studies prepared by the American Battlefield Protection Program ("ABPP"), an arm of the National Park Service. These robust reports commissioned by Congress examined the more than 13,000 battles and skirmishes in which the Revolutionary War, War of 1812 and Civil War were decided and identified the 627 principle sites most worthy of preservation.

Once we determine whether a prospective property is part of an ABPP-listed site, we utilize our Geographic Information System ("GIS") computerized mapping capabilities to locate the property in relation to the historic landscape. If a property is within the recognized boundary of an eligible battlefield, we next determine what conservation strategy is best suited to the project, recognizing that each opportunity presents a unique situation. Thus, we oversee each prospective land deal on a case-by-case basis.

Fee Simple Transactions transfer full ownership of a property. The Trust generally pays fair market value for land, but landowners can sell for less and receive tax benefits from their charitable contribution of the difference. Some landowner choose to

negotiate a life estate, meaning they retain the right to live at and use the property until their death, or a leaseback option; land trust gains control upon death of landowner. We also work to identify conservation buyers who take ownership of the property after placing permanent restrictions on its development potential.

Conservation Easements are legal agreements wherein a qualified land trust or state entity formally restricts future activities on the land to protect its conservation values in perpetuity. Ownership of the land does not change hands. These are an attractive option that protects family land in perpetuity without selling it, while also providing benefits on federal and state income taxes, estate taxes and property taxes. Each easement is negotiated individually, but in general, they disallow new structures not necessary for an agricultural operation, restrict changes to topography and limit the ability to subdivide a property.

Once the American Battlefield Trust determines the best preservation strategy, the Trust must determine how to pay for the transaction. Funding for battlefield preservation projects generally comes from member donations being leveraged against federal and state matching grants — most notably National Park Service Battlefield Land Acquisition Grants. However, contributions by other nonprofit organizations, foundation grants and landowner donations also play significant roles.

For more information about our current preservation efforts, please visit our website www.battlefields.org.

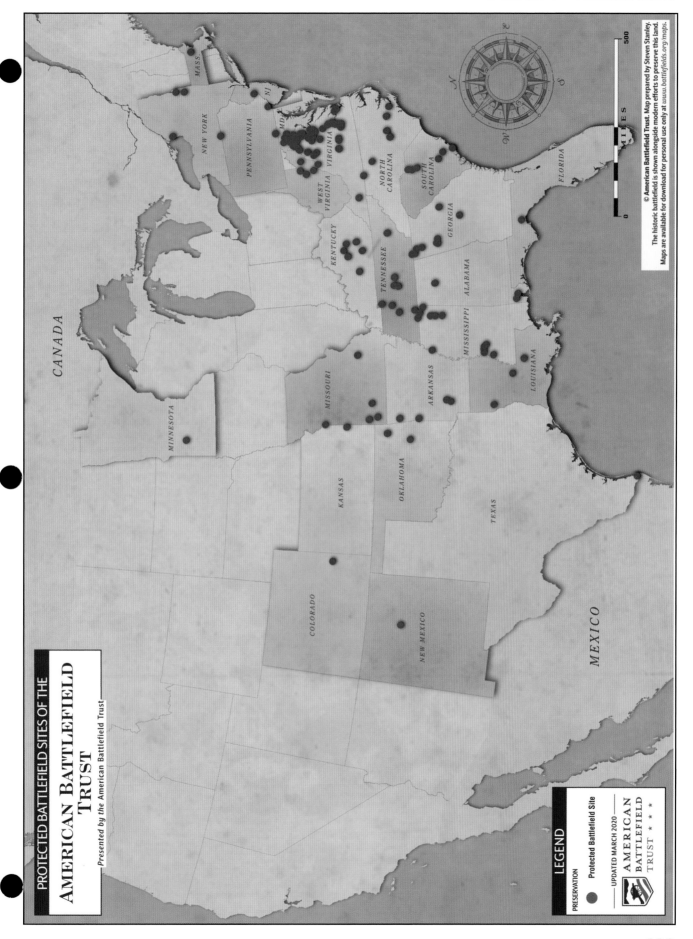

PROTECTED BATTLEFIELD SITES OF THE
AMERICAN BATTLEFIELD TRUST
Presented by the American Battlefield Trust

LEGEND

PRESERVATION

● Protected Battlefield Site

UPDATED MARCH 2020

AMERICAN
BATTLEFIELD
TRUST ★ ★ ★

© American Battlefield Trust. Map prepared by Steven Stanley.
The historic battlefield is shown alongside modern efforts to preserve this land.
Maps are available or download for personal use only at *www.battlefields.org/maps*.

BATTLE MAPS OF THE CIVIL WAR: THE EASTERN THEATER VOLUME 1

PROJECT TEAM

ADMINISTRATION AND MANAGEMENT DEPARTMENT

David Duncan

President

Steve Wyngarden

Chief Administrative Officer

Ruth Hudspeth

Chief Financial Officer

DEVELOPMENT DEPARTMENT

Amanda Murray

Deputy Director of Development

POLICY & COMMUNICATIONS DEPARTMENT

Mary Koik

Director of Communications

DIGITAL OPERATIONS DEPARTMENT

Wendy Woodford

Design Lead

REAL ESTATE DEPARTMENT

Jon Mitchell

GIS Specialist

HISTORY & EDUCATION DEPARTMENT

Kristopher White

Deputy Director of Education

Steven Stanley

Historical Map Designer

Antietam National Battlefield
Sharpsburg, Md.
MATT BRANT

YOU'VE SEEN THE MAPS.
NOW HELP US
SAVE THE LAND.

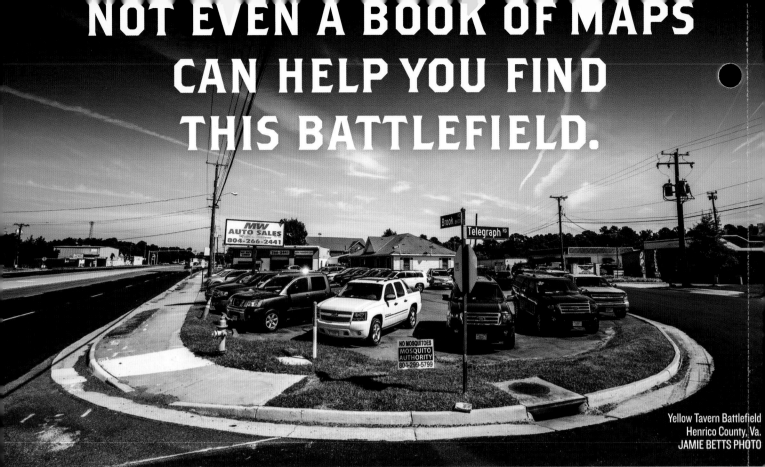